Day Breaks Over Dharamsala

ALSO BY JANET THOMAS

At Home in Hostel Territory

The Battle in Seattle
The Story Behind and Beyond the WTO Demonstrations

www.battleinseattlebook.com

Day Breaks Over Dharamsala

A Memoir of Life Lost and Found

Dear Norm,
Here's to Freedom!
Love,
Janet

Janet Thomas

First Edition

Nutshell Books
P.O. Box 2333, Friday Harbor, WA 98250
www.nutshell-books.com

Cover design and interior layout by Bruce Conway
Cover and interior photos by Janet Thomas (unless otherwise noted)

Printed in the U.S.A. on recycled paper

ISBN: 978-0-615-32921-5

Library of Congress Control Number: 2009939243

Dedication

To my son, Colin.
To the Tibetan people.
To all who struggle with spirit and self.

Emancipate yourselves from mental slavery,
none but ourselves can free our minds.

Won't you help to sing
these songs of freedom...

—Bob Marley, *Redemption Song*

CONTENTS

Foreword by Andrew Harvey IX

Day Breaks Over Dharamsala 1

Afterword 351

Acknowledgments 355

Credits 357

Foreword

I am honored to write the foreword to *Day Breaks Over Dharamsala* by Janet Thomas for three reasons: I have known Janet for four of the many years she has been working on the book and have been an intimate and awed witness to her unflinching heroic struggle with the material she presents. I was born in the sacred world of India and the lessons of my childhood's exposure to India's mystical cauldron of chaos and the wonder born from it have infused everything I have done and written. I find in Janet's marvelous descriptions of India and in her stunned and transformational reactions to it the richest kind of confirmation. The third reason I am honored to be writing in praise of *Day Breaks Over Dharamsala* is that it is a masterpiece on many levels—as travel writing; as a passionate and wise account of inner revelation; and as an account, at once restrained and searing, of a great healing from the kind of extreme and prolonged abuse that most of us would have been annihilated by. This is the rarest kind of book, an accessible, utterly human and wonderfully unsparing and intelligent description of the hardest task that faces a human being—that of transmuting, through surrender and great longing, horror into grace, soul-stealing brutality into universal, active joyful compassion, and unbearable trauma into a burning sacred passion for all life and all beings.

For all of us who are coming to know that our times are plunging the world into its final ordeal in which human destiny will be decided, Janet Thomas's telling of the story of one woman's wrestling of illumination from the deepest and darkest despair will give us all the kind of hope we need. This hope does not thrive on denial but on the knowledge of the secret resurrection—the power of dogged faith and the divine blessing it draws down. This hope, rooted as it is in the growing experience of a love beyond reason and a mercy beyond judgment, cannot be withered by any cruelty, destroyed or downhearted by any defeat, or diverted by any ferocious assault or misery from flowering in a passion of compassionate action on behalf of all sentient beings. Grounded in, and empowered by such rugged hope that springs in full strength from the heart of divine reality, *Day Breaks Over Dharamsala* shows us that there is no atrocity we cannot forgive, no depth of abuse we cannot heal from, and no grueling inner and outer work we need be afraid of and cannot bring, with the ever present help from grace, to a consummation both more dazzling and effective than anything we could imagine as prisoners of self-love and despair.

Janet's evolution into such hope began in horror. Her childhood was sacrificed on the obscene altar of a satanic cult in which both her parents were active and enthusiastic participants. Janet was used in child pornography and farmed out as a child prostitute. She experienced electric shocks, drugs, acute and terrifying sensory deprivation and was repeatedly experimented upon for medical and mind control purposes by the very people she would normally have turned to for love and tenderness. Surviving this meant dissociating from the pain, the abuse, the defilement, the shame, the hatred and the nihilism it bred—and dissociating in such a way that burdened her with an isolating multiple personality "disorder," profound self-loathing, and a deep terror of life.

In a recent letter to me, Janet wrote: *We live in an age of abuse and a culture of denial. Evil exists. And nothing is more evil than the destruction of the fundamental innocence of a child. When deviant thought systems attempt to shape minds into obedience and hearts into shame and defilement, a great rage arises. This is a rage that can play itself out through insanity, through nihilistic cynicism, through sociopathic behavior, through unending hatreds, addictions and despairs, and through barren isolation. It can also play itself out through love. And love is a hard taskmaster. It demands that we love back.*

Not without extreme difficulty—and with many detours, dead-ends, and collapses—Janet made the life-saving decision to "love back" and put her whole being, in fear and trembling, into the hard taskmaster, "love." One of the greatest and most helpful strengths of this book is that it shows that such a healing journey demands of the one brave enough to undertake it every ounce of courage, every capacity for persistence, every ability to endure often harrowing insight, every form of difficult surrender to the rigors of an alchemy that remains both ferocious and mysterious in its operations. Janet's extraordinary and, I believe, archetypal journey weaves through twenty years of psychotherapy, battering and bruising failed love affairs, poverty and ungrateful work, battles for social and political causes, a healing in island quiet surrounded by whales, wild turkeys and hummingbirds, and a system of multiple selves each competing for recognition, attention and respect and threatening at times to tear her finally apart.

What has saved Janet—and for once "saved" is not too rhetorical and theatrical a word—is that, through all the ordeals her childhood inflicted on her and bequeathed to her, she never completely lost her faith in a capacity for infinite transformation, a faith that crystallizes in this book around the down-home but diamond radiance of His Holiness the Dalai Lama. Janet never surrendered the longing that lives in her like a wild crackling fire to be whole, to be her true self, to love life despite its crucifixions, to believe in the reality of the creation of a world order rooted in justice and compassion, to come at last into the blessing of what she calls "the greatest miracle of all, the miracle of the holy ordinary." It is the ordinary that knows that making a rich cup of tea, eating pizza with a loved friend, seeing a dog asleep in the sun are revelations of what Gerard Manley Hopkins called "the dearest freshness that lives deep down things."

Perhaps only those who have exhausted in their inmost selves the various fires of hell on earth can see as brilliantly clearly as Janet comes in *Day Breaks Over Dharamsala* to do, the "dearest freshness" of the "heaven" that also lies shining all around us in the subtle details of ordinary pleasure, delight and communion with others and with nature that we are all too often blind to, or too rushed to savor, or too addicted to victimhood or grandiosity to be grateful for. Rumi wrote: "True lovers use their shattered selves and heartbreak as a torch to burn away the darkness and light up the whole creation." No reader who is lucky enough to come to this book will doubt that she has become, in Rumi's high sense, "a true lover," someone who has been resurrected from a death far worse than any physical extinction and found the courage and fierce compassion to see and take on not only the system of cold evil that nearly destroyed her but also all those systems of mind and corporate control that are now threatening the survival of our world. The journey *Day Breaks Over Dharamsala* unravels and enshrines has not left Janet merely "healed," it has forged her into a gentle but fearless warrior for a whole host of causes—environmental, political, sexual, social—that she holds dear at heart. It has made her a convinced and authentic sacred activist, someone who has fused within herself a profound love of the sacred with a resolute determination to stand up for the poor, abused and voiceless whenever and wherever justice and compassion demand it.

None of us in a time like ours are going to escape the ferocious alchemy of the "hard taskmaster, love." Few of us, of course, will have personal journeys as extreme as Janet's but all of us are going to be shaken to our roots by the onrushing collapse of civilization as we know it and by the ever-more destructive eruption of a perfect storm of interlinked crisis that will compel us either to change the way we think about and do everything, or die out. Millions are now awakening to this truth, its terror and the possibility of an amazing, unprecedented, difficult rebirth. Janet's great book and the archetypal journey it so movingly depicts will shine out like a great torch of hope for all of us who know that nothing less than an unconditional surrender to divine love and grace can possibly transform us enough to rise to the challenge we face, not with denial or paralysis or despair, but with the great heartbroken bliss of compassion and the unstoppable energy of divinely inspired and empowered action.

Day Breaks Over Dharamsala is a book of the highest seriousness of purpose, but it is also a delight. It is a book not just for survivors of abuse and for all travelers and spiritual seekers; it is written with such nakedness and such grit and wit and jeweled panache that it is also a book for dog lovers, people passionate about pizza, gourmets of eccentricity, bookworms hungry for arcane information about British churches in the Himalayas, and all battered survivors everywhere of post-modern cynicism, corporate nihilism, consumerist fantasy, and religious fundamentalism, for anyone, in fact, who in Janet Thomas's words, "wants to know I have been alive before I die."

Janet Thomas has cooked up a literary Babette's Feast with enough pungent, spicy and enticing dishes to delight any palate. To have done so with such a shrewd and exuberant generosity of soul and such directness of heart is the greatest proof of the depth of her healing and the most blatant sign that she has learnt well from her soul mentor His Holiness the Dalai Lama how to open her arms to everyone in the telling of her story and how to enchant them to rediscover—or discover for the first time—the holy enchantment of an ordinary illumined life. I once asked His Holiness at the end of an interview I had with him, "Why are we here?" He flung back his head and roared with laughter at the bald naiveté of my question. But he knew I was asking him seriously and so, when he had finished laughing, he said, very calmly and quietly, "We are here to embody the transcendent."

Day Breaks Over Dharamsala "embodies the transcendent" in the journey it incarnates with such wisdom and in so lithe, dancing, elegant a prose, it helps us start to sing our own songs of redemption and begin living and acting from their radical wisdom.

—Andrew Harvey, September 1, 2009, Oak Park, Illinois

ONE

I t was midnight at 35,000 feet when my good friend and traveling companion, Thrinley, insisted she could smell Delhi. As we still had two hours and about a thousand miles to go, I assumed she was simply too exhausted to differentiate between the Korean food being served on the plane and her imagination. But I was wrong; she really did smell Delhi.

Immediately upon landing, her obsession to describe precisely how Delhi smells becomes mine, too. Yes, it is like exhaust fumes; but from what? Big diesel trucks, for sure, but from other things, too: something sweet that is barely decipherable; burning rubber and other things it is illegal to burn back where I come from; something sweaty and forbidden; something else that is on the verge of being unbearable.

Thrinley is grinning. "It smells so much better than last time I was here," she says. I'm wondering what else she has in her arsenal of surprises about India.

Thrinley and I are on pilgrimage. Her reasons are distinct. As the manager of a Tibetan Buddhist retreat center on the island where we live, Thrinley was invited to attend the long-life ceremony for His Holiness Sakya Trizin in Rajpur, a small town just on the edge of Dehradun in northern India. Sakya Trizin is one of her Tibetan Buddhist teachers. I'm going along for the ride, which isn't quite true. What is true is that I was compelled to come to India for reasons I could neither articulate nor fully comprehend. And it wasn't so much India that drew me; it was Dharamsala, the small hill town in the foothills of the Himalayas where the Dalai Lama has established the Tibetan government-in-exile. I love the Dalai Lama; I want to be where he is. But right now I am in Delhi and it smells bad.

Back in the sixties and seventies, my friends who went to India went mostly for drugs and levitation. Everybody lusted after gurus and good dope and India supposedly had both. The Beatles went there, too. But in those days I was a young, responsible mother and recently divorced. I taught Montessori school and protested the war in Vietnam. If I was passed a joint at a party, I took a toke or two but could never quite identify what it was that was supposed to happen. India influenced my wardrobe with dangly earrings, bright and flimsy cotton skirts and shirts, and patchouli incense; but my mind and its whereabouts remained tightly under my control. Now, more than thirty years later, I am in India looking for something that I'm not sure I will recognize. But first of all, it appears, I am to line up.

It is four long lines for security, immigration, customs and something known only to the Indian government, before we get to our luggage. I have dragged my security pouch out of my pants so often that I no longer worry about appearing masturbatory. Besides, I've already seen several Indian men grabbing their genitals with fevered appreciation; why shouldn't I?

Suddenly Thrinley looks confused. "I could swear I remember that this airport was made of concrete," she says.

It is stark, white, unadorned, and unmistakably marble. All the better to see the ravishing, unrestrained colors of the clothes worn by the Indian women. I had known about the flowing colors from films and photographs, but the elegance only comes through in person. Even the exhausted mothers with toddlers, who've been our traveling companions since Seattle, look serenely graceful and composed. Thrinley and I, weighted down with a couple of old canvas backpacks, hope only that we don't look American.

It is the first of December, 2004. George W. Bush is back in office and both Thrinley and I are devastated by the thought of four more years. It wasn't supposed to happen. I'd traveled from the Northwest to Columbus, Ohio, as a volunteer voting monitor on Election Day. The experience left me shocked and shaken. I'd gone there on principle to participate with Election Protection. I'm not a U.S. citizen but because I care so much about the country, I had to do something. Columbus, Ohio, however, became a lesson in how America had gone wrong. At the polling station where I was assigned, two of the five voting machines were out of order within fifteen minutes of opening. African Americans, who had been in line since before daybreak in order to vote before going to work, had to leave in order to get to their jobs. I watched the subtle and not-so-subtle ways in which voters were disenfranchised. Even so, when I went to bed that night, John Kerry was predicted to win Ohio, and consequently the Presidency. Waking up to a re-elected George W. Bush was shocking and heartbreaking. Suddenly it felt like the right time to leave the country, even though it felt like the wrong time to be perceived as American.

At first, Thrinley was going to get a Canadian flag to sew on to her backpack. I, the non-American and always paranoid about being deported, was afraid that was too deceptive and so I suggested we take a couple of old canvas backpacks that look more Tyrolean than Eddie Bauer. If we avoid the outdoor fashion statement look, perhaps we'll avoid the stigma of George W. Bush. Our packs have strings and buckles instead of zippers. The pouches are bulky; the straps are lined with fleece; and they're weighty even on empty. If they get wet we'll be on our knees. For sure we won't look American.

It was a calling to come here to India; and in some way, inevitable, even as it seemed utterly impossible. Mostly because I have no money. In the past, most of my travel has been job-related. As editor of *SPA* magazine I'd been invited to resorts of great luxury and indulgence in places like France and Italy; I'd gone to a private spa in Hawaii with Fabio; I'd also written guides to hostels and traveled to places of no-frills practicality. I'd gone to canyon country in the Southwest via the Green Tortoise bus with its on-board beds and barely above-board protocols. I'd biked and camped in Alaska with only a lousy boyfriend and a herd of mosquitoes for company. In some way they were all travel adventures prescribed by circumstance to be somewhat predictable. India, however, was otherwise. At the outset, exactly how I would pay for this trip was totally unpredictable.

Money is not my strong suit. Ever since I was a little girl and my services were sold to strangers, I've had trouble touching the stuff. There is no subtle way to say this. My childhood experience imprinted me with a shame about money that has permeated all my life. Although I've had 25 years of therapy and several lifetimes of struggle with the honorable concept of self-worth and financial entitlement, I've come to the conclusion that money and I are tainted, once and for all, ad infinitum. Which is why I really love the Dalai Lama. He went to a meeting with George W. Bush wearing his patched robes and plastic flip flops. He obviously has trouble with money, too.

My friend, Thrinley, wondered if he did it on purpose—the plastic flip-flop encounter with the President of the U.S.A. I know he did. The Dalai Lama does everything on purpose; that's his purpose. I've been trying to do one thing, anything, on purpose my whole life. But when you've been trained to believe that if you want something it automatically means you can't have it, purpose ends up in the non-existent money jar with the non-existent money. Just like money, purpose has to be a sleight-of-hand experience in my life. Which is why going to India in search of the Dalai Lama on purpose had to happen by accident.

And, of course, it did; even the money part. I told Thrinley that I was thinking about going to India with her only after she'd told me that no-one was lining up to go with her on this trip. So my life-long yearning to actually *want* to go to India became an act of altruism, a sacrifice. I was off to a good and accidental start. Then a credit card arrived in the mail, then another one. This astounded me as I've resisted life-by-credit card since I was married to the dentist more than 30 years ago. I've also been quite happily ineligible simply because I never had the credit to apply for credit. But it turned out that my last two get-through-the-winter bank loans, which I had dutifully repaid, put me in the pink with a couple of credit companies. Voila! Just as my altruistic juices were lining up India as a possibility, the plastic showed up.

I called Thrinley immediately. "If the plane ticket goes through on the VISA card, I'm going with you," I announced, not quite on purpose. And it did. And here I am. On pilgrimage.

To my untrusting ear the word "pilgrimage" sounds pretentious and implausible to consider in this post-post-modern world. It rings of age-old goings-on and of something dignified and restrained, somber perhaps, and much too private to be named. When I look it up online I find references of old to pilgrimages to the Holy Land, to Waterloo, to Paradise and Palestine. There's the pilgrimage of perfection, and *The pylgremage of the sowle* penned somewhere in the region of 1400. There are New Age pilgrimages, virtual pilgrimages to holy places from the comfort of the computer screen, pilgrimages to the Beatles, to wildflowers, to steam baths and to Glastonbury. To Google "pilgrimage" brings nearly three million possibilities. The dictionary offers up penance, worship, historic or sentimental journey. And finally a few words that catch a deeper attention, "a search for mental and spiritual values."

The word "pilgrim," it turns out, is easier. "One who journeys, especially in alien lands," is Webster's first take; followed by "a person who passes through life in exile from a heavenly homeland or in search of it or some high goal (as truth)."

For many years, my green card said I was a registered alien. Now I am an alien journeying in an alien land. If I am on any kind of a pilgrimage, it is in search of my self; not the grown-up self in search of realization and accomplishment, but the childhood self that simply deserves to be. I want to know that I have been alive before I die. I want to come in out of exile.

My first attempt to write myself home was in 1991, when I moved to San Juan Island in the far northwest corner of Washington State where there was a Tibetan Buddhist Center as well as a Buddhist Vipassana Center. To move to an island means to be on the lookout for signs of spiritual compatibility; otherwise the isolation gets you if the insulation doesn't. Islands are not easy places and my life has been full of them. Like Buddhism, they have linked together the fragments of my past, all the life lived and unlived.

When I contemplated this island move, the Buddhist centers beckoned. Even if I didn't go to them, they were there and it meant something. Even if I didn't get the book written, it was there and it meant something. This there and not-there experience prescribes the life of someone who survives things that should never have happened. Vigilance takes over and it restrains the body, suspends it in space, and keeps it safely out of sight of the world. There are no day-dreams, no wants and wishes; there is no future that can be named. Life happens and parts of us, if we are lucky, are around when it does. This alienation is what I want you to understand. The trauma is simply the trauma; the aftermath goes on forever. And when we begin to see the toll taken, when we begin to heal, it is into the unbearable awareness of all that has been lost. It is an awakening to grief. To suffering. In Buddhism, the number one wake-up call is to suffering. The cessation of suffering is the goal but the path goes right through the suffering. And there is no way out but through. So how could I avoid moving to a small island with two Buddhist centers in order to write a book about suffering?

So I moved to a house on the water and the book got started in beauty. It was quiet and the light was miraculous on sea and sky. The red currant bushes brought the first hummingbirds of the spring; the whales swam by. Sometimes I heard them breathing from across the still waters. Sometimes the wind and the waves crashed around the house in a fury. I found perfect stones on the beach and the odd and ancient shells of chitins; the waters rose with the moon and the moon with the waters. I lived in beauty and wrote 300 pages about suffering. I also got my first dog. He, too, was an accident, a want I had without wanting.

Buck was a two-year-old black lab who survived a sail through the Panama Canal and up the west coast all the way to Roche Harbor on San Juan Island. His owner was working off the after-effects of a bitter divorce; he hadn't treated Buck very well and two women working at the resort took it upon themselves to rescue him. When the fellow started making plans to leave, they kidnapped Buck, hid him, and waited to see if his erstwhile owner cared. He didn't, and sailed off without him.

A few weeks later some friends and their black Lab came to visit. I took them for a winter stroll through the Roche Harbor gardens. A woman came out of the office, took one look at the dog, another look at me and said, "I have a dog just like that one and he needs a home. His name is Buck." She turned quickly, went back to the hotel and brought him out. Before I knew what was happening, he was mine.

The only problem was that I didn't know how to have a dog. My partner at that time did, however, and when he was around he gave me lessons. But he wasn't around a lot. As a merchant marine, he went offshore for weeks at a time. When he was away, Buck, himself, took over my training. I was an awkward student because I didn't know how to talk to him, how to say his name. Our journey to full conversation took a long time. I thought about this many years later when Buck went deaf and didn't seem to mind. It was a return to our early years when it was long stretches of silence that rang out between us, punctuated only by food and long, quiet walks.

Somebody once said that the most valuable thing about marriage is the witnessing of one another's lives. As a complete failure in the longevity of my relationships with men, let alone my inability to get and stay married after my early foray into the institution, Buck became the witness to my life as it unfolded, with me and without me, for the next thirteen years. Even now, after nearly two years without him, I often wonder, "What would Buck think?" His presence, the way he would peruse the world and its inhabitants without raising his head from whatever soft spot he could find, was masterful.

Throughout the years of writing and not writing this book, Buck taught me about unconditional love and loyalty. His frailties reminded me of my own and as I struggled to recover my self, soul and sanity from the violations of my childhood, his dogged devotion to me—no matter what—finally got under my skin and made a difference. When it was time for him to die I was devastated. For help, I called Thrinley. She was my friend, she had experienced the loss of a long beloved dog, and she knew some blessings. After all, Buck was a Buddhist. He knew suffering; he knew compassion; he knew better than I how to be here now; he also knew impermanence, particularly when it came to food. He was my own private bodhisattva.

A bodhisattva is an enlightened being who makes sacrifices to benefit other beings. It is a Sanskrit word and it applies to Buddha as well as to Buck. At the end of his life, Buck kept getting up for my sake. Early in his life, the Buddha renounced the insular comforts of wealth to learn something that might help those who were less fortunate. He sacrificed his fortune for enlightenment. But on the path to enlightenment, he had no idea what enlightenment was; neither did Buck. He just kept getting up. The Buddha just kept sitting down.

Buck did something else that was astonishing. When we were out in the world, he had a philosophy of life that never failed him, even when it did. He assumed everybody loved him. Unlike his perceptive protectiveness within the confines of hearth and home, when he was out, he reveled in the possibility of love-at-first-smell. He approached everyone he met with big surging licks of tail-wagging affection. Over the years I grew more and more in awe of this unabashed display of undisciplined love for humankind. It never wavered. Even after brusque, sometimes repulsed, responses, he never missed a Buck beat. With inherent dignity he would turn to whoever was next and try again. His was an assumption of love that was majestic in its optimism.

Yet there was a moment in his daily life that reflected an opposite view. He always flinched when I went to pet him. It got less over the years but until he died he never completely trusted the hand that fed him. And loved him. And never, ever hurt him. Buck's early experiences with the fellow on the boat had left him with an inherent mistrust of the person who was supposed to love him most of all. At first, I thought he would outgrow this instinctive flinch and it hurt to see it so entrenched. After all, I might not have known how to have a dog, but I knew I loved Buck. I knew he had been abandoned and treated cruelly; I knew we had shared the worst of times at times in our lives; I knew we were soul mates. He knew this, too; but those early beatings had left him helpless under his skin, as had mine. We both know how to dazzle strangers; neither of us knew how to trust our friends.

I am a survivor of deviant abuse of my mind, my body and my soul. My abuse at the hands of others was supported and perpetrated by my parents. It started in England when I was perhaps four years old. It continued in Montreal, Canada, until I was twelve. It stopped when I was around fourteen, after our family moved to Vancouver, British Columbia. I know this because that is when my memory starts. And herein lays a dilemma of enormous proportion. It is everything I don't remember that drives my life and its losses. The empty black hole of my childhood that was at the heart of me. Into it was sucked everything—the joy as well as the terror, the innocence as well as the guilt, the knowledge of self as well as the self.

Memory is a moving target. Sometimes we recognize it: "I must remember to buy cat food." Sometimes we don't: "I must remember to breathe." In my own uncovering, and recovering, of memories, I had to start by acknowledging that I had a memory. This was, and is, difficult because all of my surviving life I have forgotten. I learned how to forget everything, the bad, the good, and the indifferent. I can't remember where I slept up until the age of fourteen; even though I know I slept somewhere. I can't remember sitting down for a meal with my family, even though I did for nineteen years. Sometimes there is a suggestion of activity but there is no feeling of it, nothing that tells me I was really there, that it really happened.

This has, of course, created doubt and dismay as I've healed from the electric shocks that could never happen but did regularly; the slavery as a child that went far too long into adulthood; the experiments that happened to someone else who just happened to be me; the days and nights in the dark that made indistinguishable my self from all that did not exist; the places where I became an animal, where being debased for the enjoyment of others was my charm and my glory. I heal from it all, even as I know it could never have happened to me. It is what I was afraid to know that both saved me and condemned me. And it seems, at times, as though there is no difference.

I do bear a visible scar. It's four inches long and reaches down the inside of my left forearm. On my left hand are five-year-old fingers and a thumb that does not bend. There is not much feeling in this hand. It is a hand that is always cold, always numb, always looked after by my other hand—the right one, the one that writes, that does everything. "The scar is real," it writes. It is a huge scar. It is connected to medical experiments and electric shocks to see if the severed nerve would grow, and electric shocks to make sure I didn't remember the electric shocks. If I don't "remember" being cut, does it make the scar unreal? This is what I would ask those who think recovered memory is a hoax, that there is only truth in the literal and sequential naming of memory and recognition. The scar on my arm is as real as the reasons it is there.

Many children were experimented on in the 40s and 50s; they still are. Many children were used for child prostitution and pornography; they still are. Many children, and adults, too, had their minds experimented upon through electric shock and drugs and by the destruction of the bonds that make life possible. It is everywhere. Yet it is ultimately our healing that matters. Only in healing is there hope.

Reclaiming spiritual grace is the hardest and most harrowing part of the healing journey. It takes the greatest toll—inside and out—and it insists on coming first, last and always. If spiritual healing isn't tended to, all the techniques in the psychotherapeutic band-aid business are doomed to expensive and shameful failure. It's not only about healing the body and the mind; in fact, the mind can take care of itself. It's about healing the spirit and restoring the soul.

In working through my years of recovery, the ongoing psychobabble about memory, false memory and recovered memory was a pain in the butt, as well as a pain in the brain. Any self-respecting survivor of trauma and abuse will tell you that the experts are only experts in their own experience. If they could enter into, for a moment, the place where mind and body separate to survive, they would know the emptiness of their conjecture and the inherent limitations of their perceptions. A few begin to get it; those who do usually keep very quiet. Admitting that knowledge is rooted in spiritual experience is a blithering no-no in the realms of academia—psychological academia most of all.

Because I was trained never to want anything, particularly in the realm of spiritual yearning, some other shape of wanting led me through my life. I call it "feeling drawn." It saved me until I learned how to save myself. It drew me to special people, to poetry, to Buddhism, to labyrinths and folk-dancing, to playing soccer and playing cards, to playwriting and the streets of WTO Seattle, to Jesus and Mary, to bad movies and good books; to my dog, Buck, to my therapist, my love of nature and my love affair with the Dalai Lama. It drew me out and drew me in. Now it has drawn me to India and I am in search of its name. What is it that saves us when we can't save ourselves? It is a question that has taken me my whole life to ask.

As I've reclaimed the innocence of my birthright, along with great gains have come great losses. Realizing how deeply and profoundly the damage settled, how terribly it informed my life before I learned how to recognize its power, is a challenge sometimes greater than healing. Child abuse most of all abuses the adult we become. The vile acts of abuse happen and are over. The effects of the abuse shape a life and the lives of those we love. This is its deadliest legacy. As survivors, we perpetrate hatred, shame, mistrust and fear; even as we live good lives and become good people. As individuals we reflect the parallel realities of abuse and denial that mark these times. And they do mark these times; we are awash in the destruction of the human spirit.

This trip to India is a lark, a burst of freedom into greater freedom. I knew this as soon as I knew I would go. I also knew that the great draw was at work again. There was something yet to realize. After so many years of therapy, so much grief and despair, so many healing corners turned; there is still one left. As Thrinley and I find ourselves funneling out through the airport towards the real Delhi, a sensation seeps in to me and there is the first hint of a great and thought-less landscape of possibility. Perhaps India itself is a drug. And here I am, about to swallow it hook, line and synchronicity.

It's Thrinley's friend, Pema, who is supposed to meet us at the Delhi airport and save us from ourselves and our luggage. He's been a travel guide to many Tibetan teachers as well as to Westerners who travel to sacred sites in India. Thrinley met him on her last trip here. So far there's no sign of him and I'm feeling no small anxiety as the end of airport security closes behind us and we walk through a silent crowd gathered in waiting for their loved ones. None of whom are us.

Suddenly Thrinley shouts out from behind me, "There he is."

It is three o'clock in the morning and our man Pema looks as fresh as a man can look. His crisply ironed grayish mauve shirt, his freshly-pressed trousers and his polished loafers reflect London's Fleet Street more than the bowels and bedlam of Delhi. Yet it is to this world that he most enthusiastically delivers us.

Stumbling in the wake of Pema's confident stride across the airport parking lot is an experience in high-stakes sensory overload. It is dark. It is beyond smelly; whatever it was that Thrinley smelled at 35,000 feet was nothing compared to the blasts of freshly and not-so-freshly pissed urine rising up from underfoot. It is loud; the silence of the loved ones-in-waiting gives way to the barrage of offers and requests of the unloved: the porters, the cab drivers, the beggars, the drivers trying to get their cars out of the whirling mess of traffic—human and otherwise—in the parking lot. It is extremely touchy-feely; hands grabbing arms to take luggage or reach out for money, bodies bumping suggestively yet seemingly by accident, the continual brush of something mechanical approaching the kneecaps. The air feels thick in my mouth; it tastes bad. By the time we reach Pema's car, no part of my body, mind or spirit remains untrammeled.

We load the luggage wherever it will fit; Thrinley climbs into the front; I climb into the back and we become part of the incoherent flow of vehicles looking for a way out. We escape into a street and turn right into a left lane. It's a wrong way country. The Brits were here.

"We'll take the long way," says Pema. "It's more interesting."

Taking the long way is not exactly what I have in mind. Besides, it's dark for god's sake. What the hell are we supposed to see? Nasty, judgmental thoughts go scrambling across my mind. I feel like I'm failing India already. In Buddhism, thoughts are perceived as pesky little creatures that insist upon marring the vast expansive clarity of our perfect minds. They deserve to be watched, but that's about all. Taking them seriously is a sure-fire way to a muddy mind. This means that for more than 30 years, ever since I took my first baby Buddhist breath, I've been in a messy mud-wrestling match with my thoughts.

This is where religious skills of discernment fail me. I find it impossible to believe that the world's religions don't, at some very critical place, join up in a celebration of unity. Nothing else makes sense. Which is why, perhaps, I am a pilgrim who is not on a pilgrimage. I am an alien in an alien land. It is Thrinley who is on a pilgrimage. She knows what she believes, and why. Her reasons for being in India at this precise moment are clear with responsibility and intention. My beliefs are obscure and unintentional. They veer from Jesus to Buddha and back again. They go to God, to God in us all, to God beyond us all. To a God that doesn't do religion of any name.

"The smog isn't as bad as last time," Thrinley says to Pema.

"No," he answers. "They make all the trucks drive in at night."

We are in the truck lane because it is all trucks. Through the smoggy haze of night they each glow with color; sometimes from reckless and garish paint jobs, sometimes from colored lights flashing out from within the cab of the truck, sometimes from something sparkly added outside in decoration. The trucks lumber through the city like motorized circus elephants, almost animate with personality. Fatigue ripples through my body, but so does stimulation. Drivers don't stop for red lights at night because the police are in bed, says Pema. There are no turn signals in evidence, and no rules of the road, even the lanes are arbitrary; rarely do I see one vehicle lined up behind another. It is like being on a wild ride at a carnival; but in reality it is just another night of traffic as usual. Pema never slows down. He navigates with composure, engaging us in bright conversation, telling us about Delhi.

"It is many cities in one," he says. "And each city has a gate."

He points one out, and then another. Through the dark I glimpse a large stone arch. An arch is a gate. It is the very first moment in India in which I hear one thing and experience another. *Nothing is as it seems and nor is it otherwise.* It's an old Zen Buddhist saying I heard many years ago; I memorized it because in some profound way it put a stamp on my experience that I could understand.

Nothing is ever as it appears to be and nor is it otherwise. It's the mantra of a child survivor of childhood abuse. Our child stays with us, with eyes open only to the possibility of violation in all the glances of life. It is as though a veil of threat is permanently in place and life is experienced through it. Everything, even love, is tinted with fear. Like my old dog Buck, I experience even the most trustworthy affection with a flinch. There is always a threat-in-hiding. Unlike Buck, I never mastered the exquisite skill of assuming, first of all and no matter what, that everybody loves me. Even watching him face the odds for thirteen years didn't put a dent in my veil.

As we drive around Delhi in the early dark hours of the morning going who knows where, I feel no fear. Everything is a threat; but nothing is in hiding. It's the hiding, the presentation of one thing being a mask for something else that I am always on the lookout for and consequently always see. The trickery of love that seduces the innocent faith and hope of a child and then twists it until it hurts. It's a veil I'm always trying to make friends with; I know its reason for being, I just don't like being it. We are working on our relationship. As Pema points out the high walls of the Red Fort, an ancient palace that was also a fort, complete with a moat, I think of this, my sixtieth year. Somewhere inside, I, too, am a palace. Maybe one day before I die I'll get over the moat.

The massive red sandstone wall around the Red Fort stretches a mile and a half; it reaches anywhere from 60 to 110 feet high. Even at four o'clock in the morning I am impressed. But, finally, I'm even more impressed that Pema, who graciously met us at such an ungodly hour at the airport, is so enthusiastically going the long way around to show us sites he loves, and that we can barely see.

It's 4:30 when we finally get to our destination, Majnu-ka-Tilla, the Tibetan Camp tucked away somewhere in the middle of Old Delhi. The word "camp" is misleading; there are no tents. Camp simply means an official place of exile; and in India, camps are the only thing Tibetans know as home.

Pema pulls up on the side of the street, gives us strict instructions to stay where we are, and walks off towards a row of derelict looking buildings and disappears. When he returns, he's accompanied by a young man, tousled and sleepy, who looks to be about sixteen years old. We all tackle our luggage and with the young fellow in the lead, wearing the mother of all suitcases on his head, we head off to wherever it is our beds will be for the next couple of nights. Our environs are dark and I make out shuttered buildings and a feeling of ghostly emptiness. We turn down yet another alley and the young man with the big burden climbs the stairs to the Himalayan Guest House. Pema ushers us in and quickly up to a room, bypassing registration as well as any other form of hotel decorum.

"It's okay," he says. "You can sign-in in the morning."

Pema gives a quick but efficient look around our room, checks the bathroom, announces it clean, and briskly wishes us goodnight. He will meet us tomorrow afternoon, he says, and show us the sights. As we haven't gone to bed yet I don't know what he means by tomorrow, but I'm way too tired to ask. All I know is that it's quiet and at the moment there is no other prerequisite for perfection. Thrinley and I stumble, each towards a bed, and sit gaping at one another. We're in India and nobody can tell us otherwise. I drop off to sleep not even minding the small smears of snot on the wall beside my pillow.

It's the sound of children being tortured that has me bolt upright in bed a few hours later. Alarm ripples under my skin. After a closer listen, I hear that they are playing, teasing one another in a furious race through the halls of the guest house. Terror and delight. They must live here, I think. Somebody loves them. I go back to sleep to the reassuring sounds of a couple of happy kids who couldn't care less about someone sleeping in the next room.

I love the way love works; how it expands the sense of self in quiet and unassuming ways. How it makes a home in the body. How lovely and unselfconscious is the self when it doesn't have to question its existence, or where it belongs, or whether it belongs. The healthy self is always at home in the halls of its embodied world. Then, when it's time, it knows when to let go, when to join the deeper flow of existence, the flow of awakened enlightenment that is the promise of Buddhism and a realized mind. Through the years, as my own mind fragmented under the pressure of denial and delusion that was my world, I devoured books about the Buddhist mind and tried to make it my own. But my Buddhist journey up the mountain of spiritual life was paved with grief long before I knew the words, the journey or the destination. The words came through poetry, the grief through the birth of one son and the loss of another.

In 1966, when Colin was only a few weeks old, we flew across the country to join his father, a captain stationed at Fort Dix, New Jersey. It was the decade in which the spiritual landscape of the country was eviscerated by the violence of the Vietnam War abroad, race riots at home, and the assassinations of President John F. Kennedy Jr., Martin Luther King Jr., and Robert F. Kennedy. The first hint of what was to become of my own life came in the middle of that first hot and muggy New Jersey summer.

I lost my bearings. It happened suddenly, in an instant. There was no substance; it was as though everything turned to water. Terror rose through me and I remember controlling my panic by pinching myself hard. It was a familiar technique. Ever since I could remember, a childhood fear of eternity had sent me into similar panics and I would hurt myself to get back to the feeling of things. It felt as though I was actually in eternity, my mind stretching out ad infinitum with no embodied reality. This time, however, it was happening outside my mind as well. The world was dissolving.

Colin was three months old. Up until that moment, being his mom had made me as happy as I could ever remember. But when my world dissolved, he did, too. I worried that I might drop him on purpose, that I might put him in the clothes dryer, that I might die and no-one would notice. The irrational and destructive thoughts combined with the way everything outside became foreign and un-familiar rendered me helpless and terrified. I remember my hus-band coming home. I was curled up on a chair and couldn't stop crying. He called our neighbor, Mel, a physician. He came over and I cried harder and couldn't stop. I was desperate to speak and there was no language.

Sometime over the next few days, I went to the hospital and was prescribed a tranquilizer of some sort. I took it and was terrified it would get into my milk and hurt Colin. So I pretended to take it. The waves of incipient insanity defined my days and nights. I was terrified of trees. I was terrified I would lose my son. At the same time I was terrified about the meaningless world he had entered. Every moment became a struggle between reason memorized and the descent into a cracked and disintegrating present. So I decided to get pregnant again. We needed a complete family, I thought. One child is not a complete family. So through the new baby I grew pur-pose and meaning.

Thomas was born on May 29, 1967, at the Fort Dix hospital. He was bellowing before he was fully delivered. "Look at that," said the doctor. Everyone was impressed. The following morning I was phoned in my room. Would I please go down to the nursery to get my son? When I got there, they told me to return to my room, they would bring him to me. A half hour later, two men came in and told me he had expired. They called my physician and he arrived drunk. It was Memorial Day, a day of BBQ, beer and car racing. "Don't worry," my doctor said. "You can have another one."

When I go back to that moment in time I am struck most of all by the inarticulate helplessness that was my response. I didn't ask, "Why?" I didn't even wonder, "Why?" My son was dead. Two strange men in suits—why weren't they in military uniform?—had informed me that my son had "expired." Only minutes earlier I'd been told to go to the nursery and get him. Yet I didn't question anything about any of it. I didn't know how to ask. I didn't even know how to want to know. From the far reaches of healing this is incomprehensible to me. Yet it defines precisely who I was—and who I wasn't. I did not inhabit my own life.

I didn't even question why my mother was suddenly there. She came three thousand miles to the scene of this loss; yet a year earlier when Colin was born, she didn't even travel two miles to the hospital to see me and her new grandson. After Thomas died she did insist, much to my surprise, that I go back home for comfort and recovery. But when I got there, her cruelty increased with my grief. I was twenty-two years old; I had a year-old son; I had just lost an infant son; I was exhausted and grief-stricken; and my mother ridiculed me for crying and refused to care for Colin so I could get some rest. Going back to Fort Dix was a relief.

I now had a real reason to sink under the waves of harrowing sorrow that marked my life even before I lost Thomas. The strange dissembling world that had come upon me nine months earlier was replaced with the justified bereavement of a parent. Thomas was a lost child; lost, perhaps, because he couldn't bear the burden of his conception. His being had brought me out of despair; his death brought me to grief, to a suffering that was real. It was the beginning of my self. It was also a mystery. How he died, why he died. Eventually, even, if he died.

During that last year at Fort Dix, two days a week I volunteered at the hospital where soldiers from the Vietnam War returned in pieces. It was the only place I felt comfortable. There was humor on those wards and in those halls; there were moments of joy; there was recovery; there was loneliness. The young captain who came back with malaria and had been in isolation for six months is still vivid in my memory. He had given up any effort to see the world as it had been. I can remember how he looked at me, a bouncy candy-striper without a clue. But I did have a clue. I had lost my son. I knew about suffering.

Suffering gave me a stature that I could identify; and from it came a moment of unadulterated wanting. I wanted to go to college. My parents had not allowed me to go to college when I graduated from high school even though unbeknownst to them I'd secretly managed to get myself admitted. Instead I was to get married. I see this as extremely difficult to understand: Why didn't I simply leave home and go to college? Simply because I couldn't. My will was not to be found. The experiments upon me in my childhood, the sexual exploitation, the mind-control, they had all worked. The elimination of a-self-as-one-knows-it was complete. I'd married a man I didn't love and lived a life prescribed from without. I don't even know whether or not it was an arranged marriage. It had all the indications of something I felt freely forced to do. The circumstances, however, from this region of time, appear suspect. But that is too circumstantial for this story, which explores only what I know.

It is hard to look back and see the ways in which the most important thing in the world to me—the birth of my son, Colin—happened within the terrible sterility of the life I was experiencing. I want to tell him he was born of love, but I can't. His father came into my life under odd circumstances. He asked me to marry him. I said, "Yes" without feeling either passion or affection. There was no other answer. My husband was emotionally and psychologically abusive and often threatened to, and sometimes did, telephone my father to come and take me away. I couldn't communicate "about" anything—how I felt, what I thought, where we should go, what we should do. My husband was burdened with a woman who didn't exist. My passivity was pathological and psychological. But I had a pretty face and a nice shapely body. He could have sex with me. I, however, was anesthetized to the experience. Passion would only come many years later, provoking a massive crisis of its own

What I knew, when we returned to the Northwest, was that grieving the death of my infant son, Thomas, linked me to the living, to yearning. I took a drawing class and the teacher, painter Paul Havas, read us Kenneth Rexroth's poems. I fell in love with language and went out and bought Rexroth's *Natural Numbers*. I read about the "nymphomaniacs of the imagination," and the anguish of "O heart, heart, so singularly intransient and corruptible," and the beauty of "The Reflecting Trees of Being and Not Being."

I fell in love with the world to which Paul Havas introduced me. The poetic presence, the world as art, gave me a parallel reality, a way of being an outsider that had its own place in the world. A life that made sense without having to make money. It was a recognition that served me through the following years when, in the face of great odds, I left my abusive marriage and continued to find my way.

I actually had to get divorced twice. The first time, after agonizing months of waiting, I was sitting in the court room with my attorney waiting to be called in front of the judge when my attorney whispered to me that he couldn't go through with it and got up and left the court room. Shocked and bewildered, I followed him out. It turned out that my father had been to see him that morning. What ensued between them my attorney never said, but he effectively removed himself from my divorce proceedings. So I started the whole thing over again.

I never questioned the ways in which my life was controlled. I never asked my father why he did what he did—ever—about anything. From many years later I look back in amazement at my unconscious and complete compliance to the reality created within my family. I was the caregiver for my four younger brothers, the housecleaner, the dutiful daughter who never ever had a thought or an inclination of her own. Before the emergence of my adolescent self, which was the first part of me to have some continuity through time, I remember only one moment of defiance. I was five, perhaps six years old; it was in England and I was out for dinner in a restaurant with my family and some friends of my parents. I was having an amazing and wonderful time. I was "out." I'd never seen or felt anything like it. Then my brother began to misbehave and I was told to take him to the car and stay with him. I remember the shocking power of "No" coming out of my small being. I wanted to stay. It was freedom. And my five-year-old self wielded it with a five-year-old vengeance. I loved being in that restaurant where there were other people. I could sense a normal world, a world of people engaging with one another, the sound of talking back and forth and over one another. There was ease and safety in that room and I wanted to stay right there in the middle of it. I couldn't, of course. My brother and I were carried out to the car and I could feel what was to come.

There really was no childhood in my childhood. In England, I was in some kind of training school, maybe for days, weeks at a time. I was getting electric shocks. I was an experiment. In piecing it all together, at first I assumed it was simply to do with polio experimentation on the severed nerve in my arm. But because I was also made into a small sexual object, obliterating my memory through shock treatment was most convenient. And I was a mind-control experiment. But there was also something else going on, something inside me that recognized that restaurant and my defiant "No" as the divine light of freedom. That defiant little girl who knew "No" was real. It took me a long time, but I have come to love her with great passion and admiration.

Adolescence brought with it some wanting but it could only happen in secret. And when it did, like the dream of going to college, I acted secretly. And I never questioned this either. When I told my parents that I had been accepted at a small college a few hundred miles away, in central Washington, they simply said no, I couldn't go. Then they said I could instead go to another university, the University of Washington, because it was closer. My father made a big show of going to see the admissions officer then reported back that because of my schooling in Canada I was ineligible to go to the university. I hid my heartbreak and never questioned the information.

This might be the most impossible thing to communicate about my story. I had no mind of my own—literally. There was no questioning out loud and there was no questioning inside my mind. It was a mind of pure obedience. My world was controlled and my mind was controlled. But what couldn't be controlled was something that runs deeper than mind—grief. When my infant son died, I was propelled into a grief that poured out of my body. And this bodily grieving began to put a crack in the dam of control that had been my life.

In grieving I began to feel a small part of my real self, and a heartbeat of entitlement. It was this that aroused the small barely breathing desire in me to go to school and take art classes. We had just returned from our two years at Fort Dix and we moved into a neighborhood where there were families with small children, women who were educated, and couples who communicated. I was a stay-at-home mom. The incipient madness that was my breakdown after Colin was born hovered around my edges. I took art classes because they were "frivolous" and non-threatening to the circumstances prescribed for me. But those art classes introduced me to the freedom in art and in the life of an artist. The hidden seeds of my self felt the ray of light that began to lead my way. That moment, when Paul Havas stepped into that classroom, wielding a disheveled appearance and an ironic sense of humor was like being back in that restaurant so many years ago. It was freedom. Those art classes became the foundation of my future.

When Buddhism took my hand it was a convergence zone: Paul Havas got me to Rexroth and Zen which got me to Kerouac and Ginsberg and Snyder and the politics and poetics of Zen rage. Art got me to the Seattle Art Museum, where the Asian collection led me to buy a poster of the famous brush and ink painting of Bodhidharma descending the mountain. The aesthetics of Zen, the space between things, the orderliness, the understatement, the simple being-ness and the empty grace of both Zen art and writing appealed to me in ways I was a long time from recognizing. And that is what defines a spiritual path; it is a path we walk long before recognizing it. It's why I'm here, in India, nearly forty years later.

Two

I have no idea what time it is when I wake up in Majnu-ka-Tilla but Thrinley's already up and investigating.

"There's water all over the bathroom floor," she says. "I wonder if we should tell someone."

Upon examination of the various drains and faucets, pipes and other plumbing contrivances, it appears that the water on the bathroom floor is where it's supposed to be. We decide not to tell anyone and to go and have breakfast instead. And perhaps we should register. But first maybe we should count our money.

At the airport, during the long ominous wait for our luggage, I had spied a money changing operation. We'd each changed $450 of traveler's checks into rupees, resulting in a wad too thick to count in the condition we were in. Upon waking, and with a semblance of common-sense restored, we realize how totally stupid we'd been. Before we even get our teeth brushed, the count is underway; after each reaching the 18,000 rupees mark we both relax. Close enough. Eighteen thousand of anything should last awhile.

When I was thirty-two, blind to my past and ignorant of my future, I faced my fear about money and asked my father for a loan. It was September, 1976; my birthday was in October. It seemed safe enough, and timely. Earlier in the summer I'd attended the writers' conference at Fort Worden in Port Townsend on Washington State's Olympic Peninsula. The poets in residence were Philip Levine, Kenneth Rexroth and Madeline DeFrees; Tom Robbins was there, too.

I made friends with Rexroth that summer; he was an irascible fellow well into his seventies, but he flirted like a teenager and was shameless about veering our affectionate goodbye hugs into attempts at sloppy and searching French kisses. I resisted in amusement; he would grin and bear it. Throughout the years that followed, even though he never got over his amorous inclinations towards me—and towards every other woman writer born and unborn—he never wavered from supporting what it was in me that made me a writer. During that summer workshop he listened to my poems as we sat on the beach. "Solitude," he told me. "They are all about solitude."

He told me something else that summer and his words rang with mystery and meaning: "The entire universe depends upon a monk meditating in silence and solitude on the top of a mountain." Rexroth knew Buddhism and its teachers. I had yet to meet a monk, any monk. It was poetry that took me by the hand in those days.

At that writing workshop, Rexroth and Levine both swept me away with their fierce politics of poetry. Levine laughed at himself a lot; he was also a caustic critic of pretension in poetry and recognized it right away when he heard it. Rexroth held nothing back; he hissed loudly during a reading by a Canadian poet whom he thought wrote in error about the Japanese in the Second World War.

I got to be good friends with Kenneth and his wife, Carol Tinker, whose love and loyalty for him knew no bounds. I'd visit them in Santa Barbara and stay in their library, a separate building out behind their house, where I would sit in tears at the beauty of so many books and so much love for the written word. Kenneth Rexroth's poems were an invocation to both revolution and reverence. His very presence was a daunting dance of brilliance that knew no bounds. Years later, I recognized how his ferocious love of language, of the written word, of nature, of the redemption that was art, all conspired to keep me alive. Years later, I would also recognize the facility of my "front system," the vital and vivacious parts of me that were "out" in those years, engaging with the power of poetry, celebrating the freedom of poets, and searching out the promise of the written word.

But after that first summer poetry workshop, it was Philip Levine who would be teaching at the University of Cincinnati. And if I could get myself there, he said I could sit in his classes for free. This is why I was asking my father for something for the first time in my life—a loan of a hundred dollars to enable me to buy a round-trip plane ticket to a poetry workshop.

When he said "no," the spinning despair went deeper even than the fear. It was still eight years before collapse completely took me over, ten years before I began to remember, but the heart of memory takes many forms. An anguished irreparable grief is a body memory of enormous, articulate proportion.

Much later, after many years of therapy, I could put words to that experience. It was the beginning of breakthrough. I had wanted something and I had asked for it—from the very man who made sure I would never ever ask for anything. And even though he said "no," I had wanted something, I had asked. I had begun to break the code. I also found a way to get to that workshop in Cincinnati and the poetry of Philip Levine became a lifelong friend, "where angels come toward us without laughter, without tears."

Now I'm in India with 18,000 rupees piled high on my bed. I am thrilled and can hardly wait to go outside, to see things, to feel however it is India feels, to hear it, to taste it. So after not showering because we can't figure out how, Thrinley and I go downstairs to find breakfast. A young Tibetan woman is behind the desk intently looking at the computer. She is dressed in a traditional chuba, a colorful Tibetan dress that wraps around her body and is long to the ground. She is playing computer solitaire and she laughs with us when we notice.

Our room is 250 rupees per night, which translates to about five dollars. No payment is required ahead of time, nor will payment by credit card be accepted. We are, however, asked to produce our passports and the young woman records all the necessary information in a large ledger.

During this transaction, we notice that the guest house has a restaurant and we head there for breakfast. And in this small Tibetan owned and operated guest house in the midst of Old Delhi, I get my first glimpse of old colonialism. The restaurant has a very high ceiling and there's a small balcony, piano-shaped, curving gracefully out over the dining-room. It has a wooden balustrade and the look is elegant and reminiscent of a smoky lounge full of careless, carefree Brits, the men dressed in khaki and the women in gossamer white. All wiling away a hot Indian summer's eve to the tune of something that is equally as careless and carefree. I can feel it, as though it's still going on.

On our table are some vivid red and yellow roses; small drops of dew are sprinkled across their petals. Until I touch the flowers, I think they are real. Until I touch the dew, I think it is real, too, perhaps a little water sprinkled on for effect. But it's all plastic. I imagine an entire industry somewhere, where women drop plastic drops of dew onto plastic flowers. It seems like an act of tenderness in terrible times. A moment of mercy.

Our attendant, a young earnest Tibetan boy of about fourteen, brings us menus and paper and pencil. It seems we are to write down our own orders. We have pancakes and milk tea. Each swallow is an adventure; I am in India. I am slowly waking up to this astonishing adventure of being somewhere I have always wanted to go and was never able to ask. An immense feeling of freedom infuses my every bite and breath. I am hugely grateful to be here.

When we get out to Majnu-ka-Tilla's main street, there is no sign of last night's desolateness. Vendors, Indian and Tibetan, have set up their daily wares. Beautiful turquoise and orange and silver jewelry is arranged across makeshift tables along with brightly striped blankets and shawls, athletic shoes, prayer flags, bananas, backpacks, plastic flip-flops and T-shirts. There is a long wooden bench where old and young people drink chai and watch; a small band of shoe-shine boys ready to polish anything that moves; signs and announcements on walls, trees, and propped up against anything that remains stationary. And our first beggar. He is sitting at the end of the alley as it goes out to the street where we arrived only a few hours ago. He is looking for people coming in and looks surprised as we come up from the other direction. His smile is both pleading and accepting.

"No," says Thrinley sharply, more to me than to him. "We'll give him something just before we leave. Otherwise we'll be in trouble." She recounts her stories from her last trip to India, when she was mobbed whenever she gave anything.

By the time we finish walking the length of main street Majnu-ka-Tilla I am exhausted. So, too, is Thrinley. It is two o'clock in the afternoon and we go back to our room to rest before dinner.

It was "trouble with men" that first got me into therapy with Brian. I was forty years old and had been seduced by a younger man. It spun me into a maelstrom of feelings that gathered destructive force like an avalanche gathers snow. Although I'd "had sex", I'd never experienced passion. And it was this that blind-sided me. Many years later, I recognized that my life included the localized clitoral pleasure of sex going back to when I was a small child. But I had no language for the deep visceral feelings of sexual passion. I didn't know that my sexuality had been hijacked. I just knew sex. I knew orgasm as masturbation. I knew submission to sex. I knew the performance of sex. I didn't know that sexuality had joy and power and playfulness and abandonment and laughing. I didn't know love. I was living inside a self-created world that had no way of recognizing my authentic sexual self.

Within the vast community of pedophiles there is this self-congratulatory philosophy that children enjoy sex. As a child who was trained to enjoy sex from a very young age, I can also testify that it destroys sexuality. Right after it destroys the soul.

The man who introduced me to this place called passion was thirty years old. David was a theatre artist with a brilliant mind and a tortured and endearing vulnerability. His seductive urgency was at first entertaining as well as rather preposterous. He was ten years younger than I. His pursuit was hot, playful and romantic. I was astounded, flattered, and then swamped by the power and grief of erupting sex. I had yet to know my history, but it wielded me like a breath in the wind. I was blown apart. I was also involved with another man, who just happened to be married.

The journal entry from the day I called for help reads:

"I'm standing in the middle of my kitchen early in the morning sometime between Christmas and New Years, 1985. All I know is I'm in trouble. Dead. I can't find myself."

There was nothing romantic about my feelings. I wanted to kill myself. I remember stiffness to my perceptions—as though I was seeing each second of time as if it was the face of a playing card that would be turned face down and never looked at again. I was making myself up from second to second and I could no longer keep up.

I remember that day with essential clarity. The fear and depression were so immobilizing that I literally could barely move. I stood alone in that kitchen and knew I needed help. Trouble with men. Okay. This time better get a male therapist. Okay. Who did I know who'd had a male therapist who had helped quickly and efficiently? An old friend from years ago came to mind. He'd seen somebody and in a fairly short time seemed to be happily on with his life. He'd told me his therapist's name but I'd forgotten and I was too paralyzed to call and ask my friend who it was. To do so would be to acknowledge that I was in trouble and I could face neither the sympathy nor the empathy.

I simply hoped the therapist's name would appear in my mind. All day I hoped. My body moving as though it was alive and all the time I was dead cold watching the phenomena of intentions without meaning. I'd just survived another Christmas with my family. This time, however, without my son who had graduated from high school and moved to California. I'd moved off the island, where we'd lived for so long, to Seattle where I had an administrative job at a hospital. I was sharing a house with a physician friend who was always working. I was writing a new play about deaf culture and the holocaust and I was involved with two men at once. One fit me into his life subversively and sporadically. The other one loved me over the edge of the abyss. Deep inside, I was aware that I was psychically and psychologically on the skids; but even the aware bits and pieces of me were paralyzed. There was no-one to reach out and no-one to reach out to. I wanted a quick-fix stranger to zap me with some tough-love magic wand and get me back on my feet, in the saddle, on track, or wherever the hell it was I was supposed to actually "be." But I wasn't capable of making a phone call.

When, after hours of immobilizing fear, the recommended therapist's name surfaced to recognition, my fingers did some quick walking. He was, of course, fully booked. Could I wait a month or two? "No," I told the woman. She gave me the name of another therapist in the building. "Is he good?" I asked. She said something inane and professional.

When I finally made that fateful call and made an appointment, I had no idea that my life as I had known it would never be again.

Brian was tall and handsome. His manner was gentle and his spirit quietly present. "Oh no," I thought, immediately upon meeting him. "Just what I need: another attractive man." But my pain knew better. I started to cry minutes into our first session. And it was only the beginning. There would be no quick fix. There would be nothing as simple as "trouble with men." I was about to go over the falls and it would be a twenty-year drop.

The night after that first therapy session I had a dream:

I'm at a large and elegant gathering in a yard. Someone drops an ash and a small fire starts. Someone else puts the fire out but it jumps up again around its edges. I get a hose and stretch it out and spray the fire from a distance. It seems to work. Then the fire goes underground. It travels along a duct to a coffin area where it bursts into flames. Suddenly the flames are jumping from place to place. I try to get help but no-one takes me seriously. There is something evil about some of the participants. A sense that they have something invested in the existence of the fire. I go to look in the coffin area and find it full of flame and the worst, the most vicious, primeval creatures. An existence of utter evil. I am terrified. I make a decision to call the fire department even though the atmosphere among those present is a "macho" one. They think they can take care of it. But I know they can't. I race into the house and the electricity is out. I stumble to find a telephone and take it to a room where there is privacy. I'm afraid that if someone hears me calling for help they won't let me call. In the dark I find the outlet for the phone. There's a small girl huddled in the corner. I call 911 and tell them there's a fire and give them my address. Please, come quickly. Suddenly I'm on the fire engine. It has arrived. I turn my head and there is a smiling fireman. I realize help had already been on the way and soon my own request for help will also arrive. I try to cancel the order but realize that the extra help will be fine. I watch from a distance as the work is carried out. A lot of techniques are being used. I am reassured. I wake up.

I knew the dream was of great significance. I had no idea why.

During that first year of therapy I cried with such desolation that I thought there could be no greater grief. The sobbing was uncontrollable and wracking. I'd come out of Brian's office with eyes swollen shut, my chest aching and hollow, my entire body hurting from the mysterious and profound grieving that began to mark my life. Although the "trouble with men" continued, it was obvious even to me that the grief was out of context. Its enormity was overwhelming.

My love thrilling affair with the "younger man" became an agony of anguish. He was the first man with whom I ever experienced a kind of sexual ecstasy—a loss of control. It triggered thundering fear, burning shame and a regression into infantile loss and abandonment. From this distance, looking back I see a woman unmoored. I had raised my son as a single parent and now he had finished high school and moved to California to go to college. My day-to-day role as a mother had moved with him. It was a role that had anchored me to life, to being somebody. Then I fell head-over-psyche into passion. As my very own deep sexuality was aroused, it brought with it all the feelings of terror, degradation and humiliation that had marked my childhood. The arising of something pure in me gave rise to all that was defiled. These are understandings that I came to only years later, when sex was no longer the issue.

Our room in the Himalayan House is spare; our two small beds are separated by a table with no light and when I wake up it is very dark and very quiet. This was supposed to be a nap; but now I don't know what to call it. I still have on my clothes so I don't feel like I've officially gone to bed yet. I don't know the time so I don't know if I should still be tired or not. I don't even know what day it is. My mind flits around the edges of time and the rest of me feels all cozy with anticipation. There is something delicious about this feeling of being suspended on the edge of an adventure, of not knowing what lies ahead. Most of my travels have had purposes: to visit someone, or to write about someplace, or to see a landscape I love. But I have no agenda on this trip and no expectations I can name.

Suddenly, I hear Thrinley rustling around.

"You awake?" I ask.

"Yes," she says. "Do you mind if I turn on the light?"

It's eight o'clock—in the evening.

Six hours is a weird amount of time for a nap so we decide to go to bed for real. I get into my pajamas, think about brushing my teeth, and pop an acetaminophen-P.M. to counteract my growing enthusiasm for this venture. I'm back asleep before the pill goes into effect.

It's about three in the morning when next I wake. Armed with a flashlight, I duck under the covers to read my mystery. Thrinley surfaces about six. We evaluate the past sixteen hours and decide we've had enough sleep. Then she asks if I mind if she does her Buddhist practice. Nope, I say; and lie back down for a little rest.

It is comforting to hear Thrinley recite her prayers. Some are in Tibetan and the sound of certain syllables repeated over and over in a soft murmur is soothing. Other phrases, in English, catch my surfacing attention. Because I was raised with the lying violation of the spoken word, letting myself be soothed by sounds is a really big deal. I never trust the kind word because as a kid it was always a trick. This has caused me a few problems throughout my adult life. Recently, a friend who has known me through it all asked if I'd learned to tell the difference between real kindness and trick kindness. I had to answer, "No." But I'm not sure if this is really true.

There is kindness that manipulates, sometimes in innocence. There is kindness that condescends, kindness that dismisses, kindness that is convenient, kindness that is careless, kindness that precedes a kill. In my world, kindness is complicated. But I know Thrinley. We have been friends for a long time. There isn't anything complicated about the sound of her voice rippling with prayers. I wish mine could do the same.

Instead I read to myself the poem from the current *New Yorker* that I'd brought aboard in Seattle. At 35,000 feet, somewhere after leaving Korea, the poem had jumped out at me as though it knew I was there. I tore it out and tucked it into my address book. Every line spoke to this trip. It's a poem that unfolds into pain and pleasure in Bombay and Calcutta and ultimately into the fabric of grief and joy that make up our lives. It has a title: *A Brief for the Defense*, and an author, Jack Gilbert. If the Dalai Lama won't have me, maybe Jack Gilbert will, I'm thinking, as I read it over and over.

Then, just as we are getting ready to leave our room and go for breakfast, I ask Thrinley if she would like to hear it. It's an offering, I say. Kind of like a prayer. I want to contribute something, too.

> *Sorrow everywhere. Slaughter everywhere. If babies*
> *are not starving someplace, they are starving*
> *somewhere else. With flies in their nostrils.*
> *But we enjoy our lives because that's what God wants.*
> *Otherwise the mornings before summer dawn would not*
> *be made so fine. The Bengal tiger would not*
> *be fashioned so miraculously well.*

It is the raging of opposites that keeps us alive. The shock of what shames us and inspires us, all together in these few lines being read aloud in this room without windows. There is always snot on some wall somewhere; and there is always the grace of being here, too.

> *The poor women*
> *at the fountain are laughing together between*
> *the suffering they have known and the awfulness*
> *in their future, smiling and laughing while somebody*
> *in the village is very sick. There is laughter*
> *every day in the terrible streets of Calcutta,*
> *and the women laugh in the cages in Bombay.*

It is laughter that saves us. And I think of all the years in which I could not laugh, even when I did. And I wonder if true laughter can only come when the suffering and the awfulness is together, in communion one with one another, the shared fate, the shared laughter. If only I could have shared, I am thinking as the words rise from the page.

> *If we deny our happiness, resist our satisfaction,*
> *we lessen the importance of their deprivation.*
> *We must risk delight. We can do without pleasure,*
> *but not delight. Not enjoyment. We must have*

the stubbornness to accept our gladness in the ruthless
furnace of this world. To make injustice the only
measure of our attention is to praise the Devil.

This is where the poem grabs me by my spiritual short hairs and doesn't let me go. *"To make injustice the only measure of our attention is to praise the devil."* Ha! I am drawn and quartered by these words. Injustice has been my life's blood. I have seen it everywhere and all the time have I lessened the importance of suffering by immersing myself in the importance of suffering? Have I been praising the Devil? Have I undermined the importance of the suffering of the women in cages in Calcutta by neglecting delight? And I see, in this blinding instant, that it is not my suffering that weights me with meaning; it is delight in life that is the final revenge.

If the locomotive of the Lord runs us down,
we should give thanks that the end had magnitude.
We must admit there will be music despite everything.

The locomotive of the Lord. It's an image that defies a Christianity too-long restrained by passivity and control. It's a fierce Lord, a Lord of action and passion, unswerving with commitment and vigor. How can we end our lives with magnitude? And can we die knowing there will be music, whether we hear it or not.

We stand at the prow again of a small ship
anchored late at night in the tiny port
looking over to the sleeping island: the waterfront
is three shuttered cafes and one naked light burning.
To hear the faint sound of oars in the silence as a rowboat
comes slowly out and then goes back is truly worth
all the years of sorrow that are to come

This is where the poem becomes a mystery. I have no idea what Jack Gilbert really means. It feels personal, as though written for a loved one just met, under a circumstance of silence and watching. To be present just once as oars dip into the sound of water, to be fully present in time, fully aware of everything there is, is worth all the pain of the future. And I suddenly feel something else. To be fully present, just once, is worth all the pain of the past.

I once lived on an island to which I had to row. And I've lived on islands requiring ferries for more than 30 years. An island is safe. And sometimes it is a prison. This poem came to me by accident, 35,000 feet over the Pacific Ocean, on the way to this place, India, and in its lines rests my entire life. I read it out loud, twice, like Robert Bly does when he reads his poems.

Over tea and toast, Thrinley outlines our tasks for the morning; most of all they involve lightening the mother load of all suitcases. Thrinley has brought stuff from people in the U.S. to be delivered to Tibetan friends and relations in India. Our first stop is right here in Majnu-ka-Tilla, where someone knows someone who might be going to Lumbini in Nepal where someone else lives. Because of the Chinese invasion of their country, Tibetans live in exile all over the world. They network in all sorts of practical ways, as well as in a seamless spirituality symbolized by the man I love, His Holiness the Dalai Lama.

I know I have no business loving the Dalai Lama. He belongs to the Tibetan people and I am nothing but a half-baked Buddhist white woman haunted by all the confusion of being a quasi-Christian in a born-again world. I don't belong anywhere and I know it. But if I were to belong somewhere, it would be in the lap of the Dalai Lama, where I know all my emotional anguish, psychic distress and spiritual confusion could come to rest—at least for a minute.

My first awareness of His Holiness the Dalai Lama was in 1959, the year he escaped from Tibet. I remember hearing about his journey, his youth, and his burden. I remember because it was not long after the birth of my remembering self. I was fourteen. I had started to know where I slept, where I went to school, that I had brothers, that I had parents, that I existed. Before that, the landscape of my memory is barren, littered only with fragments of place and possibility. There is no "I" that can remember where I slept, that knows who I was for the first thirteen years of my life.

The Dalai Lama's escape to India happened when I was still living in Canada and it was widely covered in the media. It was his youth, his escape and his responsibility in exile that made him my friend. At that time I knew nothing about Buddhism. It was, in fact, another ten years before I knew its name and all these years later I am still learning about it. Buddhism is named a religion but is more often known by me as a philosophy, a psychology, a science of mind.

Buddhism has as many faces as Christianity; and like Christianity, it offers itself ready-to-wear by anyone with a half-dressed inclination in its direction. This means that the messenger, no matter how well-dressed, is often mistaken for the message. This is a dilemma shared by all the great traditions in religion. They begin in the pure land of perfection, where compassion reigns for all beings, born, hatched or planted. Life is an unfolding gift to be treasured and protected. We are to love one another, and treat one another accordingly. The basics. Then the human mind gets involved and it become treacherous with conditions, either-ors, and ways of being.

Christianity comes in many guises. More than 1200 denominations, according to one reputable website. They fall under five branches: Roman Catholicism, Eastern Orthodoxy, Oriental Orthodox and Assyrian Churches, Protestantism, and—the ubiquitous Others. The breakdown continues: Jehovah's Witness, Mormon, Southern Baptist, conservative, mainline, liberal, Lutheran, Adventist, Episcopalian and on and on. Globally, it is estimated that there are some 34,000 different Christian groups all huddled under the big umbrella of Christianity, all interpreting the teachings of Christ in their own way.

Buddhism has its own big umbrella, too. Theravadan, Mahayana, Tibetan, Zen, they each break down into various schools and approaches and interpret the teachings of Buddha in different ways. Tibetan Buddhism itself comes in four different schools: Gelugpa, Nyigma, Sakya and Kagyu; the teachings are further delineated into such categories as the ten excellent qualities, the five blissful clans, the ten outer and the ten inner abilities, the eighteen heavens, the five certainties, the six kinds of beings, the eight worldly concerns and on, and on. Like Christianity, Buddhism has a very big vocabulary; they both lend themselves to lots of wordplay.

Tibetan Buddhism is also big into hats. The Sakya school is known as the red hats; the Gelukpa as the yellow hats. The Dalai Lama is a Yellow Hat; the Sakya Trizin, to whose birthday party we will go at the end of our trip, is a Red Hat. Today, it is off to the Sakya Guest House we go in our efforts to deliver the goods.

When we get there, and the Tibetan fellow who answers the door gets the gist of our visit, we are greeted like long lost relatives. Yes, he knows the recipient of the goods. Yes, he is thrilled to facilitate the delivery to Nepal. Yes, we must come for lunch. It turns out that today is the big opening of the new Sakya Guest House—we are obviously now in the old one—and dignitaries are coming to cast prayers upon the premises. We must be there, he says. We must.

We'll see, we say. We'll see.

Sometime this afternoon, Pema is coming to take us out on the town. Tomorrow we leave for Rajpur. Our time in Majnu-ka-Tilla is short. The sights, sounds, smells and feel of this place have my senses aroused and I want time to explore before we leave. This is one way in which I am not a good traveler; I fall in love with where I am and want to stay there. As we leave the old Sakya Guest House, I mutter my reservations to Thrinley.

"I might not want to go to lunch," I say. "But you can."

"I'll see," she says.

It's always tricky traveling with a friend. We think we know one another and find out otherwise; or we think we know ourselves and find out otherwise. No matter what, traveling is a learning curve, often in several directions at once.

I remember a trip to Wales a few years ago. I was on assignment for the travel magazine I worked for; it was also a pilgrimage home. I was born in Wales and I wanted to see where. I also wanted to get a copy of my birth certificate. My parents had always claimed they didn't have a copy and I held the deep fear that perhaps there wasn't one. I am a wreck about where I officially belong. Even armed with passport and "Green" card (it is now pink) I carry anxiety and fear in my bones that perhaps I don't exist. My friend, Martha, went to Wales with me and was there when we went to the records office and the woman happily handed me my birth certificate.

"Here you go, luvvie. Exciting, isn't it? You've come home."

I cried. Martha, who knew why I was there, cried, too.

We were the best of friends but on that trip, whenever we went off for long hikes along the Pembrokeshire Coast trail, she'd go one way and I'd go another. We'd arrange to meet back at the car, four or six or eight hours later. It was a way to refresh ourselves as well as our on-the-road relationship. Both of us liked to be alone.

I'm suspecting as much about Thrinley. In Wales, alone-time was easy to negotiate because the culture was familiar and the language shared; but here it's all different. Being alone in India is what everyone warns you about. So Thrinley and I wander the shops together, eyeing the colors of things, the textures and the odd assortment of goods. The Tibetan faces are open and welcoming, shy, too. It feels intimate to be here. As the prayer beads turn through fingers and the hush of "O Mani Padme Hum" is whispered under the breath, the inner world is made manifest. Our pace slows to that of our surroundings. It feels almost like a ritual walk, with room for thought and inner solitude. Perhaps this is what it will be like to be alone in India. When Thrinley and I get back to our guest house to meet Pema he's left word that he'll be late. It's after one o'clock and we're hungry so we decide to go and find the new Sakya Guest House, maybe there's still some lunch left.

The new Sakya House is so different from the old one that it's like some sort of paradigm shift. The big neon sign reads in big red letters, "New Sakya House, Restaurant and Shopping Mall." There are posters of glamorous women, a sign about a coming beauty parlor, and all indications of much to buy. It looks like a mini mall.

For some reason, all I can think is "Richard Gere." This is what happens when movie stars strut the path of Tibetan Buddhism, I think. Most uncharitable of me, I know. But I am not the Dalai Lama, I just happen to love him. Maybe I'd love Richard Gere, too, if he wore flip-flops to meet George W. Bush. Right now, however, all I see is Los Angeles glitz in the midst of Majnu-ka-Tilla. I have to laugh. Thrinley laughs, too. Nobody ever said it would be simple.

We climb up many flights of stairs until we get to the roof, where the luncheon festivities are in full swing. The rooftop has the look of a garden party: flowers and food under a billowing saffron tent; Tibetan and Indian people dressed in their most colorful finery; women in flowing saris and long dresses; men in tailored suits; monks in maroon robes. We are the only two Westerners.

One of the members of the welcoming committee tries to usher us to the front of the food line. This is way too embarrassing and we both demur. When we finally get to the food table, a lovely young Tibetan woman gives us a plate and some cutlery. My plate has a few drops of water on it and I notice each one. My fork, too, shows signs of a most recent washing. Thrinley and I have agreed on very few rules, but water is one of them.

When news of our trip to India reached our small community, the advice was forthcoming: Don't eat the food; don't drink the water; don't breathe the air. Our spiritual transformation would be complete; we'd be dead. We did, however, agree about the water and decided to avoid ingesting water from the tap, including brushing our teeth with it and eating fresh uncooked vegetables which might or might not have been washed in it. Now there's water out of the tap dripping on the plates and on the forks.

The mind can be a terrible thing. Suddenly I am in the throes of a plague full of possibilities. I'd had a pause or two at all the tea-drinking we'd done since arriving but rationalized it away because at some point there must've been a moment of boiling. And we all know boiling is bad for bacteria. When I'm being a Buddhist, I can accept the plague-full possibilities with equanimity. But after being a Buddhist for more than thirty years, one thing I do know: I am not a Buddhist very often. My mind invariably gets the better of me, especially when there is something to fear.

Thrinley's more practical. She surreptitiously digs into her bag and takes out two packages, each containing a small hand-sized antiseptic paper towel; she gives me one and wipes off her plate with the other. We do this while unceasingly looking up and around so that hopefully no-one will notice what our hands are doing. God forbid we should appear rude. Now all I have to do is eat the food.

There is an array of vegetables in an array of sauces, steamed breads, assorted salads, and a huge barrel of fine rice, all presented beautifully on decorated tables set out under the saffron tent. Whatever reservations Thrinley might have had about the evidence of tap water are not at all evident. She is eating with gusto; I pretend I am, too. But the drops of water, presumably out of the much-maligned tap, have ignited my intestinal paranoia. The food tastes delicious and my mind destroys every bite.

Suddenly, without a moment's notice, Thrinley is exchanging an excited greeting with someone she obviously knows and likes, which plunges me into a moment of profound disorientation. There are no old friends here; we're in India, for god's sake. But there's Tsering Dorje, and I know him, too. Some cosmic accident has found the three of us on the same rooftop on top of the New Sakya House in old Delhi on the same day in December, 2004.

More than ten years ago, Tsering Dorje was sent to our small island by Sakya Trizin to paint the thankas on the walls inside the shrine room at the gonpa. A thanka is a sacred painting depicting the various realms and realities of Tibetan Buddhism in which no reality is left unpainted. Heavenly landscapes, hell realms, beatific buddhas, power buddhas, ferocious animal-like deities, consorting males and females, serene and wild animals are all rendered in meticulous and colorful intricacy. Buddhism is supposed to be a religion without a deity but the Tibetan version has a deity for every occasion. This has always amazed me; how did I ever get from Zen Buddhism, which has all the aesthetic intricacy of a baked potato, to Tibetan Buddhism, which unabashedly celebrates an opulence of color and design in endless repertoire of ritual and imagery.

I don't do ritual because ritual was done to me; I don't do secrets because secrets were done to me; I don't do power because power was done to me. Secrets, rituals and power are part of Tibetan Buddhism in ways that I refuse to let become familiar. We're on a need-to-know basis and I don't need to know. This doesn't mean that ten years ago, when Tsering Dorje asked me to wield a paintbrush and help paint the outside borders of the gonpa that I refused to do it. I painted away with great enthusiasm and loved every minute. I loved the fact that a Tibetan thanka painter was sent from India to paint the walls of a small gonpa on a small island in the far reaches of the northwest corner of the United States. It meant something; and when meaningless is the ground of one's being, such brash and unequivocal gestures of meaning are great beacons of existential delight. Wielding a paintbrush gave me yet another opportunity to paint myself back to life.

So now here we are on the rooftop in a frenzy of excited recognition. Tsering Dorje, who lives at the Sakya Podung (Palace) in Rajpur, about ten hours drive north, is here for the big opening. We're here by accident, even though Thrinley planned to see him in a few days anyways. Time just did a shortcut.

We are a bit late getting back to the guest house to meet Pema; but so is he. While we wait, I scan all the potential symptoms of dysentery that might be arising from inside my body. This sudden preoccupation of my mind is unnerving. Because I don't believe in doctors, I've never really believed in germs. "Everybody gets sick in India," I was told over and over. But I don't want to get sick in India. It would be a colossal waste of time. It would also be life-threatening. My fear of doctors, born out of my childhood, knows no bounds; I would die of fright long before I'd die of diarrhea.

In the midst of this intestinal reverie, the phone rings to announce that Pema is in the lobby. Today he's wearing a crisply ironed royal blue shirt of some very high quality cotton. His sleeves are folded up just so. There is something very cosmopolitan about this fellow; he knows whereof he thinks.

Pema leads us out to the street to the tuk-tuks, which are peculiarly modified three-wheelers with a small covered seating area in the back. He enters into colorful negotiation with several drivers about where we're going, who will take us there, and how much it will cost. Pretty soon we are careening our way through streets that are a mere suggestion of possibility. As the near misses mount up, I start to feel slightly hysterical; but it's not an unpleasant feeling. In fact, it feels as though I am about to burst out into uncontrollable laughter. I am letting go because my life depends upon it; I am having a moment of Buddhism. If I don't, I will die of shock. I am here and now on the mad streets of Delhi and there is no other way to get there, wherever it is we are going.

There is nothing but now—it's the message we are always left with when Buddhism has its way with us. And now does not exist. That's the next part, where the great emptiness raises its non-existent head. Emptiness is a big deal in Buddhism and what it really means is that everything is too full to count. The emptiness part has to do with independent meaning; everything is empty of independent meaning because it all depends on something. These words depend upon your reading, the book depends upon a tree, the tree depends upon the earth, the earth depends upon the sky, the sky depends upon space, and on and on. Nothing exists in and of itself all by itself. Buddhist books are full of writing about emptiness. Emptiness is overflowing with rhetoric. Describing emptiness is the ultimate koan. It's empty of its own meaning. It is, because it isn't.

As a kid who spent a lot of time suspended in timeless terror I had a lot of experience with emptiness. I learned that my mind can just as easily wrap itself around what is not happening. I learned that I can forget things even before they happen, as well as while they are happening and after they have happened. I learned about the great emptiness of forgetting. It served me well.

Right now, driving through Delhi is delivering me to the edges of my own mind and it is much more fun than rage and regret. It is an exhilarating experience, like being at sea in a hurricane. There's great beauty in the nature of it all; at the same time it renders life very precarious. And there is great beauty in the streets of Delhi, an uprising of life, a chaos of creativity that makes room for everyone all at once. It is dazzling to behold: every vendor with their few square feet of organized capitalism at their feet, be it selling food, shoes, tools, silks, motorcycle parts, gold and diamonds, strung-up chickens, Hindu icons, haircuts and shaves, ear-wax cleaning, glasses of hot sweet chai, along with every other product and service required to get through a day and a life. Pema is on the lookout for shock absorbers for his car and sure enough, we ride by a row of street-level stalls, all selling shock absorbers. He takes note for further reference and on we go. Our destination is the Red Fort, in daylight.

I'm not usually drawn to tourist attractions—not because of the attractions but because of the tourists—and I probably wouldn't have gone out of my way to go to the Red Fort. As usual, my expectations are thwarted. I'm glad I'm here and grateful to Pema for leading the way. The Red Fort is impressive, not only because of its great red sandstone spires and turrets but because of its great calm in the heart of the chaos that is Delhi. It is a huge collective breath of relief to walk through the gates, past the small tourist shops with their accompanying hawkers and into the old space where elegant lawns and old stone lattice walls and arches preserve time and space.

I've felt this before, at Tintern Abbey in Wales, where grass grows under ancient arches and where the outside and the inside come together in grace; at St. Peter's Basilica in Paris, where height takes on a whole new meaning, shaping and enclosing the sacred space of possibility; in ancient dwellings in the southwest United States where the spirit is caught up in the landscape of old adobe. These places tell us where we are from, what we loved, and the treasured ways we re-constructed the sacred in both building and not-building. I think of our rapacious ways with the land these days, and wonder what exactly it is we are saying about what we love to those who will come beyond us.

Then we head off for dinner. Pema expresses his enthusiasm about the restaurant we are going to and given his sophistication I am expecting a place with a door and some windows. But the restaurant opens right onto an alley with no particular indication of where the dining area begins and the alley ends. The tables are unadorned, the floors dirty, the décor missing. We are in a restaurant called "Dysentry Meets Malaria," I am thinking, my faith in Pema wavering just for an instant.

The place must be all about food because there is no service. We find our way to a messy table towards the back wall. A man shows up and wipes off the table without even noticing we are there. Pema acts as though it's all business as usual and busies himself with the menu. Looking around I notice a sign that says we are at Karim's, and that the place was born in 1913. Nothing much has changed since, including the waiters and their aprons. My imperious Western standards are at full throttle and I feel like throttling myself. I wonder if Pema is reading my unpleasant mind as he peruses the menu.

Some teachers teach us all we need to know without teaching us a thing. Somehow being with Pema falls into this category. He is from Bhutan; he speaks fluent Tibetan, Hindi, English, and is learning French. There is something slightly surreptitious about him, as though he's leading us very carefully along a chosen path and is watching to see how we choose our way. But he gives no indication of watching; his attention is always forward and right now. So he informs us about the food on the menu and we tell him to order away. It's all Hindi to us.

And so unfolds a delicious meal. It really is all about the food, most of which is prepared in outdoor kitchen areas in the alley where the breads are freshly made by men squatting up on stone platforms kneading a variety of *nan*, *roti* and *paratha* fresh for the meal. In another corner of the alley, strips of chicken are pounded to the thinness of paper, stretched over hot rods, and barbecued to perfection. We have tandoori chicken, too; its slow clay-baked flavor unequaled in my memory. The dal, which is a soupy mix of lentils, has strips of ginger and a taste buttery and delicious. There is a creamed vegetable dish, spinach maybe, with a square of white buttery cheese in the middle. And meat, mutton I think, wrapped in thin, almost translucent pastry and deep-fried to perfection. The food is not made to look pretty and so each bite carries with it the taste of surprising beauty. The flavors are delicate and intricate; it is simply a wonderful meal.

To go with our auspicious repast, we drink Coke. I'm sure it was freshly produced but it was bottled in what looks like a collector's item vintage. The label is barely readable and the glass is scratched and opaque. To prove its viability as a live drink, the waiter pops the lids off at the table and the Cokes fizz accordingly. My activist life flashes before my eyes. The Coca Cola Company is destroying the lives of many people in this country because its bottling factories drain the water tables, denying farmers the water they need to grow food and villagers the water they need to drink. Back home I get emails from "Stop Killer Coke;" in India I am drinking it.

It's dark when we leave Karim's. Pema retraces our steps to the bicycle rickshaw corner and bargains us a ride to the tuk-tuk corner. His confidence is complete, even when negotiating his way through the chaos on the streets. Jesus may have walked on water but Pema cuts through traffic like it is butter; and he never looks back. He trusts that we're behind him, trusting blindly as we go.

When we get back to Majnu-ka-Tilla, the alleys are quiet and peaceful. We say goodbye to Pema and give him a card of thanks. Tomorrow we leave for Rajpur and I feel sad already. Getting to know Delhi would be a triumph of no small proportion. A pilgrimage, not into the aesthetics of the spirit, but into the heart and soul of humanity.

There are all kinds of clinical terms and theories about what happens when we suffer abuse at the hands of those whom we are supposed to trust the most. My shelves are full of books chronicling every detail of recovery and lack of recovery known in the analytical language of psychology. But I've never seen a chapter on the broken heart.

In his poem, *The Descent*, William Carlos Williams writes:

*For what we cannot accomplish, what
is denied to love,
what we have lost in the anticipation—
a descent follows,
endless and indestructible*

It is a poem I have returned to for thirty years, long before I understood why. It opens with my life:

*The descent beckons
as the ascent beckoned.
Memory is a kind
of accomplishment,
a sort of renewal
even
an initiation, since the spaces it opens are new places
inhabited by hordes
heretofore unrealized*

Of everything I have lost to my childhood trauma, losing love hurt the most. It was a descent endless and indestructible. It was also a secret. Nobody ever knew. My loves happened beyond my reach, their possibility a myth, the wanting a curse, the attaining a tragedy. Love was soaked with loss before it even began. I turned away from the promise of passion and love just as it became possible. Because I wanted it so much. And wanting was the end of possibility. Over the years I have thought about this a lot.

I know what "real" love means. It means to love our children most of all. And it takes a lot of different forms: like caring and worrying and cooking and attending and listening and hearing and sacrificing and laughing and crying and always, always loving. I recognize that feeling for my son, even as I know I failed him. I remember his joys and how happy they made me feel; how proud I was at his accomplishments—and still am; I remember my heartbreak at his losses—be they big or small; I remember his first day at school and how I cried as he went off on his own; I remember when he didn't make the soccer team and was all alone while I was off with one of my plays in San Francisco; I remember watching him in his sleep his whole life, marveling at his presence; I remember knowing how I could never knowingly hurt him, even when I was a young Army wife, disintegrating into fear and despair. As unconscious as I was about my life, I knew I loved my son. But how did I know? When I, myself, had never been loved by my mother? The answer is many years long.

It was my two sons, Colin and Thomas, who brought me alive. When Colin was born there was a joy and fulfillment that cast in dark shadow the indifference of my own mother. When I collapsed into fear after his birth, it was born out of the love that had never been felt for me. When my son Thomas died, it brought me to grief. Uncontrollable love and uncontrollable grief came out of the parts of me that I could not control and could not be controlled. My two sons were the beginning of my freedom. These were realizations that came long after love and grief had their way with me. In the meantime, I had my mother.

The Dalai Lama has a refrain that comes up in his teachings. It says that everybody has, at one time or another, been our mother; so we should treat them accordingly. This is a test I fail, an image that I cannot use to anyone's benefit. Turning away from my mother and father when I was 42 years old meant turning towards life. It seemed like a decision made *for* me. Certainly not by Brian, who was meticulous with not giving advice, but by an inner guide, an old wisdom, a guiding soul. He sighs inside as I say this. (He is a "he.")

"When will you ever get it?" he wants to know. He's a reclusive guide, tired of being there for me. Resigned. But he wants me to make it. He wants me to live.

How do we know when we are not loved as children? For me, it took a very long time. Only after years of being unable to *feel* loved did it begin to occur to me that I was *incapable* of feeling loved. That something about it held such visceral terror that even when it was there, clearly and completely, I could not, would not, feel it.

"You must have been loved by someone somewhere," Brian said to me many years after our work had started. He'd seen me through so much; he trusted me.

I had an insight about this when I'd gone on my private pilgrimage to Wales to find out if I'd been born. During my few weeks there, I felt as though I was in a culture of love. "Luvvie" this and "luvvie" that, was part of the national lexicon. It was a language of love, of curiosity, of caring. For those few weeks I was in a culture of affection and it felt familiar. Later I realized that it had been part of my childhood. So, too, had the love of my Welsh aunts, my mother's younger sisters. The youngest was only fifteen when I was born. She liked to comb my hair when I was little and she did it with gentleness and affection. And my jolly Welsh grandmother was warm and embracing. It was years after writing the play, *Ten Minutes for Twenty-Five Cents*, when I realized that I had named the loving, wise, blind woman in that play, "Lottie," after my grandmother. Love, too, had been forgotten.

Like memory, reality shifts its shape to accommodate life. This is another reason I love Buddhism. It doesn't believe in any one reality; it knows the mind as a pure stream of consciousness upon which reality plays out but is never really "real." It goes beyond the mind as we know it to a place of timeless perfection. *Om Mani Padme Hum*, chant the Tibetans. It translates reluctantly into English: The jewel nestled in the heart of the lotus; the perfection found in the heart of perfection. To someone so thoroughly defiled in this life that there is nothing but shame, the image of a mind beyond the mind is paradise. It shimmers with a possibility of the self beyond the self. It gives hope.

The heart, however, remains broken. I have come to recognize this as a good thing. Only by being broken open can the heart be shared. Only through suffering can we know suffering and envision the end of suffering. I think of the Dalai Lama, his rolling belly laugh and the overwhelming loss of his people, their land and culture, history and hope. When he sees the ever-fleeing new refugees who come every day into India, he tells them to study and learn, and then to return to Tibet, to heartbreak. It is the only hope the Tibetan people have to heal.

THREE

It is eight o'clock on our last morning in Majnu-ka-Tilla. Our cab will be here at ten. Thrinley does her morning practice; I go out for a morning walk. The air is mild and still and the sun sends a warm glow along the alley, lighting up the beginning of business-as-usual. In the hotel, two young men are washing windows. Outside, the dirt streets are being swept clean with brooms made of sticks, then sprinkled with water to keep down the daily dust. The benches are full of tea-drinking Indians and Tibetans watching the morning manifest itself. They are relaxed and cheerful. A beggar woman goes by; she folds her hands together in prayer, looks me right in the eye and says, "I love you." She doesn't ask for money. I don't give her any, either. We both smile.

After my morning chai, I find Thrinley and we eat a last banana pancake breakfast at the Himalayan House and dash to the cyber stall to send off emails to friends and relatives. Somehow, while traveling vast distances away from home, it seems important to email just before departing for anywhere, as well as just after getting there. Whether or not anyone cares we have no idea; we're just following the rules we taught our kids.

Thrinley has six kids, three girls and three boys, including a set of twins; she is a ceramic artist as well as the manager of a retreat center. Like me, she was a single mom most of the time, with a passion for the creative life all of the time. This means that one way or another, our relationships with our kids is complicated. We juggled jobs, creativity and men as we raised our kids, which meant they felt juggled, too. Throughout our long friendship we have talked about this a lot. Our regrets pile high; the "if only we'd known" mantra is a familiar refrain between us.

Curiously, we haven't talked much about our kids so far on this trip. It seems that we are doing what all working moms on pilgrimage are likely to do when released from the responsibilities of everyday life. We are sleeping until we wake up and we're not cooking. The obligatory email home is the only link to the illustrious ways in which we've failed, and to the kids we love beyond life.

When we get back to meet the cab there is no sign of it or the cab driver. As an occasional cab driver myself, I wonder what being on-time means in India. As Dr. Einstein reported, time is relative, and never more so than when it comes to getting somewhere. By ten-thirty, Thrinley has gone out to call the cab company, which is in Rajpur, eight hours away. In India, distance is relative, too. Miles are meaningless; it's getting there that's the point and it all comes down to how long it takes.

Thrinley reports back that our cab driver should have been here hours ago and we go once again to quiz the woman behind the desk. She shakes her head and then stops in mid-shake when she hears me say Thrinley's name.

"Thrinley," she asks. "You named Thrinley?"

"Yes," says Thrinley.

"Oh," she says. "The driver was here waiting for Thrinley and said maybe he was supposed to be here at ten tonight and so he left. We thought Thrinley was a monk."

But Thrinley is not a monk, she's Lois. And when she took refuge as a Buddhist from a Tibetan Buddhist teacher, she was, as is the tradition, given a Tibetan dharma name. Turns out that "Thrinley," which means action, is a name freely given to both men and women and often to monks. The guest house management had been waiting for a monk to show up for his cab ride.

From our driving experiences in Delhi we knew that driving at night was really suicidal so we had planned our trip to Rajpur for daytime. The panic on our faces when we hear that our driver might have disappeared until ten p.m. sends our desk clerk running. She thinks she might know where he is, she says, half way out the door. Turns out, she does.

We're on the road to Rajpur by eleven. By 11:15, I'm hoping it's all over quickly because there's no way we are going to survive this trip. I'm actually nostalgic for our time with Pema in downtown Delhi. At least a head-on collision at twenty miles an hour gives you half a chance. We have eight hours to go to get to Rajpur and getting through the next thirty seconds will be some sort of Judeo-Christian-Buddhist-Hindu-Muslim miracle. I notice that Thrinley's on the most dangerous side of the car and I feel better, until my higher mind raps me on my very un-Buddhist-like knuckles, which by now are as white-knuckled as one white person's knuckles can get. This can't be as bad as it is, I am thinking. If it was, nobody in the country would be alive.

Our driver, who speaks no English, is concentrating in a way I recognize from my bus and cab driving experience. There is a "zone" which one can enter where time, speed, space and consequence feel totally controllable from behind the wheel. It's quite possible that it's a deluded state-of-mind but I know it well. It's a kind of Zen suspension of the ordinary; a place where the driver really does know best and it is best not to chirp up with any advice or instructions while he or she is zoning

I notice the clever positioning of the mirror. With a slight adjustment of his position our driver can take a quick glance at us without us noticing. All we get to see is the top of his head. I am familiar with this technique. Some drivers like to flirt into the rear view mirror, others like to twist it off and stash it under the seat; real drivers, however, like to have total control over its behavior. Our fellow might not speak English but I understand his driving language. He's got two white broads in the back seat for at least the next eight hours; the last thing he wants is to have us either in his sight, or out of his sight.

This brings us to the sound of our voices. Like a mind, a voice can be a terrible thing. People talk in taxis and on buses as though being deaf comes with the job of being the driver. It's easy to look deaf, and we do. But folks have no idea how much we hear and what

49

we think about it. Having been in the driver's seat with everyone from a load of screaming kids to one whining tourist behind me, I'll take the kids every time.

The class system might be alive and well in India but it's also in full view inside any cab and bus in the U.S. The most difficult to take are the passengers who get in after landing in their private plane or disembarking from their private yacht and assume the cab is driving itself. To them, the driver is simply not there. When I first encountered this passenger life-form, I tried to prove my existence by being friendly. This inevitably ruined the rest of my day so I quickly learned to assume they didn't exist either. It turns out that such people don't want to know we exist; our particular life-form reminds them of something they'd rather not know about—being of service. A bus driver buddy of mine coined a phrase for such folk, "yacht trash."

Well, there goes my mind again. I hate myself for hating rich people. As much as I can blame it on the way money was made off me as a kid, I know better. And as a Buddhist, I'm supposed to *be* better. When it comes right down to it, it's really money that I hate. The way it defines life, and lack of life, worth and lack of worth. What I have learned to do is accept the conundrum of it all, the way money does and doesn't show up, the way people I truly love do and do not have money; the way money does and does not mean something; the way it talks and what it says.

This gets me back inside our fateful cab ride to Rajpur, where, for the most part Thrinley and I are being very quiet. And when we do say something, it's said quietly. Not as though we're whispering, mind you, but softly, so as not to interfere with our driver's concentration, or the privacy of his experience as he drives us through the transportation hell realm of our shared fate. The outskirts of Delhi go on for a long time; they are a hell realm of wonder.

I've never before seen anything like the poverty I see driving through the countryside between Delhi and Rajpur. It is a culture beyond poverty, a place where there's no light at the end of the tunnel because there's no tunnel. It's a way of life that begins and ends in a state of destitution so complete that any other possibility is impossible. The only way out is rebirth into another time, place and body. Suddenly I understand why reincarnation is rooted into the very cultural fabric of India. It represents hope when there is none available in this lifetime.

This poverty manifests as disintegration. In downtown Delhi, the roadside capitalism is well-organized and tidy—similar goods offered in specifically identified areas; people know the limits of space and abide by the spoken and unspoken agreements that make life work for as many people as possible at once. The few square feet of commerce are orderly and so is the appearance of those buying, selling and/or trading goods, services and every other want, need, desire known to humankind. In the outskirts of the city order prevails. Beautiful women in their signature saris work the piles of cow dung into shapely mounds; the stalls are still recognizable as shops. But further into the countryside the divisions break down; the boundaries collapse. The dung piles are a random mess, often cluttered beside wood fires where food is being prepared; the clutter of one activity becomes the clutter of another; the garbage has no distinct place to be, it is simply everywhere. The people, too, look formless, as though they don't distinguish themselves from the filth and stench of their environment.

It is poverty blind to its own poverty. It is poverty deprived of even that which makes even the worst poverty bearable, a moment of nature. The air is thick with drifts of smog; local smoke from cooking fires and burning rubber; the rank smells of animal, human and vegetable waste; and that strange pervasive odor of something sweet and repulsive. There seems to be no plant life left, nothing green and growing as a reminder of the intrinsic regenerative nature of life.

Poverty is a word that I've never been able to fully understand. In *Webster's*, the first definition has to do with lack or relative lack of money or material possessions; meagerness of supply comes next; with debility due to malnutrition as the third. In my own personal wrestle with the meaning of money, poverty has somehow seemed unrelated. I know that my income has often fallen below the "poverty line" as far as the U.S. government is concerned, but I've never in my life felt poor. Even when I was stone broke. As I've registered this over the years, and tried to think about it, two things surfaced. The first has to do with living with poetry; the second with living in nature.

A poem is an articulation of the inarticulate wealth in and of the world. It is a representation of riches, an abundance of excess in a world sinking beneath the weight of materialistic mayhem. A poem is a salute to the spirit. In 1963, British poet, novelist, literary scholar and traumatized World War I veteran, Robert Graves, gave a speech to the London School of Economics in which he said, "If there's no money in poetry, neither is there poetry in money." Poetry doesn't need money. Money, if it's going to have any meaning at all, needs poetry to remind it of its true worth, which is always momentary.

There is no poverty in nature, either. Throughout my years of healing, no matter how impoverished my spirit, how despairing my mind, or how empty my bank account, nature always offered a restorative hand. A breath of salt air, a glimpse of stars, a bird's quick song, the wind everywhere—nature always gave me a wealth of reasons to live.

Later, when the language of my recovery took hold, I could see that the guiding instincts that took me to live on islands made sure that I never knew poverty. How could poverty exist within the beauty of nature's grace? How could there not be poetry? Any artist will tell you that there is something more important than money, even if they can't quite tell you what it is. God, too, is nameless.

But here, on the road to Rajpur, God appears to be missing. There is no poetry on the streets, there is no nature. I don't sense any story but despair. Even the wild street life in Delhi overflowed with stories, with listening. Here it is rough with alienation, dust, dirt and the very roots of deprivation. I look over at Thrinley and she is looking quietly ahead, neither on the road nor towards its burdened shoulders. There is nothing to say.

About four hours into our day-long cab ride, when my heart, mind and bladder are all on overload, we pull into what is apparently the designated oasis for travelers such as Thrinley and me. The place has a name, Cheetal Grande. There are gates and we are allowed to enter. It's a world of nature at its manicured best. All the red and golden shades of marigolds and chrysanthemums are elegantly placed in pots on patios; there are sculpted bushes, waving palm trees, golf-green lawns and white wrought iron furniture. I am aware of deep relief at being spared the poverty-stricken sights that have jarred my psyche for the past few hours. It feels like we've entered the palace life the Buddha sacrificed so much to leave. No wonder he's the Buddha.

We eat lunch out on the patio. Our meal is delicious: chicken curry, spicy vegetables, soft bread stuffed with cauliflower and cheese, bottled water and strong tea in a teapot with a tea-cosy. Over our meal we talk about managing our minds and wonder what day it is. I'm not particularly curious but Thrinley is so she asks the waiter. "Thursday," he says, not batting an eyelash.

Then the joyride continues. Slowly, finally, the countryside opens up to sugar cane fields and the occasional small stand of small trees. The clusters of poverty are still there but not as unrelentingly as before. We turn off onto a less traveled road and even the traffic thins a bit. It's finally possible to relax. Until it starts to get dark and I wonder why we're driving without headlights. Perhaps we don't have any. Then I notice that they come on at intervals. It appears that night driving, too, has its own set of protocols. I look over and see Thrinley softly saying prayers under her breath.

It's almost eight when we arrive in Rajpur. The trip has taken nine hours and we are exquisitely relieved to have arrived alive. We're also beginning to realize the extent of our driver's skill and stamina. In spite of not being able to talk to him, our road trip has bonded us to him in a way that goes far beyond words. We each tip him 500 rupees. An enormous smile breaks out across his face and he gives us a shy bow; then he turns to drive himself all the way home. Five hundred rupees equals a bit more than ten dollars.

FOUR

About 20 years ago, I stopped seeing my family and my family stopped seeing me. It wasn't supposed to turn out that way. A separation from my parents was supposed to help heal things. Instead it began a slide into isolation that continues to this day. So I have found my family with those with whom I am familiar—in friendship, affection and loyalty. I have a family of friends. I always felt odd saying that until I looked up the meaning and origins of "family." According to *Webster's*, the nuclear family as we know it, "the basic biosocial unit in society" is number five in the list of definitions. The first one, the oldest, has to do with slavery, military service, shared convictions and employment. In between, there are families of plants, languages, instruments and typefaces; rocks, comets, asteroids and soils and on and on. To be family can happen anywhere in the universe; and it does.

It was 1986 and I was more than a year into therapy with Brian when I was compelled to take a break from my parents. Christmas was planned as usual since my parents' divorce—twice: Christmas Eve with my father, and Christmas Day with my mother, and both events at my house where I cooked, baked, made, bought and generally created Christmas cheer for my bitterly divorced parents and my brothers and their families. This was a role long familiar to me, both before and after their divorce. But my mother did an odd, uncharacteristic thing that year; she invited me over to help her wrap the family presents. I was touched as such a gesture was unknown in our relationship. A skilled seamstress and knitter, she owned and managed a fiber arts shop and when I arrived there to wrap presents, the counters were filled with heavy wool sweaters hand-knitted into Northwest Coast Native American designs. Known as Cowichan sweaters, she'd had one on display for a couple of years and whenever I went into the shop I expressed my admiration for it and told her I would buy it when she no longer wanted it as a sample. Now she'd knitted a dozen of them for Christmas presents and we spent the afternoon wrapping them for my brothers, their wives, partners and children. I knew there was one for me, too, but I didn't say anything as we would be opening presents at my house and I wanted to be part of the surprise.

On Christmas Day, the present-opening concluded with the gifts from my mother. Everyone got a beautiful Cowichan sweater but me. They all donned their new sweaters and my mother asked me to take a group photograph with her in the middle. There was something gloating on her face as she looked at me in expectation. I, long-practiced at ignoring abuse of every description, slapped a big smile on my face and took the photo. Then I went into the basement, closed myself into a closet and sobbed uncontrollably for ten minutes. Afterwards I fixed my make-up and went back upstairs to finish fixing Christmas dinner. Nobody said a word about my exclusion from this collective family gift and photograph, and neither did I.

But, as so often in my life, grace was right over my shoulder. A few weeks earlier I had gone to a Native American craft sale with a close friend. I had exclaimed about my love of a Cowichan sweater on display. Unbeknownst to me, he bought it for me and as we were eating our Christmas dessert he arrived with his gift. I was stunned. So was my mother. She gave me a look of profound hatred. Later, I realized that she thought perhaps I had manufactured the event in response to what I suspected might happen. But I was still far too helpless to have seen such betrayal coming, let alone prepare for it.

My distress spilled out in Brian's office. This time I actually had an event to process. Up until then, simple overwhelming grief had defined my therapy. It was grief without cause, without connection to anything or anyone. I was immobilized with it from the moment

I entered Brian's office, which was often three times a week. And when there was no role to fulfill in my out-of-his-office life, I would be curled up in uncontrollable crying, often visceral and heaving. In between, I went to work at the hospital where I had a job and began to write a play about abortion.

If there is one thing that I know for sure about healing, it's that grieving gets you there. And there is no short-cut. For whatever reasons—be they Brian's caution, wisdom, knowledge or stupefaction—he witnessed my grief respectfully and empathetically, without trying to "fix" it; and somewhere inside, after a year of feeling witnessed, I began to trust him. The Cowichan sweater incident was real and in real time. We had a circumstance to explore.

Brian gave me homework: ask my mother to knit me a Cowichan sweater and ask her to tell me she loved me. I couldn't get close. As the weeks went by my inability to ask these questions threw me into deeper and deeper anguish and greater and greater regression. All because of a lousy rotten Christmas present. But it was a present that unearthed the past. It was the watershed event that started the landslide of recognition that things were not as they appeared—in my life, in my family, in my self. It was the beginning of remembering the life that had lived me. This was the Christmas when my lack of memory started to take on meaning and not remembering became a memory in itself.

Anyone who has entered the post-traumatic stress healing process will attest to its inarticulate emotional helplessness. It's not the mind, with all its verbal virtuosity and reasoning skills that has the memory; it's the body. It's a physical and emotional remembering in which the concept of time and circumstance is replaced by a visceral experience of strangely disembodied feelings. The body in fear takes over the body in time and all gets consumed in a state of timeless terror. As I slipped into remembering what I did not remember, all my survival skills began to slip over the edge.

My appointments with Brian increased in number and in intensity. But my visceral pain and panic had no language whatsoever. His voice insisted itself through the fear: "Where are you, Janet?

Who's there? How old are you? What's happening?" And out of the fear came answers. There were people around me, things were happening to my body. I couldn't breathe. I was five years old. I couldn't move. I couldn't breathe. Most of all I couldn't breathe. Over weeks of entering and re-entering these sensations a kind of coherence of events began to take place and a great awe of questioning began. At the same time that I, as a forty-one-year-old woman was unable to ask my mother to tell me she loved me, as a five-year-old girl I began to remember. And as Brian kept asking me to ask my mother those two simple questions it finally burst out in helpless rage: "She doesn't deserve to know she hurt me."

I remember being stunned by these words. *She doesn't deserve to know she hurt me.* This is a complicated sentence, ringing of layers of meaning that speak to pain deeply hidden from me and from her. As this maelstrom of feeling and memory unfolded, along with it came the realization that my mother was getting money for me. I was being sold. I felt it. I knew it. And it all fell into place. The organized nature of my abuse, the presence of onlookers and participators, of being watched as things happened to me, of my exploding body, of needing to be helped and no-one helping. The strange fascination in people's eyes, the exposure, the pain and the violation, the sense that I was watching it happen to me as it was happening. It was incomprehensible to me because five-year-olds don't know the words. And with my adult comprehension came the conundrum of knowing what I was never, ever, supposed to know. Not only were the words unformed, they were lies. Whatever I remembered was a lie. The truth was a lie. This became the mantra of my healing journey. It was all a lie. And if I named it I would die.

I went down for the count. What was surfacing was beyond a shock. It was incomprehensible. I had no vocabulary, no frame of reference, no context for the reality and the realizations that were surfacing. A great and physical fugue set in. I isolated myself from friends, from all the things I did, and from everything that had ever had meaning to me. It was a hell-realm in which I had lost the Invincible One—the part of me that had triumphed our way through life with a smile, a bouncy step and an irrepressible sense of responsibility. She lost her place to the Emerging Ones and it would be a very long time before I saw her again.

After three or four months of hard therapy trying to reconcile the irreconcilable events of the holiday season, I ran away to Oakland, California, to work in a friend's public relations business where my survival self went into overdrive to keep me alive. I made enough money to fly back to Seattle for therapy almost weekly. And I was terrified of flying. I was also terrified of everything about the past I had known; because it appeared as though nothing that I had experienced as real was real. I was up against the wall of the truth and the truth of the wall I had created as the truth.

In California, when I wasn't cranking out propaganda for the banking industry or flying to Seattle for therapy, I high-tailed it to the coast. There, sometime that spring, somewhere on the coast between San Francisco and Santa Cruz, I sat in my old Volvo, Ethyl, and wrote a simple paragraph to my parents. "I am having a hard time," I wrote. "So I won't be in touch with you for awhile." To my four brothers I wrote a letter of love and explanation. "I don't want to be out of touch with you," I wrote. "I'm just taking a break from our parents for awhile."

It was a shock to find out that I didn't matter. I did not hear one word back from either of my parents or any of my brothers. I was barely hanging on to life and there was not a word of concern, or even curiosity. Years later, I would understand the dynamics of things that go on when somebody breaks the code of silence that defines a family. At the time, however, I was simply a sister in distress.

In word families there are form-based and meaning-based versions. When I think back about my function within the family, I see it as bringing meaning. When my parents separated, I helped my mother find meaning as she raged at and ravaged everyone she could reach. As my younger brothers each left home, they often stayed with me for various lengths of time as they looked for meaning in their worlds. My youngest brother was like a son. I was fifteen years old when he was born. What I didn't tell him was that our parents told us that they might give him up for adoption.

Our family was a closed system. There was no continuity in the outside world. We lived in at least five places in Wales and England before we moved to Montreal when I was seven. We lived in four places in Montreal before moving to Vancouver when I was twelve. We lived in two places in Vancouver. It was in the second place where my very first memory of self was born, where I remembered my own bed, the street upon which I lived, and some friends. I remember being thirteen.

Life changed for our family after we moved to the U.S. when I was sixteen. Continuity of place served my brothers with neighborhood friends, continuous schools, and a familiar landscape. I, however, faced my last year of high school in a new place and was heartbroken to leave behind the beginning of friendships in Vancouver. But I discovered there was an exciting extracurricular possibility in my new school; I could join the after-school Drama Club. But my parents got me a job babysitting and it was arranged that my "free" period would be scheduled last in the day so I could leave school even before the final bell. Drama Club fell by the wayside as quickly as it had aroused my excitement.

My role in the family continued in subservience. I did not know how to know I was imprisoned in a system of mind control that left me no freedom of will. After graduation, when I was not allowed to go to college, I got a job working for an insurance company. Most of my salary went to my parents for my room and board. At some point, a friend at work asked me to share an apartment with her. I marveled at the idea. But I did not know how to want to do it, or how to do it. These are odd words. So were the circumstances.

What do I know about my family? Mostly I know that I created what I know. And it surfaced in all kinds of ways. In a magazine article, I described how my father took me to soccer games in England when I was a little girl. After the article was published, I overheard my father telling a brother that he "never took me anywhere of the kind." And even though I heard this, I didn't have the psychological independence to ask my father what he meant or to wonder how and why I created the experience.

Whatever it was—the electro-shocks, the day-in and day-out behavior towards me, the mind-control experimentation, or the part of me that created a world in which no such thing was possible—I was unable to look at my life, evaluate it, and make decisions on my own behalf. What I did know was how to be the bearer of holiday gatherings; it was at my home the family gathered, and for birthdays, too. I rose dutifully to each occasion, facilitating peace and possibility, bringing meaning. Afterwards, for at least a week I would be stunned with depression and deadness through and through. These are words that work only later, when the "I" has surfaced and can see. At the time I was simply a robot of responsibility. It was my job to always make everything better for everyone around me and I especially made things better at Christmas.

Now I will be in India for Christmas; it is the first Christmas away from the responsibility of Christmas. Even after I lost my birth family, I didn't lose my ways. The burden of having to make everything alright continued and reached its pinnacle of expectation at Christmas, even when there was no-one around to make happy. As this trip was in the planning, being in India at Christmas was not my decision. The celebration of Sakya Trizin's sixtieth birthday is to happen on the 29th of December. It only made sense to be in India for Christmas. For years I have been determined to be "away" at Christmas, to sidestep the angst of my lost family at the time when I traditionally brought everyone together. For years, I have failed to get away. Instead, I tried to tame my internal chaos by creating Christmas for all my friends with no place to go. I re-created the frenzy of responsibility for a good cause; it was exhausting. The alternative was overwhelming loneliness and loss. I have no idea how this Christmas will translate, how I will feel, where I will be, whether or not the burden of Christmas will be lifted, here, half way around the world.

It is possible, if one looks at life very closely, to see the invisibility of things become visible. The hidden ripple effect of each moment's existence that brings us to the here and the now. It is then we discover that it is the things that happen outside our control that put fate into our future. When I think back through the great waste of my life, the years lost to fear and isolation and grief, I see the moments of grace that kept me going. It was nothing short of divine intervention; and I don't believe in divine intervention. To believe in divine intervention means to believe in someone else's control over my life. To me, that had always meant being held hostage to evil. But someone inside had learned to control my life, in spite of me.

I started to get a clue about this at the first conference on ritual abuse I went to at the University of California at Berkeley in 1988. It was sponsored by survivor-organized Healing Hearts and was geared towards both survivors and the professional support community. I had simply heard it was happening and was compelled to go. It was more than three years into therapy with Brian. He told me that I was courageous to attend. At the time I had no feelings about it. The urge was intellectual - the Therapist inside me wanted more information, the Philosopher was curious.

The trip was rich with opportunities for my multiplicity. At the time I was working for a magazine, *Seafood Leader*, so the Writer would work on an article about Bay Area seafood restaurants. The Mother would visit Colin who was living in San Francisco at the time, the Adventurer would get away from home; I did not yet know precisely who would be attending the ritual abuse conference. It was a distant, science fiction event that had nothing to do with me.

But a few years of therapy had made me smarter. I booked a bed-and-breakfast in Berkeley for the time of the conference. I wanted privacy and quiet. By then I was beginning to understand that I was seriously dissociative. Or, as it was named in those days, I was a "multiple." No matter how much I hated and feared that word, it named me. Because I couldn't name my self.

We're all on the spectrum of dissociation, shifting from one role to another as the circumstances of our lives shift. We behave differently in the boardroom than we do in the bedroom. The role we play as the parent of a five-year-old is not the same as the role we play when we're out for martinis with our girlfriends or a few beers with the guys. It's a shift that is made within the framework of consciousness. We know we are doing it and why. There is a conscious partnership between the self and the circumstances.

In dissociative disorder, there is no such partnership. Life is a series of isolated roles without the continuity of "I" weaving them together in consciousness or in memory. When I found myself paralyzed in the middle of the kitchen at Christmas in 1984, I was like the pack of identity cards that could no longer be shuffled together. My parts went splat, face down, all over the kitchen floor and I didn't even know how to look down and see them, let alone how to pick them up.

This fragmentation of who I had been was starting, somewhere inside, to make sense. And I began what in many ways became the signature of my life—I went into hiding. I was beginning to know what had happened to me as a child. I knew how easily I would be distracted by socializing at this conference, and how it would instantly arouse the complete state of disassociated denial that was the trademark of my life.

It's hard to describe the shifting states-of-being that defined those years. There really was no relationship between my distinct and valiant parts inside, yet they ruled my very existence. When I was in therapy with Brian, my Little Ones spilled out into the room in hordes. I cried and sobbed and howled and raged, re-entering the life that had destroyed me. With everyone else, I was a shadow self of competence and model behavior.

For the first few days in San Francisco I stayed with an old friend who helped me with my restaurant research. With Colin I explored Sausalito. He gave me a tape of Bonnie Raitt, "You'll like this song, Mom," he said.

"Hey, shut uuuup…." Raitt crooned as we drove over the Golden Gate Bridge. I was on a great eating assignment in San Francisco, I was getting to visit my son, and oh yes, I just happened to be going to a conference on ritual abuse.

Colin drove me over to Berkeley. He was cheerful and supportive. He didn't say much about the conference and neither did I. Our pact was both spoken and unspoken. I told him almost as soon as I knew about the possibility of cult abuse within my family. Colin's response was instant: "Mom, if that goes on in the world, I know your parents could be involved." I was shocked at how intuitively he responded. Later, it became clear that he, too, had a story. And this is where it gets intolerable. What I didn't know about my life meant that he was too often alone with my parents. So my agreement with Colin was that I would answer any questions but I would not burden him with my process and my predicament. A lot of things came to pass in this regard but they are not mine to tell. I would simply say that I have the most amazing son in the world and I love him beyond life. I would also say that I am unbearably sorry.

When Colin left me at Cecilia's Bed & Breakfast that day I felt as though I'd been abandoned in space. But Cecilia had kindly left me a key and I let myself in. My room was full of frills and lace and midday sun. After looking around, I lay down on the bed and felt the familiar paralysis settle around me. No form, no thought, no substance. If there is any one word that describes so much of my life through those years, it is "paralysis." And this is weird because in my outside life I was really active. I wrote plays, raised my son, supported us both by myself, played soccer, socialized—but when I wasn't "out" and "on," I was immobilized. It was as though my existence was defined by the expectations around me; otherwise I literally had no sense of my own existence. I couldn't feel myself.

When Cecilia arrived she was a warm, friendly matter-of-fact woman who worked as a therapist in the public schools. Inside, all my parts breathed relief. I told her I was there for a writing project and to attend a conference. She didn't ask me any questions and I was grateful. She said she left early each morning and that I was her only guest at the time so I would have plenty of privacy.

Once again I felt the familiar reassurance of grief hovering close by. Cecilia was a loving, kind woman. She showed me a gentle kindness and all my own lost children rose to the surface. That night I had a bath and cried into the night. I had one more day before the conference started. One more opportunity to open my heart to what I was about to do.

A few years earlier, during my self-exile in Oakland, I came across Stephen Mitchell's, *The Book of Job*. Its power of rhythm and reason, and its irrational despairing faith rang deep chords in me and I wrote Stephen a letter. We subsequently met in Berkeley for tea and talk. The Playwright in me wanted to hear his book from the ancient voices of Native Americans. I could see the theatre piece—a cluster of Elders gathered around a fire sounding out the language of Job and his challengers. It seemed that only out of the great ancestral silence of our indigenous people could the words be spoken and the authority real. We talked about a possible play.

Over the years we had kept in touch, Stephen and I. He would come to Seattle to read from each new book. He was succeeding in his writing. I was receding with each new uncovering of my truth. Yet I continued to attach myself to Stephen's work. Through his writing and translating he held out the possibility of faith. And he had told me about his wife, Vicki Chang, an acupuncturist and a healer.

Her office was only blocks from Cecilia's house where I was staying. Just before leaving Seattle I made an appointment to see her.

I was without feelings, yet I *knew* I was without feelings. That was the victory in those days—to recognize the paralysis. I was going to a ritual abuse conference that did not exist, staying in a B&B that did not exist, visiting a son who did not exist. The denial was complete. But somewhere inside I was learning and the fact that I had made an appointment with Vicki Chang before I left Seattle was a sign. I had anticipated my dissociation and had known that I would need help.

The trouble with dissociation is that when you're in it you don't feel it. Years of lying dead still on couches and beds while all around me I would be able to do things and be things. Yet inside, the paralysis was complete. There was no being, no doing, but simply a blankness broken only by outside events, a phone call, an obligatory play to write, a complex magazine to edit. I felt no personal identification with any of it. There were no threads of relationship to any of the accomplishments in my life. It was the only way I could keep the past at bay.

Occasionally, past and present would converge and I'd imagine a moment of reconciliation between my accomplishing self and my dissembling selves. During one particularly busy period of time while I was going back and forth between Seattle and Long Beach, California, where I was organizing the California Seafood Festival, I also had a commission to write a play. It was for Open Door Theatre, an Everett, Washington-based theatre company that focused on the complex issues of sexual abuse. They already had plays in production for elementary-aged kids, mine was written for an older audience—junior high students—the average age at which the first sexual offense is perpetrated. The night before I was scheduled to go to Long Beach, the actors had their first read-through of the script for the theater board members, including Seth Dawson, the Snohomish County Prosecutor who was the board chair. Except for the artistic director, who was a friend of mine, nobody knew the struggle I was having with my history.

The reading went well. It was a good play and I knew it. The board was impressed. The discussion afterwards was invigorating. There were some adjustments to be made, and some suggestions, but they were welcome and enriching. The two male actors were concerned about the portrayal of the adolescent boys. They wanted a greater complexity. They wanted ambivalence to be part of the boy's experience of sexuality. We talked about how it could happen without sabotaging the focus of the forty-five minute play that must captivate, as well as educate, an unrelenting adolescent audience.

I was articulate, assertive, confident. Afterwards I drove home in a sob of tears. I could barely breathe. I was sick. Something happened during the evening that I had never experienced. I was articulate, assertive, confident. I wasn't pretending to be, I was. I was really feeling those things. I really did know what I was doing. I knew my work. I knew its truth. I was being who I was without fear. I felt it. It was me. It was a miracle.

Then I thought about Seth Dawson, the Snohomish County Prosecutor. I felt a kind of secret excitement because I suspected he liked the play and was impressed by my competence. And if he was, then I would be able to ask him about his experience with cult-related crime. But even as I thought about getting help, I was swamped with terror. Someone inside who had bridged the gap between past and present didn't yet trust either my inner, or my outer, resources. I felt a clamp across the back of my head. A vise. And as I climbed up into the loft where I slept I expected to see my son's severed head staring at me from my pillow.

The threat of life. The threat of death. They were the same. Breathing fear into my skin, my bones, the blood circulating through the pores of me. I was beginning to recognize fear simply because it was no longer constantly there.

When I woke up the next morning, there was no new play, no Seth Dawson, no miracle, no loneliness, no son. I was the traveler, packing up Ethyl (my trusty '67 Volvo) to go to California. I headed off downtown to get money from the bank and a latte from the espresso stand next door. Then I hit the freeway and headed south, dissociation complete.

I was four years into therapy when I went on that trip. And I didn't even have the ability to call Brian for help. The adult controlling all our needs was unaware that dependence was one of them. She kept a tight reign over us. "Us." Who were we anyway? Only sometimes could I feel the yearning ones. The ones bone-tired of being "protected" from their own knowledge of one another. The "adult" Janet kept us all in line. Un-needing, independent even from our knowledge of one another.

It would be many more years before I could make that simple call—to connect, to ask for guidance, to get reassurance, to get simple affirmation that my struggle was real, that it meant something, and that I meant something.

In my work with Brian we worked relentlessly on this disconnect. Many people with dissociated disorders lose great chunks of time. They come to consciousness in strange places, not knowing how they got there or why. My loss of time happened differently. If time can be measured a foot deep in experience, I was remembering and absorbing but the top quarter inch. The relatedness between my experiences and their relationship to my core self was aborted even as they happened. "I" was somewhere else. In hiding from a life that was unbearable, "I" was still occupying a child's mind suspended in terror. From this writing, it seems so simple to understand. But back then there was no way out but through the terror.

When my parts first started coming awake, the fear was constant and immobilizing. The Little Ones were terrified. They didn't even know how to walk. They'd never been out in public. They'd never been known. They fought me on the inside, stiffening my body with fear so that I could barely tie my shoes to go outside. But I had started to recognize the paralysis and was determined to do something, anything. So I learned to walk around Green Lake in Seattle.

I parked my old Volvo, Ethyl, on a side-street and walked bravely to the edge of the lake where the trail was alive with walkers, joggers, strollers, roller-skaters. Children splashed in the pool, fed the ducks and geese on the lake, and played with their parents. Windsurfers skimmed across the lake's surface and an occasional fisherman, rod in hand, dozed in the sun. "See how easy it is," I told the Little Ones inside. "We just walk. One foot in front of the other. Simple."

It was like walking for the first time. Around me everywhere was naturalness, an ease that felt like an exquisite painting I would never be part of. But we walked all around the lake that day. Nearly three miles. I had forced a dent in the dissociation. We had gone for a walk. And survived. It would be the reporting highlight of my next visit to Brian.

This seems crazy. I was a mother; I could give an impassioned presentation; write plays; give press conferences and do restaurant reviews. But inside the descent into my past, "I" as I knew myself did not exist. And those hidden parts I was meeting had none of my experience in life. Over the months I attacked the dissociation with more walks round the lake. I was re-entering the physical feeling of being and it was a place filled with fear and shame. At first I walked alone and later with friends. Then I started taking an aerobics class and persevered through months of hot shame and humiliation. It was not just me who was stretching and jumping in front of others—it was us. Some of us were suspended in shame; others simply didn't know how to move. "I" knew how to be graceful and physically present. "They" didn't. This time, life was for them. I was guided inside to let the Competent One who'd carried us through life rest. And let the others—with all their shame and fear—begin to breathe and come alive.

Multiplicity happens in the mind; the body is an afterthought. Yes, I had a body. But I didn't inhabit it because it held too much fear. Until I was 45, fear was something I was. It had no word, no form, no cause, no beginning or end. When you are born into terror and your mind has been splintered apart by that which you cannot tolerate, there is no safe place. A frightened animal does not stop to chat about its fear. It flees. We flee. I fled. Fled into space. Into the vast silence outside my body.

So, many months later, when I knew I would go to the conference, I knew I would dissociate. I knew I would be afraid. And I knew I would need help.

Vicki Chang was as startled as I, that, out of the blue, I would make this appointment with her. She had regular local clients; I lived far away in Seattle. What am I doing there? We told her. The Little Ones cried out their grief while the Competent One made sense of it all. The Spiritual One offered a silent connection. The Voice knew, ushering us along and through our visit with Vicki.

"I have to go to this conference," I told her. "About ritual abuse. I am a survivor of cult abuse." The words science fiction, the grief choking and bottomless. She physically recoiled.

"I'm shut down and frozen," I said. "I want to feel. I want to be there. I want to be spiritually strong. And open to the experience."

I lay fully clothed on her table. Her voice soothed me into re-laxation. She used a gentle touch and meditation. The grief poured out of me like a river. I was afraid the evil around and in me would poison the air she was breathing.

Describing the amorphous, elusive details of spiritual experience is like describing the life of a river. It can pool in great stillness, cas-cade recklessly over stones and flow with a purposeful maturity to-wards the sea. It never stays the same. Being with Vicki, her presence a finely honed reflection of a long and refined spiritual practice, gave hope to my own struggling spirit. "You are more than half way there," she told me. "It's just what's in the way." I had heard that before.

"There is a darkness here, and here," as she gestured across my body. "But you can do it. You can know."

I was exhausted after our hour-and-a-half together but, as usual, grief had washed me awake. On the way back to Cecilia's I stopped in a little dress shop and bought a skirt for seven dollars. Then a piece of chocolate. I walked by stately houses and felt like the little match girl looking for a home. I bought a book of poems at the bookstore and noticed a restaurant where I could go for dinner. I thought about how I wanted to look. Whether I should wear jeans or a skirt - look respectable or like a writer. The conference would begin in the morn-ing and all I could think about was my appearance. Who would be appearing? What would they wear? I had no idea.

That night I had a dream:

> I am small - six or seven. Two women are paying nice attention to me. They bring me into a room and there are two men there - one older, one younger. The women tell me they will do some things to me and I say very sweetly - innocently, "But I won't have to take my clothes off, will I?" They don't answer and I know I will have to but I can't accept it so I pretend I don't have to. They smile at each other and I pretend I don't see. I know the men will be there and I pretend I don't. There will also be other men there and I pretend there won't be.

When I woke up I was on the verge of an orgasm and so I did. One part of my body all pleasure. Everything else – inside and out – was hell and terror.

It gets complicated when sexual exploitation is combined with sexual stimulation. As a small child, the imminence of being used sexually sent me out of my body and out of my mind. I pretended myself out of existence. Yet I'd been trained with the pleasure of part of my own body. In specific purpose and for specific reasons, my little clitoris was stroked over and over and over. But it had nothing to do with my sexuality. It was all done for the perverted sexuality of others. So this dream, in which I was terrified out of existence, left me with a stimulated clitoris. It felt good. As I awoke, I was feeling it all—the immediate arousal of that very small sexual place in my body and the immediate arousal of the terror that sent me off into disassociation.

At breakfast I encountered the inevitable from Cecilia.

"What conference is it?" she asked.

"About abuse," I answered. Then I plunged into the truth. "Cult abuse."

"Oh."

"Are you familiar with the issue?"

"Yes," she said. "I work with abused kids in the schools."

And she went on to speak about how extensive child abuse is, about the hurt children in her care, about the Presidio day care case in San Francisco. This was a federal case that surfaced in 1986 and grew to involve more than fifty children between the ages of three and seven, many with Chlamydia, a sexually-transmitted disease, as well as bruised and hurt sexual parts of their small bodies. They all attended preschool and hourly care programs operated by the U.S. Army at the Presidio in San Francisco. Eventually one teacher was found guilty of abusing one child. But there was indication of a much more extensive network of abusers as well as satanic ritual practice. It was a case fraught with complexity because the children were so young. Their testimony about weird ritual was suspect, even if there was documented medical evidence of sexual abuse, including rape, sodomy and venereal disease. And it appeared they were taken off-base to be abused as well, which made jurisdiction complicated.

A name that surfaced during the investigation was that of Lt. Col. Michael Aquino who had joined the Church of Satan, founded by Anton LaVey, in 1969. Aquino went on to found his own satanic church, The Temple of Set, in 1975. It was reported that while on a NATO tour of Europe in 1982, Aquino performed a satanic ritual in the Westphalian castle that had been used as an occult sanctuary by Heinrich Himmler's SS elite in Nazi Germany. Other U.S. Army day care centers were also investigated for child abuse—including at Fort Dix, New Jersey.

Cecilia and I commiserated about the drastically sad state of affairs in the world and then both cheerfully wished one another a good day and went our separate ways. I was grateful to her for not probing. She left my conference motives untouched, unexamined. I could feel her discretion at work—and her curiosity. She became a link to the world and as I waited for the bus I realized that I might be able to tell her who I was and not feel ashamed.

The conference was on the fifth floor in the Student Union Building at the University of California, Berkeley. The bus ride had taken longer than I thought and so I was late. I rushed up the stairs instead of waiting for the elevator and arrived out of breath as well as full of anxiety. There was a relaxed crowd milling in the hallway outside the conference room and I instantly knew I'd read the schedule wrong. Registration, not presentation, would take the entire first hour. I actually had forty-five minutes to spare. I went back outside in search of a cup of coffee and a dose of equilibrium.

A year earlier, I had been self-exiled in Oakland with paralysis so profound that I could do nothing but work in a desperate job at an advertising agency owned by a desperate friend. Berkeley bookstores and coffeehouses had been but a BART ride away. They could have been on another planet.

I was now in Berkeley to become more aware of the death in my life, yet I could feel the measure of difference that the last year of chipping away at denial had made. I could feel the place. I could look around Berkeley and see it. Notice it. The sixties had survived intact. Beads and incense were still for sale on the streets. Political opinions were still free of charge. Loose limbed hippies in flowing fabrics were now joined by skinhead skateboarders and the new sub-culture—the homeless. Those days in Berkeley you could buy food coupons and pass them out instead of cash.

I was wearing jeans, a turtleneck sweater, a vest and my favorite earrings. I carried a cup of coffee. I was going to a conference on ritual abuse. This time I waited for the elevator. At the last moment a woman jumped through the closing doors. She was bright and attractive.

She smiled at me. "Are you going to the conference?"

"Yes." I smiled back.

"I'm Alana," she said.

"I'm Janet."

"Mind if I sit with you?"

She had come all the way from Boston to attend. She was a writer, a nurse, married with children. A survivor. This was her first conference also. We took seats close to the front.

What I remember so vividly about the next few days was the language—both spoken and unspoken. I understood it. For the first time in my life I was with a large group of people who were either directly or indirectly experienced with ritual abuse. The words used, the grief and confusion expressed by survivors, the serious presentations by professionals, it all rang through me like a bell.

Tears of relief at hearing about memory loss and multiple personality disorder. How one "grows" an MPD. It is a biological capacity to dissociate. A survival mechanism when a child is not provided with restorative experiences after being traumatized. The systematic disinformation that is part of the brainwashing and mind control. The "fuzzed out" psyches of ritual abuse survivors. The blanks and suspended terror. The societal denial because ritual abuse is outside the realm of shared reality. All the information that I knew without "knowing" reverberated through the stone self that made my presence possible. This was the truth, the language of my life.

For three days I learned about the sophisticated workings of ritual abuse. How the mind is manipulated until the "self" is lost under layers of torture and fear. How language is contaminated until it becomes a tool of complete destruction.

"I torture you because I love you."

"If you remember, you will die."

"If you tell someone you trust, they will die."

"You have no thoughts that are yours."

"You don't have the right to exist."

"Everything you do is bad. Good girl. You are guilty"

"Everything you are is bad. Good girl. You are shameful."

Father Kent Burtner, a Catholic priest from Portland, Oregon, spoke about programming and thought reform.

"Satanic cults demand the surrender of humanity."

"Communication is destroyed within both the outer and the inner world."

"One's own thinking and feeling becomes the enemy."

"Compassion is punished."

It was a whirl of hearing out loud the conundrum of my own life. I was there and not there at the same time. A few women sat with stuffed animals on their laps. I thought they were stupid. I did not respect the "acting out" in public. When one of them stood and spoke as a mature woman who shared soundly and profoundly about her struggle, I was shocked. My own inner children, who would have loved to hang on to a teddy bear for dear life, were not yet allowed to co-exist with the adult.

Inside, it was my Controller who was suddenly learning about his existence. The blueprint was laid out and looked at.

"The Controller must be on the therapist's side," said Marjorie Toomin, Ph.D.

"Huh?" My Controller has not thought about being on anyone's side.

"The skills must be re-directed to allow help from the outside. The Controller must not keep protecting the system from help as well as harm. The therapist and the Controller must work together."

My Controller recognized many colleagues in that room. He was also startled to see that some of the other Controllers were allowing their systems to need help. To be vulnerable. To be spiritual.

One woman spoke about her spiritual recovery. My lost, lonely disenfranchised spirit jumped with recognition. "Yes," the soul in me yearned. "Yes, I am here. See me. Know me."

For more than twenty years I'd been more spiritual than most of my friends, but the fragmentation inside meant an isolated spirit— detached from the Controller, the Little Ones, Pieces of Personality, the Mother, the Intellect, the Shamed, the Writer. All of them creating an as-needed existential response to the minute-to-minute needs of my day-to-day life. None of them were touched by the spiritual grace trapped inside me. It was a grace born out of a yearning for justice—but always on behalf of someone else. I can trace it back

to meeting that young lieutenant with malaria, who had just returned from Vietnam and was isolated alone in the hospital at Fort
Dix. Although there were many men on those wards with serious
and disfiguring wounds, something about him, the look in his eyes,
the great sad resignation that enveloped him, woke me up to war. I
was not yet ready to wake up to my own suffering; but I could take
on his. It was a moral indignation that partnered with the grief at
losing my son and it started me on a spiritual path that led through
my whole life.

It opened me up to the causes that were embraced by those whose
faith fueled their activism: Jim Douglass, a Catholic theologian who
went to jail for protesting the Vietnam War and started Ground Zero,
the Christian-based organization that fought the Trident Nuclear
Submarine base in my back yard; the Japanese Buddhist monks who
came to the Northwest to build a Peace Pagoda next to the nuclear
submarine naval base; a prayer gathering for world peace at Chief
Sealth's grave that brought together Steve Old Coyote and his Cre-
ator, a Lutheran priest and his God, the Japanese monks and their
Buddha. From Jim Douglass and Ground Zero, I learned about the
spiritual power of non-violence and the partnership of faiths that
saw beyond the limitations of definition. I gathered constantly with
others in prayer and meditation but it was for world peace not for
personal peace. I had a long way to go before I could name my self as
a person in need of spiritual solace and sacred recognition. At that
conference, that need was articulated. It gave voice to the personal
struggle I was finally beginning to recognize.

There was another voice at that conference, too—the voice of a
man who loved a woman like me. At the conference, William Koehler talked about "Surviving a Survivor." I'd experienced years of
failed attempts to connect with men—some lovely gentle men, some
destructive and disturbed. I had watched my sexual personal life disintegrate as quickly as it was born. There was no discriminating. Fate
brought me men, I brought my selves. The landscape was strewn
with debris. I did not know that attraction could become love, and
that love and sex, sex and caring, passion, respect and real unconditional loving could be a home for the relationship between a man
and a woman. I felt sex as sordid, which soured my romantic life as
quickly as it was born.

William Koehler spoke about another possibility. As the husband of a ritual abuse survivor, he spent seven years actively participating in his wife's recovery process while at the same time alleviating the impact of ritual abuse on his life and the lives of their children. He was funny and wise. His patience and understanding offered a beacon of possibility. But his presentation held a particularly chilling moment. "The most difficult thing," he said, "was when it became apparent, after years of therapy, that the person I had fallen in love with was not the original self." The walls of my Stone Self shuddered in recognition.

In some way he talked, not to my loneliness and the absence of a man in my life, but more to the inner Judge who reigned so imperious above and beyond the Shame, Fear and Helplessness that took up most of our time. I wanted a William Koehler in my life. It seemed that he should be cloned and sent as an emissary of healing into all our lives.

Patti Hills, a nurse, lecturer, educator—and survivor—from Portland, spoke with grace and composure about her own personal history. As a child she was prostituted and used in pornography. She told how her family was looked upon with such respect for taking their daughter to the symphony when she was young. The only problem was that she never got to hear the symphony. Her mother and step-father would turn her over to a pedophile for a few hours of work as a child prostitute while they listened to classical music.

She then spoke at length about child pornography and the insidious underground that makes it so prevalent and profitable—more than a five billion dollar a year industry in the U.S. alone. On and on—facts compiled from law enforcement statistics, facts spoken by respected experts, facts "I" could not believe. I was completely split. Nobody could do such a thing to a child. The truth is a lie. Only lies are the truth.

This recognized expert on ritual abuse, and also a survivor, spoke eloquently about the horrific. As a child her step-father would show her a photograph of herself involved in an act of bestiality. He would say to her, "See what a sick person you are? See how weird?" Her own personal history laid claim to the most savage abuse and humiliation. Yet she stood before us as a thoughtful, attractive woman offering a gentle, loving expression of hope and recovery. Her life had been fouled by deviancy but she wasn't. This message, simple and unreachable, laid the groundwork for the next few years of my recovery.

During those three days of conference activity, my elevator friend, Alana, and I kept each other in the world. I introduced her to City Lights Bookstore in San Francisco's North Beach district. We ate ice cream and drank coffee and marveled at the sisterhood we felt. If she had not been there I would have lifted my leaden body back and forth—my grief and joy banished—only my Intellect working the information, taking it in while everything else in me was left out in the cold, icy outpost that had become my body.

After the conference was over, Colin picked me up and took me back to my friend's place in San Francisco where I borrowed a car and a sleeping bag and drove to Half Moon Bay to my secret sushi spot. On the way I listened to tapes I had bought at the conference. The implications of community, of understanding, of support, linked me to a world of my own. I was a survivor of ritual abuse and I was not alone. That the acceptance of such a horrific reality could bring such sweet joy is something only God and a survivor could begin to understand.

It was dark when I reached the hostel at Pigeon Point, about twenty miles north of Santa Cruz. I found a spot to park along the dirt road at the edge of the sea a few hundred yards from the hostel – which was already closed for the night. The Survivor wanted to stretch out and sleep on the beach but the consensus inside voted to stay in the car, fold back the seat and open the windows just a bit so we could hear the sea. It was an uncomfortable night for the Body and a night of flying exhilaration for the Mind, which seemed to open out and into the pulse of the universe. It felt as though it belonged out there—beyond the imaginings of this life and the bindings of this earth. I watched from a distance, awed by its power, sorry, in a way, that all it had to come back to was pieces—pieces of me.

I don't know quite what happened that night. It was as though there was a fleeting release from the prison of this body. A moment of reunion for a Mind that had been long cut off from its source. As though it went back to see its family for a moment. To let them know it was alright, that the job was taking a little longer than usual but it was well and would be back soon. A moment of communion that had nothing to do with me.

In the morning some of us ate oranges, some ate chocolate. We were stiff and the euphoria of the night before gave way to scathing self-consciousness. "What are you doing here anyway? Who do you think you are? What a puny and stupid gesture - to come out here and be holier-than-thou alone. Who cares? You really are pathetic."

The voices reigned fast and furious. "Your life is a lie. Everything you do, think, feel, are, is a lie. You might as well die." When the assault comes it is a physical one. A slumping into a feeling of physical filth—as though breath itself is mocking my existence.

It was the Mind's will that got me up and about. For awhile my senses seemed artificial, as though borrowed. I knew I was seeing, smelling and hearing the sea, but during the last few days I had come too close to the truth of me. The pulses of hatred and fear were activated almost beyond reach. I prayed. And as I struggled with the gesture of prayer, it too, became a lie.

The day was a clear sunny expanse of sky and sea. The car was a jumble of papers, books, bedding and last night's sushi. I was a crumpled, puffy-eyed creature struggling to make sense of the universe, inside and out. It seems that I remember laughing. Stumbling out of the car into the magnificence of the morning. The color of life everywhere. Something seemed ludicrous, something so grand and so much larger than I was, such a celebration of glory, that all I could do was laugh. And find a place to pee.

I drove a few miles down the road to the big driftwood "fist" that marks a trail to the beach. Over my years of self-exile and isolation in Oakland, the stretch of shoreline between San Francisco and Santa Cruz had become a friend. A park ranger had told me about the fist and its beach and it had become one of my favorite retreats. The trail stretches only about half a mile to the sea but within yards it closes out the highway with a bounty of delicate shrubs, wildflowers and dune grass. That morning the sun was just beginning to warm my back and light up the land around me as I set out.

It was a Monday in March. There was no-one in sight. The coves were sparkling, the sand still damp from tide and dew. It was a beauty all mine and I knew I must do something to honor my presence in the world, even though I could barely feel it. I knew that ritual was anathema, prayer a dangerous stranger, and language a lie. But this was real. The cove, the pools, sea, sand and stones all lifting themselves up in a celebration of light so transcendent that my eyes were forced to see and my heart to hear.

It all wrapped around me, invisible and complete. In a small hollow in rocks just above high tide I put four stones, three shells and a small piece of driftwood into some sort of purposeful proximity. Each stone chosen for a quality of light and resilience. The shells for enduring delicacy. The driftwood worn elegant by storms. The hollow itself protective, maternal. The rocks around vigorous, protective. The incipient sea, sands, and sky.

I didn't do much. Just looked at my small creation with a child's sense of satisfaction. The Little Ones all pleased. Some of the Big Ones all pooh-poohing like mean parents. But it was my very own ritual, my very own altar. In spite of the derision and disdain, in spite of the self-hatred, in spite of the disenfranchised soul, I did it! I prayed. Yet even as it was done I was forgetting. Losing the self that was leading the way. So I took a photograph to remind me of the moment. The prayer. It would be years before even the photograph was real. Now I am in India where prayer is everywhere, defining the very shape of existence.

FIVE

Our room in Rajpur has charm. There are crisp colorful curtains at the windows and wicker furniture artfully arranged around the room. After all the hours of driving, I am exhausted and collapse onto one of the beds, leaving it to Thrinley to be sociable with our hosts while I contemplate crawling under the covers completely dressed, shoes and all. But tea is on it way.

I wanted to talk to Thrinley about today's wrenching poverty-stricken drive from Delhi but there are no words to get there. I know the edges will wear off. But if there is to be any lesson at all, about life, about gratitude, about needs, about justice, I won't forget. I've breathed in all the depths of poverty in one day. I'm hoping that in some way they will breathe some new understanding into me.

It is Matthew who brings us tea, complete with a small dish of sugared chick peas. He's a very slight elderly Indian gent with a permanent bow to his posture. The tea pours out of the pot with milk already in it; it's very strong and there is a touch of spice that heightens the flavor. The tray, the cups and saucers, the charm of the room, the elegance of being served, is a great soothing. My mind, still spinning with repulsion, shock and confusion about the poverty I've seen today, is suddenly buoyed by a moment of understanding. And this, too.

"Two-faced Truth, the Either, the Or, and the Holy Both." It's a quote from Cyril Connolly, the other quote I memorized years ago. I just can never remember whether it's "Wholly Both" or "Holy Both." Perhaps it doesn't matter. Perhaps they are the same thing. Right now, I gaze around this room in astonishment. It is so normal, so much what I am used to—sheets on the bed, shelter from the storm, privacy, quiet, four walls and a few windows, a private bathroom and a light on the table between the beds. What is it that we become used to? And why us? Why not them?

I don't know how to measure the experience of driving through that endless tunnel of poverty. There is nothing I can do about it so what use is it to let it in? What good does it do to be shocked? It sure as hell doesn't make me a better traveling companion or a more congenial house guest. The inner and the outer, the suffering and the end of suffering, the anger and the acceptance, the tourist and the traveler, the pilgrim and the atheist, the haves and the have-nothings—they all ripple across my mind and leave emptiness in their wake. I am much too tired. And with no small amount of guilt and remorse, I sink into my new mystery novel, into my nice bed, and into the great warmth of escape and denial. It's the very best I can do.

When I wake at seven it is to a new day. Outside the windows are soft green hills that remind me of Marin County in California. I hear a sound like monkeys and the sky is a clear, clean blue. I remember a dream in the night of caring for a small infant. I have returned home to take care of the baby but am supposed to be back in India. The dream leaves me unsettled. I am in India. Who is the baby I have left behind? I tell Thrinley about it and she says maybe this trip is for me and that perhaps the frightened child inside, who needs so much attention, has been left behind. She knows whereof I come from, my struggles with my history, my struggle to survive. I nod, "maybe." As Thrinley does her practice, I lie back quietly and let the soothing sounds of her mantra begin my morning. Yesterday's journey is now a dream, not even a nightmare. It is now simply yet another new day in a new country.

I love waking up into the daylight of a place for the first time. I remember a first morning wake-up many years ago in Maui where I'd gone for a job interview as a Montessori teacher. Getting off the plane gave me my first smell of soft scented tropical air and my first feeling of night-time warmth. I slept that night in a screened porch and woke up early to the soft-throated sounds of some kind of dove and my first sight of palm trees. Then, wandering down to the end of the lawn, I encountered white sand and the blue reaches of the Pacific Ocean. I was dumbfounded as I didn't even know I'd slept near the sea. It was as though I suddenly didn't know how to see.

Later that year, after Colin and I had moved to Maui, he asked me, "Mom, how do our eyes make us see?" It was one of those questions only a five-year-old can ask, a question for the ages.

How do we decide what to see? Who was seeing yesterday's reaches of unending poverty? Who is seeing these soft green hills in early morning light, lawns and gardens tended with care, and a small stone deck with a chair and a clothesline, a sky free of smog? Who decides whether it's right or whether it's wrong? Who's to know? How do our eyes make us see? And not see? I am aware of the shift into this new reality where all is clean and familiar. And I am aware that I am aware. I'm also aware that the poverty has not gone away, even if I have.

Thrinley goes across the street to the Sakya Buddhist Temple compound to report her arrival and to find out where to deliver the big mama suitcase. I take my time getting up. A room open to the glories of nature is a room that does not have to be left in a hurry. I still feel wrecked, as though every tense moment from yesterday is lodged in my muscles, every grief bone deep. I do a few meager exercises and crawl back into bed to watch the light rise in the room. I take a shower, dress, and go back to bed to read. I can stay in a room a long time if I can see outside to trees and other living things.

When Thrinley gets back, we're both hungry and head out to find a meal. She knows where Rajpur village is so we head uphill past the Sakya Temple where young monks in long maroon robes are playing soccer in the courtyard. Before reaching the little village, we get to the Hotel Royal Inn, a conspicuously new-looking building with outdoor dining furniture suggesting lunch. The waitress is an attractive and gregarious young Tibetan woman wearing slightly low-slung jeans and a casual jacket over a t-shirt. She asks us lots of lively questions and is thrilled to know we will be going to Dharamsala. She escaped from Tibet, she tells us, and went to live in the Tibetan Children's Village in Dharamsala when she first got to India.

"I didn't finish school," she said. "But I studied hotel business in Mussoorie. This is my job." She gestures to the hotel and interprets the menu for us. Her English is excellent and her casual confidence striking. Our lunch is an array of Indian dishes, all tasty and unrecognizable. We eat leisurely and read the *Hindustan Times*. It's December 3rd, our fourth day in India and our first newspaper. The headlines are big: It's the twentieth anniversary of the chemical explosion at Bhopal.

Before its name became one with tragedy, Bhopal was considered one of India's most treasured cities. Like Delhi, its architecture had been enhanced by the Moghuls who built handsome palaces and stunning gardens throughout its regions. Mosques, too, embellished the landscape of the kingdom of Bhopal; it was a city of great culture and beauty, renowned for its four women rulers who developed railways, roads and running water as well as centers of philosophy, poetry and painting. Bhopal, because of its architectural and cultural elegance, was known as the "Baghdad of India."

With India's independence in 1947, Bhopal became the capital of Madhya Pradesh, a province encompassing the vast reaches of central India. It was a city thriving with renaissance zeal until December, 1984, when forty-two tons of methyl isocyanate escaped from the Union Carbide plant in a toxic gas that decimated the population.

In *Five Past Midnight in Bhopal*, their compelling account of the Bhopal tragedy, Dominique Lapierre and Javier Moro estimate the explosion caused from sixteen to thirty-thousand immediate deaths and has had lasting effects on three-quarters of the city's people.

What does it mean when we destroy sacred places and their sacred people? As I sit on the lawn of the Hotel Royal Inn, enjoying a fine meal and a leisurely indulgence in time and contemplation on this warm morning in Rajpur, my immediate mind rattles about in dismay. I feel a layer of incomprehension that refuses to be penetrated. It's a mind that doesn't get it, a mind that sees humanity dead-set on self-destruction, not only of the infrastructure of history and progress but also of that which is spiritual and timeless. What's the point? This mind wants to know. If life isn't sacred, why bother? Why are we here at all?

This is a mind that views progress as the pollution of all possibility. It marvels at the stupidity of politicians and their idiotic ego-driven deeds that defile all the potential of what it means to be fully human. It has nothing but disgust and contempt for the corporate power structure that results in the destruction of a city like Bhopal, and the sacrifice of sacred places and tender people in such places as Baghdad, all to fill the deep pockets of an oily and endless military, industrial, technological greed. It is an angry mind resolute in its desolateness. It is not a mind the Dalai Lama would approve of. It is also a mind that has kept me alive.

In the landscape of survival there are no good intentions. When trust has been betrayed on a cellular level, there is no-one to trust. Ever. This is when this mind is born; this is when it enters the body. It arrives intact, complete and completely protective. It is a mind on a mission. It's a mind that has gotten me into a lot of trouble—some of it good, some of it not-so-good. It's a mind that doesn't discern between threats large and small. It is a mind primed for it all. It doesn't trust anybody, not even me.

Through the years, as I've grappled with all the things that go on in my surviving and thriving life, this mind—insightful and inciting—has been both my biggest enemy and my biggest ally. It has kept me safe from everything perpetrated by humankind. But most of all, it has kept me safe from love.

This was not an easy realization. As I worked with Brian over the years, this mind of mistrust was with us every step of the way. It was unyielding. It is unyielding. Even now, sitting here in India, it's paying attention. And it's got its ever-watchful eye on Thrinley.

On the night before leaving for India I had gone to Fred Meyer's to get something special to wear. This is not an oxymoron. Those of us who live on small islands and frequent the local thrift shop for our next stylish look can find something special to wear almost anywhere. Along with camera batteries and Handi-Wipes, I'd found a nice fleece vest. It was crimson maroon, the color of Tibetan Buddhist monks' robes. It would be my moment of color, I thought. I can wear it over everything everywhere. On it I would put the many layered heart a dear friend had given me for my birthday. It would be my comfort zone. It would keep me safe on the plane, safe on the planet.

Yesterday morning, as we were getting ready for our drive to Rajpur, Thrinley asked if she could wear my vest because she was in need of a little color. Of course, I said. Today, she's still wearing it; and my ever-protective mind is noticing how comfortable she is in it. He is not very Buddhist; he is pissed. "She's likely to keep it," the Mighty Mind tells me. "You won't get it back."

I know better, of course. Thrinley has no intention of keeping it. But this mind is not to be reckoned with and is lashing out towards her as though she is a raiding marauder, a murderer of women and children. But only in my head, of course; outside I am quietly and happily sipping tea and reading the paper. I know what is happening. A child inside, learning from the wanting of the vest and then the actually getting of it, is wailing in despair and grief. The Mighty Mind is doing his job, protecting the desolate hordes of wee ones. They have all gathered around the wanting of the vest, the waiting to see if the one who wanted it and got it gets to keep it. Or if, perhaps, the wanting will once again be the poisonous snake in the pit of the family.

As I sink into the *Hindustan Times* and the tragedy that was, and is, Bhopal, I am aware of this inner war of worlds. And as I drink my tea and appreciate the companionable silence of being with my dear friend, I reassure the combatants inside that all is well, not to worry, we will get back the vest. They are not so sure. Living this way has grown familiar. It is the way it is.

Moments of tragedy don't go away. Twenty years away from Bhopal does not diminish the losses, or the language of loss. My own trauma, stamped timelessly on the minds of my small ones, does not go away. Like Bhopal, it gets looked at, remembered, managed, honored, explained and also, at times, forgotten. But it does not go away.

Sheepishly, I break into the companionable silence, "Thrinley," I say. "I don't want to lose the vest forever. I got it special for the trip."

The words sound absurd. Of course she won't keep it forever. But someone inside really needs to know and really needs me to say something, to lay claim.

She responds instantly, "Of course, here have it."

"Oh no," I say. "Not right now. Later is fine."

It is a brief exchange but inside I am stricken with shame and embarrassment. As much as I know about my selves and their ways, I have yet to fully pay attention, to accept them.

Much has been written about "multiple personality disorder." So much, in fact, that it has been written out of vogue; it is no longer part of the lexicon of psychotherapy. The new jargon is "dissociative disorder." The dis-association of one self from another. *Webster's* weighs in with: *The splitting off of certain mental processes from the main body of consciousness, with varying degrees of autonomy resulting.* As a definition, it comes closer than "multiple personality disorder." A personality is something superficial, something to wear to a party. My parts have character; they are characters, fully formed with minds of their own. Each has a "self," timeless and true.

Over the years, as I have worked with this complex interior world and its many selves, I have gained great respect for their hearts and minds. Even so, integrating them into my "core self," as it is named, is a delicate and precarious process. Most of all I have to stay connected to the process. I have to stay tuned to when I am being triggered by something that has nothing to do with what's happening. I have to keep an inner part of me open and free of the fears and deceptions that have formed my responses in the past. I have to ask my inner guides to rescue the parts of me stuck in the time and circumstances of their abuse. I have to make conscious and purposeful the process that has unconsciously come to my rescue throughout my life. This is an unfolding, ongoing process that challenges me every day because I want to be "normal" without having to think about it. Not a chance.

My Buddhist inclinations have been invaluable in helping me differentiate the signals of my past from the signals of my present. It remains as a kind of backdrop for my moving parts. It holds them. In his book, *Transforming the Mind*, the Dalai Lama says that we tend to assume that there is some kind of singular entity called "mind." In Buddhism this isn't the case. "If we probe a little deeper," he says, "we will see that what we call consciousness actually covers a diverse and complex world of thoughts, emotions, sensory experiences, and so forth." He writes of the luminous mind and "the beginning-less nature of consciousness."

My backdrop mind is not luminous but it is steady and true; perhaps it's what others know as the "self," the shifting self that moves through diverse and complex thoughts and emotions. Perhaps my selves are sometimes simply a bit more independent. They don't like to hang out all the time with the central self; there are too many painful images on that canvas. So they go about their merry business, free of memory and continuity. It is a comforting thought, if not for the forgetting, the isolation, and the desolation.

Contrary to popular literature, my selves didn't want names. They were states of being, not people. Even they knew that. Yet in working with, for, and in spite of my many different selves for years, becoming conscious friends with them has been a huge challenge. At all costs, I wanted to be "normal." It cost me years of my life as I did everything I could to deny the reality of my different parts. In effect, all I had to do was accept them as well as the helpers inside that could help me accept them. But like any "normal" person, I didn't want to have parts, let alone have parts with names. It is this denial that I invested in as I struggled to heal. I was my own worst enemy.

Brian would take issue with this perspective. He observed how I always wanted to personalize my struggle as "my fault." He saw the bigger picture, the one in which conditioning had most effectively succeeded in isolating me inside my own shame and guilt and responsibility. That I was a victim of a deviant and debilitating system of mind control was not something I could, or wanted to take comfort in. My parts were my enemies because they weren't "normal." I've learned that neither is "normal" normal. This has been the last bastion of my battle with the mighty tsunami of denial that kept me afloat on the waters of my life. My parts kept me alive. Why would I ever want to see them as terms in somebody's litany of clinical diagnosis?

Brian knew better. He liked all my parts right away. He knew them, respected them, and was never afraid of them. But it took me many years of emotional healing and cognitive understanding of my inner system before I could actively partner with my parts in my own psychological and spiritual recovery. I was well-trained to resist any help that might come my way. My therapy history is testimony to this—I would disappear from it for months and sometimes years at a time. I was afraid of being who I was, a woman with multiplicity, a woman who was not whom I appeared to be, to either myself or others. Most of all, I was trained never to know who I was and what had happened to me, and never to ask. As Brian and I worked together over the years he never failed all the parts of me that were split off and dissociated. Looking back I see this as a superb service. A life-saving service. Brian showed me a path that had room for us all, a path I continue to discover.

But ahhhh, the luminous mind. I got a peek at it once. In 1987, when my life as I knew it was disintegrating like smoke in the wind, I got myself a job cooking for 16 people and practically no money at a year-long silent Buddhist retreat. It was at Cloud Mountain Retreat Center, a hundred miles south of Seattle. The Tibetan Buddhist monk in residence was Gen Lamrimpa, which means "honored teacher", and he was helping a small group of retreat participants with their Shamata, or calm abiding, meditation. The Dalai Lama had approached Gen Lamrimpa in his small meditation hut in the hills high above Dharamsala, where he'd been in retreat for seventeen years, and asked him to go to the West to teach. In residence at Cloud Mountain, Gen Lamrimpa guided the year-long retreat and in doing so had a translator, Alan Wallace.

On one weekend, Alan presided over teachings and meditation. He guided us into our minds. Imagine you are in a wide open valley, he said. Imagine wildflowers and blue skies and birds flying through the warm air and the round green hills gently rising around you. Imagine backing up along a trail—a safe trail—towards a cave and seeing, hearing, smelling and feeling all the beauty reaching out in front of you as you rise higher on the hillside. See the small cottages, the people going about their daily routines, the harmony of it all. Then imagine being at the mouth of the cave and looking out over the valley one last time. Then turn into the cave and walk towards the back. Imagine a luminous stream flowing gently at the back of the cave. Take off your clothes and lie down in the stream. Feel its warm buoyancy, its purity, and its shimmering light-filled awareness. Imagine it is your mind.

I don't remember if this is precisely how Alan described this meditative journey. I do know it opened, for me, just for a moment, a window into something divine. An awareness of pure mind, the mind-stream, the luminous nature of consciousness—a consciousness that flows through everything, that buoys up the life in the valley and the valley itself. As I struggled through the next few years of dissembling, this vision of luminous mind stayed with me as a beacon of light at the back of the cave that had become my life. It was a mind upon which to rest.

Back inside my newspaper, Bhopal continues, this time on the editorial page where it's noted that 400,000 people have been seriously maimed and injured as a result of the chemical explosion and that "much more has been said than done to meet the victims' demands for compensation, medical care and rehabilitation." Arguably the worst industrial catastrophe in history, the explosion at the Union Carbide factory, known as the "Beautiful Plant," was the result of a "combination of technological, legal, organizational and human errors." The editorial continues: "Multinational corporations exploit the tempting competitive advantage that developing countries like India offer by way of low-cost labor, access to markets and lower operating costs." It concludes with a call for an international treaty that will insure compensation for those injured in industrial accidents.

A wave of helplessness comes over me, a memory from my experience inside the demonstrations against the World Trade Organization meetings in Seattle when I first began to realize the depth of the damage caused by the onslaught of multinational corporations around the world. In researching and writing, *The Battle in Seattle— The Story Behind and Beyond the WTO Demonstrations*, I had learned Too Much At Once about how these corporations, with all of the rights and none of the responsibilities of a human being, had set up shop in poverty-stricken areas where there were no irritating environmental or labor laws to contend with. If there was a moment that inspired that book it was walking in the streets of WTO Seattle behind a small group of peasant rice farmers from Japan. Finding out why they were there started the thread that unraveled every assumption of my daily life. It also led me to the winemakers of France, the coffee farmers of Brazil, the cotton farmers of India, and organic farmers everywhere.

It all comes down to seeds. Traditional farming has always been rooted in the locale as well as in the local community. Crops grow familiar with such things as the weather, the soil, the turn of a hoe, and the way the wind does, or doesn't blow. From soil to supper, there is a web of affinity that nurtures the entire process non-stop.

Seeds adjust accordingly, refining themselves to their environment and becoming invaluable in the process. Saving seeds for next year is as important as this year's crop. But in India, and other developing countries around the world, farmers have been having their seeds stolen at a terribly rapid rate. And not by bandits in the barn—by agribusiness.

At the risk of oversimplifying the equation: When a corporation genetically identifies the make-up of a seed, it gets to legally own the rights to the seed. Then it gets to build in a terminator gene to keep the seed from reproducing itself. This guarantees that every year the corporation gets to sell the seed to the very farmers who were responsible for its ongoing existence in the first place. This means that farmers, who are used to growing things rather than taking them apart, are suddenly being deprived of that which has sustained them, their community and their land for untold generations. This is why, in the streets of WTO Seattle, there were so many farmers from all corners of our food-producing planet.

In India, the results of agribusiness taking over farming are beyond tragic. Farmers, pressured by the export-based global economy, were forced to grow cotton for export instead of food crops for community. Then they were forced to shift from open-pollinated seeds, which can be saved, to high-priced hybrids that must be purchased annually. The hybrids, however, required greater amounts of pesticides. The farmers, who were expecting to make greater profits from cotton, had to take out loans to afford the pesticides and the high-priced hybrid seeds. The corporations, oh-so conveniently, offered the farmers loans. The interest and the extra costs created a burden of debt resulting in an ongoing epidemic of suicides. It is estimated that ten thousand Indian farmers a year commit suicide because they can no longer sustain their families. They kill themselves by drinking the very pesticide that was supposed to make their lives easier.

When I made plans to come on this trip, I knew all about this stuff. Trying to do something about corporate greed and its degrading effects on humanity was what WTO Seattle was all about. I was a wreck when I finished writing that book. Everywhere I looked, everything I wore, ate, drank, used and misused became a reflection of the global injustice that I'd been blind to and complicit with.

I was in a kind of shock in the years following the book's publication. The ways in which we in the West are riding on the backs of so many poor people on the planet infiltrated my very being. Suddenly, I wasn't only carrying the shame of my childhood in my bones; I was carrying the shame of the whole fucking planet. That's when I got a job driving a bus in circles around a beautiful island.

Thrinley and I finish lunch and head back to our guest house. Renee, our lovely and lively hostess, brings out shawls, pillow cases and bedspreads of glorious color and hue. She gets them from the local indigenous community renown for their handiwork, she says. We each buy four pillow cases for 450 rupees. I wonder how much she paid for these, I'm thinking as I fork over the ten bucks. Are people going blind making them for a handful of rupees a day? Is Renee a corporation, too? And if so, what does that make me? A corporate lackey? But it's not why I'm here so my callow questions get to remain unanswered.

Exhaustion settles in and I go upstairs to our room to rest. Thrinley arrives not long afterwards and we agree that we're both feeling a kind of depressed lethargy. We'd better walk. So we once again take the road up to Rajpur; this time actually we get there, passing along the way the local dumpster restaurant and its distinguished clientele of cows, dogs and monkeys. In the village, we find an email stall and check for messages from home, but neither one of us has the energy to send any. We're back in our respective beds by seven, firmly resolved to stay awake until eight o'clock. Neither of us is successful.

SIX

"Sorrow everywhere. Slaughter everywhere. If babies
are not starving someplace; they are starving
somewhere else. With flies in their nostrils.
But we enjoy our lives because that's what God wants.
Otherwise the mornings before summer dawn would not
be made so fine."

I wake to thinking about Jack Gilbert's poem. About enjoyment, pleasure, gladness, happiness and delight. How are they different? Why does he write, "We can do without pleasure, but not delight?" What is pleasure? Is sex pleasure? And is it "the mornings before summer dawn" that cause delight? Does delight happen in the mind and pleasure in the body? And what makes us glad? Can happiness just happen? And what do we do when we enjoy? And does God really want us to do it? Does God really want me to lie here, happy, while the world goes on outside the window where suffering and injustice define the day?

This is one of those weird questions that plague me without answer. I don't know how to define God but in human terms I'm pretty sure *She* has a broken open heart and I'm almost certain *He* has a big Dalai Lama belly laugh. And how else can God exist but in human terms. Even the words we use to define the inexpressible divinity of God are human. Language does that; it has the habit of coming out of the human mouth. It is conceived. Perhaps we are the language of God. We are conceived. Then, like language, we often miss the mark; we garble and get mixed-up; we dangle modifiers and reverse the order of things; we are rendered speechless. We only work well when we are understood. And there, I suspect, is the rub. How do we ever get to be understood?

My own life has been based upon a big misunderstanding. I didn't know I existed. This can be a problem, particularly in relationship to others. If I don't exist, how can I be understood? And here's the scary part. If I don't exist, how can you? This brings us to the really big word, ontological. It has everything to do with being and the experience of being. It is a word I bumped into when I was twenty and pregnant, a captive on an island in Canada, where the dentist had a job before being drafted. Even though my parents had not allowed me to go college, to be educated, it didn't mean I couldn't educate myself. I read everything and mostly hefty philosophical tomes about existence. All these years later, I understand why. Back then, it was the big Wise Guy inside who was making sure we found our way—one way or another. He's the inner guide who, through so much of my life, kept me on the track of intellect and learning. He knew I was ontologically-challenged and made sure I learned the word, even though it would be twenty years before I began to understand why.

Lying in bed under warm blankets in this gentle room with its flowered curtains and my socks hanging to dry on the ironwork at the windows, I am utterly, and momentarily, content. I am being. From the deepest place inside, I feel a familiarity with my self. There is nothing to understand in this feeling and if I try to understand it, I will begin to feel ashamed. Why me, when there is so much misery? Why do I get to be safe and warm and happy? Why me? It is also a question I ask in the darkest of times. It has about as much use in the light. Questioning the existence of God seems about as complicated as questioning the existence of ourselves. How do we know we exist? Quantum physics, with its vast exploration of inner space, is getting us closer and closer to a deeper and deeper mystery. Not only time, it appears, is relative, but space has a few twists of its own. As does matter, which apparently can be in two places at once. Believing in God means simply believing in a word that cannot be understood.

Feeling the presence of the divine, however, plunges us into delight. And this is perhaps what Jack Gilbert means in his poem. *We must risk delight. We can do without pleasure, but not delight.* Delight rises without warning; it takes us by surprise. Pleasure we can plan for. Delight seems to lay in-waiting. All we have to do is show up. This is always harder than it sounds. My mind starts to ramble through its own devising. How do I show up for today? Will I be burdened by shame and guilt about my existence or be purely and simply glad for it? Am I in search of meaning or do I let meaning come in search of me? As I lie in wait for Thrinley to finish her morning prayers I realize that mostly I am in search of breakfast. I am hungry.

It's shortly after seven when we leave the guest house. The first thing we encounter is two monkeys fussing with one another on the gate. Their ministrations to one another are gentle and thorough. Whatever crawling creatures they find are carefully plucked from under their mate's hair and popped into the mouth of the nit-picker. Suddenly I understand nit-picking. It is very, very thorough and it requires tremendous focus and concentration. Not wanting to disturb them, Thrinley and I wait respectfully for the monkeys to finish before we open the gate to the street. Around us, the early morning light is having its way with the landscape and there is a warm glow to all the colors and shades of green in the yard. It is easy to be patient.

In the midst of our monkey gazing, an elderly gent comes out of the guest house and proceeds to fuss about with an old and clunky little car parked in the driveway. He, too, is concentrating. Suddenly the whole world seems brilliantly focused and intent, even the early morning quiet seems suspended in concentration. As the fellow turns away from his car he is holding a package. He looks over at us. "Would you like to see some photos?" he asks, cheerfully. There is a sense that we are all conspiring, the monkeys and the man and us. This day is starting out like every day so far in India: There is a sense of purpose beyond our planning. All we have to do is show up.

The fellow has a British accent; he is short and compact with bright blue eyes and a no-nonsense demeanor. There's no exchange of names, he just whips out his photographs and happily shares them with us. It turns out that he lives in the mountains beyond Mussoorie, the hill town high on the ridge above Rajpur. The photographs are of his small house and the looming and lovely snow-covered mountains that are his view. His passion for the place is palpable and contagious.

"How about going in for breakfast?" he says.

Thrinley and I share a quick glance of agreement. This is a bit of a big deal for me as for some dumb reason I've equated food safety with "eating out." Perhaps I think there's a department of public health at work in the restaurant business, even as I know damn well there isn't. Suck it up, I tell myself, and hope somebody inside is listening.

At the breakfast table, our hostess, Renee, informs us that we've met Mr. King, their dear friend. Eighty-two-year-old Mr. King, it turns out, was born in India of British parents and sent to England at the age of seven to to acquire an appropriate accent. But it was too late. He was already in love with India; and except for sailing around the world, he has lived here ever since. Mr. King tried marriage but adventure held more allure. He is very funny and we are all laughing out loud before breakfast is on the table.

The scrambled eggs are great. Even at home I like them cooked until they bounce and Matthew serves me my blasphemous request accordingly. It turns out that Matthew is not Renee's or Jaant's father, he's their servant. This elderly, wizened and wise looking gent with the shy smile and mischievous eyes lives with the family and appears to have a hand in everything from eggs to babysitting. In one of our first conversations, when I was raw-nerved from our poverty ride and still exhausted, Renee had talked to us about the "servant issue."

"Yes, Mathew is our servant and everybody loves him," she said. At which point I had chomped on my tongue, barely holding it in check, and disappeared upstairs. My Buddhist brains were missing in action. I could barely contain my contempt. At least I had the sense to get my miserable self out of the room.

I am so narrow-minded and judgmental about issues I don't fully understand that they can often float moat-like around me, insulating me in the privacy of my own mind, where it is no fun at all. In the meantime, life happens "out there" to everybody else. This is where my rage has taken its greatest toll, where it has eaten whole my opportunities to connect and to love. It is a visceral rage that dismisses immediately the existence of the other, that renders them squished under the flat foot of my mind. And the worst part is that Pissed-As-Hell mind is also right. This is where it gets confusing. Because it is a mind that fueled my playwriting, a mind that gave me the courage to write about the big issues such as nuclear war, abortion and the

Holocaust as well as the easier stuff like Laundromats, sex and religion. What it hasn't learned to do is distinguish issues from people. This gives it a dangerous analytical edge that first of all sees people as threatening.

Through my many years of work with Brian, Pissed-As-Hell, an old and reliable inner self, has persevered without giving an inch—even with Brian. Perhaps I should say, particularly with Brian. Because Brian is always helping and if there's one thing Pissed-As-Hell knows, it's that helpers are hazardous to our health. He, and he is a "he," was so intent on protecting us all inside that he very rigorously protected us from getting the help we needed. And Brian was help. It took a very long time to get Pissed-As-Hell to understand there was such a thing.

This is where the real tragedy of child abuse deepens unfathomably. When the people who are supposed to care and protect us, turn upon us when we are at our most innocent, a great bruising happens. What begins as a violation upon the body becomes a violation upon the soul. It is an ontological wound. It bruises our very being. This is what only survivors know—along with the saintly and brilliant therapists who survive them.

When I think about the years of patient, loving support Brian brought to our work and the bottomless pit of resistance that I contributed—all I can do is shake my head in wonder. I wish he was here to see me in India. To see the partnership I have with Pissed-As-Hell as he tries to cut and paste people right out of my consciousness. Thanks to Buddhism and Brian, I have learned to respect Pissed-As-Hell as a Cautionary Mind, a mind that will never forget the treachery of the known world. Remembering is his job. Sometimes we wrestle and sometimes I lose. But never for very long.

It only took me half a day to get over being pissed as hell about Matthew's servitude. I am beginning to realize that there is a social structure here that I don't understand at all. Renee and Jaant are gracious and friendly, their house is open and expansive and they treat Matthew with respect. They have both instantly welcomed us to their home, without reservation. Even though Pissed-As-Hell thinks Mathew should be pissed as hell, we've successfully negotiated our way to a truce and he's letting me love Matthew and Renee and Jaant. Somewhere inside I breathe a big sigh of relief.

It's a convivial breakfast. Along with our eggs, we have toast with good butter and there's tasty jam on the table. There's another guest at the table, too. Robert is a Tibetan Buddhist monk from our backyard back home, Vancouver Island. He is an American living in Canada who is visiting India to meet his Tibetan teachers. And much to my relief, he is way more obsessed with his digestive system than I am with mine. His tales of intestinal woe, imminent woe and post-woe are hilarious. He's my favorite kind of monk—he has a good sense of humor and no sense of over-zealous spiritual propriety. He's also afraid of flying. After small plane-hopping between holy sites in India, Robert proclaims he now realizes that he has a profound attachment to life.

Through my years of ontological distress and plain old despair, I've often thought of suicide. I just never had the will. As close as I got was riding the out-breath until it stretched out before me like a wild and endless plain. It felt as though I could float away from life on that breath and just not bother to inhale. Simple. But the body has a different agenda. Not matter how expansive and inviting that freedom-seeking out-breath, the in-breath always gets the last say.

Over breakfast, we talk about life and death, toast and butter, and our various faiths, which include Buddhist, Hindu, Christian and Confused. Turns out that our servant, Matthew, is a Christian and will be leaving for a few days over Christmas to visit with his family. Thrinley and Robert are Buddhists and unequivocal about it; Renee is Hindu but doesn't go to temple; I am Confused. Even though I've considered myself Buddhist for more than thirty years, I currently go to church. I call myself either a Buddhist Episcopalian or an Episcopalian Buddhist. It all depends upon the company I keep.

This spiritual quandary is all His Holiness the Dalai Lama's fault. Many years ago I went to hear him speak in Seattle. One of the surprising things he said was that too many people were becoming Buddhist. He thought we should be cultivating our own spiritual backyards instead of jumping onto the bandwagon of Buddhism. He said this very thoughtfully and although at the time I was twenty years away from any inclination towards Christianity, his words stayed with me and meant something.

As we all sit around this Sunday breakfast table, mulling the spiritual state-of-affairs in the world-at-large, I am hugely grateful for this gregarious start to our day. It's our first bit of real social-izing in India and I feel anchored in reassuring and familiar eccen-tricity. Most of all we bring ourselves and our stories to the table. Even the spiritual ranting and raving roams the broad expanse of our lives where we all share the same fears and frustrations. And we all conspire to laugh in spite of it all. I say a silent thank-you to the two monkeys of the morning who got us to stop just long enough to keep us here for breakfast.

As we finish up with our breakfast revelry, Renee suggests to Thrinley and me that we meet up in the afternoon and go to visit the pottery district in Dehradun. Thrinley is thrilled. She has been a potter for many years; her work ranges from small production pieces to large one-of-a-kind sculptures. One of her burnished raku vessels is one of my most prized possessions.

Before we get ready for our afternoon adventure, we stroll up to the village cyber stall. Finally we have some time and energy to email home. The black keyboard on the computer I'm using is so worn out the letters have been reproduced with white correction ink in a blurry reminder of the alphabet. Cows and kids walk by; occasionally a motorcycle, its engine shut off to preserve gas, weaves silently down the hill. The electricity in the cyber stall stays on al-most the whole time. We only have to start our emails over once.

SEVEN

We decide to take a cab to Dharamsala. Actually, it was decided for us. It happened when we told our new friends that we were planning on taking the bus. Jaant could not conceal his distress. "Are you sure? You could take a cab." Shit. A cab ride is safer than a bus? And right away I knew it was.

So Thrinley and I weighed our pocketbooks against our lives and opted for our lives, even though only a few days earlier we'd taken what we swore was our last cab ride ever throughout history. The cab will cost us 4500 rupees, about a hundred dollars, to get door-to-door service to Dharamsala. Because there's something about recognizing the face you trust your life to, we asked Mr. Manjeet if we could have our same lovely driver from the Delhi delivery.

"Of course," he said.

Now it's 5:45 in the morning and I'm stacking up our luggage on the dark steps outside, all the while going through my usual bereavement at leaving a place. Sometimes I can't go to the bathroom without grieving. I really hate that part—the part that knows every departure as an inconceivable and complete loss.

At six o'clock, our driver and his cab are not yet in the driveway. From the Buddhist temple across the street I can hear the long mournful horn sounds of early morning call. Next door, the ringing bells of the Hindu Temple are calling people to prayer. Prayer, it seems under the circumstances, is not a bad idea. Because in my own personal lexicon there are no words to be trusted, I open myself to a state of prayer, a feeling I have cultivated throughout the years that starts behind my eyes and spirals downward in a kind of letting go into gratitude. This morning I give it my best shot, hoping that, if indeed the taxi ride is terminal, gratitude might be a good grace to ride out on.

Our cab is sporting only one headlight when it arrives and when I try to explain the situation to our dear driver, he shrugs and continues to stack our luggage into the trunk, where it actually fits this time. He looks around for the mother of all suitcases and gives us an, "Is this all?" look. Thrinley and I both nod, quite pleased with ourselves.

Just as we are getting into the cab, Mr. Manjeet shows up. He greets us cordially and then huddles over a map with our driver. There is much discussion and pencil-marking on the map and I wonder if our driver has ever in his life actually driven to Dharamsala.

"No problem, no problem," says Mr. Manjeet as though he's reading my mind. "He goes there many, many times."

So how come he needs a map, I try not to wonder. I can't, however, keep myself from asking Mr. Manjeet about the headlight situation. He actually takes a moment to inspect the lights and has a brief exchange with our driver. Then he pokes his head in the window and says to me, "No problem, no problem."

Okay, fine. And I turn myself over to the day.

One of the things I have learned along the road to recovery is that you don't get better, you get different. The skills that popped out of the psychic woodwork to keep you alive as a kid can make your life very interesting as an adult. And they really are skills. Not necessarily earn-a-good-living skills but real-life-is-wonderful skills. Having learned how to forget practically everything means that I have lots of psychic energy to "be here now."

It's those old acid-heads, Timothy Leary and Harvard psychologist, Dr. Richard Alpert, also known as Ram Dass, who made the phrase memorable so many years ago. They left no stone un-stoned and although my relationship to mind-altering drugs as an adult is pretty limited, my familiarity with mind-altering mind is intimate.

I "got it" back then, without knowing why. I "get it" now way better because I do know why.

The present, when fully entered, is always joyful, even when it isn't. And when it isn't, it's only when we don't go all the way into the pain, the angst, the despair, that it becomes just another hell realm. In his book, *Full Catastrophe Living*, Jon Kabat-Zinn writes about entering into the pain to get relief from the pain. Awful pain comes from straining against it. Beautiful pain comes when we let it flood us with feeling. When we welcome it as a friend. This, I know, is decidedly un-American.

Our Western attempt at civilization knows how to anesthetize us to sleep so we don't have to feel physical pain; but it completely fails the grade when it comes to waking us up to emotional pain. It means we have to really be there for one another, and most of us would rather go shopping. I know that as an adult I created two very distinct plains of existence—one was for me and one was for everyone else. In my own personal existence, I got to be non-stop desolate; in everyone else's, I got to be non-stop happy. These were two worlds that never collided into full catastrophe. I just couldn't let them.

Brian did his best to get me to open up, to ask for support from my friends. To simply tell them things were hard and I needed to know they cared about me. From this distance, the words I wish I'd had the courage to say seem so very simple: "I need a safe place to feel sad." I know I could have farmed myself out a few hours a week to a few dear friends and perhaps saved myself a few years of desolation and isolation. Most of all, I didn't need anyone to say anything. I just needed to be in proximity with normal life without having to pretend I was feeling normal. As we head off on our day-long drive to Dharamsala, normal takes a back seat and I feel wonderfully liberated from all its implications—imagined and otherwise.

We begin our journey through the early morning darkness and drive quickly into countryside full of country, not poverty. There are even large trees off on the side of the road and they immediately offer a kind of spiritual solace, a sense that the nurturing nature of nature is still preserved in this complicated country. I have always suffered from inexplicable bouts of ecstasy and they are always brought on by nature. As a kid, the whiff of freedom was the smell of salt air and all the odorous variations of low tide. My pervasive amnesia might get in the way of visual memory and the sequence of time, but my nose remembers. To this day, these smells land me in moments of ecstasy even when life itself feels like a hell realm. As a kid, it meant I was outside, where it was safe. As an adult, it means precisely the same thing. I open the window of the cab and get a dose of low tide on land about a thousand miles from the sea. Perhaps it's the smell of Delhi. I take a look at Thrinley out of the corner of my eye but she doesn't say a word.

About an hour out, we drive along the shores of a lake and the first light of day rises around us in mists of silver and shadow. And we start to climb. This is when I find out that Thrinley is afraid of heights. It's amazing how long you can know someone without knowing a critical piece of information that is essential to their life. I suddenly understood why she was so happy to let me sit near the window on the plane. Now we're veering out to the edges of cliffs a mile high and Thrinley is rigid with what might quite possibly be fear but I'm not about to ask. Luckily, as we careen around hairpin turns at impossible speeds, there's not a lot of traffic. Until we careen around a corner into a flock of sheep. Our driver stops just in time to prevent an onset of lamb stew.

We climb for a long time. It is a glorious mountainside landscape of farms, pine forests and, when a certain direction prevails, even a cactus forest. Then, without warning, we pass a group of Indian school children formally dressed in English school uniforms, book bags over their shoulders, and with no sign of where the students have come from or where they are going. As they cluster together along the road they are talking and laughing, mindless of our car as it speeds by. Our driver never slows down, he just goes fast more carefully. It is another startling picture of the rules of interdependence. Nobody gives way, everyone gets what they want. Democracy runs deep in India, and it never looks back.

About five hours into our journey, we make our lunch stop. Our driver pulls into a long driveway and stops beside a stately house with a view looking out over a vista of mountains and valleys. He gets out of the cab and enters into a discussion with a couple in the garden. He gestures towards us and so we, too, get out. There's no sign of it being a restaurant but the people are friendly and hospitable. I am desperate to take a pee and assume Thrinley is, too. We ask where the bathroom is and the fellow gestures, and says, pointing beyond the house, "Just a few yards that way." We go "that way" and end up behind the house, lost and confused. The woman picks up on our urgency and takes us into the house, where there are actually two bathrooms, one each. The woman asks us if we'd like some tea. Yes, we say. That would be lovely. I don't ask about lunch. Maybe we'll get menus. And I climb a short flight of stairs up to a shining clean bathroom.

It is an elegantly furnished home. The floors are marble tiles covered in places with handsome rugs and the chairs are upholstered in heavy brocades and clustered in tasteful seating arrangements. After hours of precipitous driving, compounded by constant readjustment of the body due to the endless variety of gravitational pulls, it is an utter blessing to be upright in a gracious house with gracious hosts.

I notice a lot of books, most of them written in English, and ask our hostess about them.

"They are my husband's," she says. "He's a writer. Would you like to see his study?"

Startled, I say yes. And off we go up more stairs to a wonderful library office nook that feels like every writer's studio everywhere. Books and papers and papers and books. The chair at the desk faces out the window to the mountain vista. I instantly want to sit down and make myself at home.

"My husband wrote those," she said, pointing proudly to a shelf of books. "He's a poet."

A thrill ripples through me. A poet. Here in the unknown and unnamed far reaches of India, in the middle of our long day's journey, our driver delivers us to a poet for lunch. I am stunned.

"Shall we have tea outside?" asks our hostess.

So we sit, drink tea, and discuss the world of poetry.

"Poetry is dying in India," says our host.

"Not in the West," I say. "Perhaps because the culture is dying. People need poetry."

I have no idea what I'm talking about, but the outpouring of the written word, the spoken word, the performed word in rap and all forms of poetic competition has been on the upswing in recent years. I tell him about the poet, Sam Hamill, who solicited anti-war poems for an "anthology of protest" and was planning to present it to Laura Bush at the White House symposium on "Poetry and the American Voice." It was an action that resulted in cancellation of the event honoring Emily Dickinson, Langston Hughes and Walt Whitman, ironically, all activist poets in one way or another. Hughes and Whitman voiced outrage and social criticism in their work. The FBI put Hughes under scrutiny during the McCarthy era and Whitman once described the White House as "bought, sold, electioneered for, prostituted, and filled with prostitutes."

When Hamill's email request went public, within weeks there were 10,000 poets posting poems against the war in Iraq on the Poets Against the War website. Laura Bush had no idea of the power of poets and poetry when she planned, and then cancelled, "Poetry and the American Voice".

I try to talk about this to our newly met poet, but there is a great sadness about him. How does it feel to be a poet in India, I wonder? To be writing about the stream of life that at once blesses and defiles, sometimes at the same moment. How does one get to poetic reconciliation? To any reconciliation at all? He speaks English with a halting reticence; I discover he writes in English, too. Somehow, I am surprised at this.

"Would it be possible to buy one of your books?" I ask.

"Of course, you can have a book. There's no need to buy one," he responds.

His wife disappears into the house and returns with two copies, one for me and one for Thrinley.

As all this is happening, I am of at least two minds. One of them doesn't quite believe it. Why a poet? Why here? Why now? Another part of me is rejoicing in the astonishing synchronicity of it all.

Our new poet friend signs his beautiful plum colored book of poems. Its title is *Cries of Anguish*. The author's name, K.V.S. Thapar, is embossed in gold on the cover. Hand-bound in handloom cloth, it lies elegantly in the hand. I look inside, it is signed "with love" followed by his name. As we get ready to leave, I am only mildly curious about our lunch. Perhaps it will be at our next break, I think, as we express our appreciation to our tea-time hosts.

When we get back to the cab, our driver looks more than mildly aggravated. "We've been too long," I mutter to Thrinley. We have no way of expressing to him how wonderful it was that we got to stop here. He goes up the driveway; we turn right, and then turn right again and go down the next driveway to the restaurant where we were supposed to be in the first place. Our wonderful literary tea-break had actually been a wrong turn.

I am stunned that I didn't get it. Thrinley had some suspicions. "It seemed a bit odd," she says. "But it was great so I just went along with it."

I am reeling at how I translated all the miscues into cues of connection and cosmic coincidence. Yet it really was a synchronicity of a higher order. Meeting Mr. Kumar in the midst of a dramatic drive through the hills of India and speaking with him about poetry and the essential sensibility of poets in difficult times was like falling into the collective language of possibility. The ways in which the human heart transcends differences of experience, culture and communication is the only hope there is. And that's what we all experienced in that short time over a cup of tea and a few cookies. Now we're the only customers in a hotel restaurant open only for us. The room is stylish with squares of black and white tiles on the floor, rattan furniture and matching china. The waiter is formal and courteous as he gives us menus. We see our driver outside, sitting on the steps, waiting yet again.

As Thrinley reads the daily news, I leaf through *Cries of Anguish* and am stopped by the last few lines of the second poem:

If only
My past
Could I sing into the present
And thus
Read my future too
Wounds would
Have
Left no scars
To heal.

What does it mean? If we sing our past alive into the present do our wounds lose their scars? It is an alluring thought. It is a Buddhist thought. Knowing suffering brings the end of suffering. It is a poetic paradox as well as a spiritual one. And all our scars are spiritual. I think about the scar running down the inside of my left arm. It's about four inches long; the place where the skin is sealed is wide and ragged. The stitches are far apart and reach wide away from the cut. In damaging me, it preserved the remnants of my childhood self. I have a tiny five-year-old forefinger to remind me of my innocence. Most of my hand is numb; that reminds me of my childhood, too. And my thumb does not bend. I was told I fell through a window. A story I'd repeated to any doctor who asked about it.

One fellow looked confused, "It looks like an incision," he said.

"No," I said. "It was an accident. I fell through a window."

Years later, when I asked my father about it, he said to me conspiratorially, "Your brother did it."

His words echoed oddly in my ears.

"Oh," I said. And said no more. I was not yet able to question my father, my past, or my present.

Our meal is much more than we can eat so we fill a plate from the various Indian dishes and I take it out to our driver. I'm a bit nervous that he might be insulted but he gives me a big smile and happily takes the plate. The waiter watches the encounter then invites our friend in and they disappear into the regions of the kitchen. Now Thrinley and I are the ones who are waiting. We go outside and stroll around the grounds. There is a sun sculpture in a small stone enclave and it reminds me of Thrinley's work. Over the last couple of hours, the work we love the most has been reflected back to us at every turn.

It is nine o'clock when we arrive in Dharamsala. We've been on the long and winding road for fifteen hours, the last three in the dark.

"Where go?" asks our driver.

As I scramble around to find the name of the place we'll be staying, Thrinley asks him if we're in upper Dharamsala.

Turns out we're not, so off we go again. The final stretch is about eight miles straight up on a road that appears to be crumbling on both sides. The death-warning road signs, most of them in a friendly rhyming cadence, such as, "Stay Alive, Watch Your Drive," increase in frequency. Thank God, it's dark, I'm thinking as the hairpin turns increase in frequency and intensity. If Thrinley could see where we are, her fear of heights would way outmatch my paltry fear of eternity. I notice that our driver gets to anchor himself with the steering wheel while we have to compensate for the wild swaying with a grab at whatever surface makes sense. It reminds me of one of those rules my boss Dan had tried to instill in his bus drivers. "Watch their heads," he told us. "If they're swaying, you're going too fast."

Dan, I'm thinking, you should be here now.

Finally, it's over. We stop in the middle of a small town square and wonder where to go. Our driver doesn't recognize the name of our lodge and I try in vain to explain to him that it's at the end of a quiet, secluded dead-end road. At least that's what it said on the Web. I'd arranged our first night ahead of time as it seemed like a smart thing to do. He asks a lone Tibetan monk for directions and we drive down a very narrow and deserted path through the small dark town of McLeod Ganj, otherwise known as Upper Dharamsala, the home-away-from-home of the Dalai Lama.

At the lodge, of course, we aren't expected. But two friendly fellows lug in our luggage and deposit it and us into a room with two beds and a bathroom. We can register in the morning, they tell us. We pay our driver and each of us tips him 500 rupees and for the second time in our relationship, he breaks out into a big smile. All I can think is that he has to drive back and I hope he doesn't have to do it right now.

I crawl into bed and stretch out my knotted body and try not to notice that it feels like I'm in a room at a Howard Johnson's just off the freeway someplace in New Jersey. It's just the lampshade, I tell myself as I drop off into sleep.

EIGHT

There is a connection somewhere between laughter and spirituality, between a sense of humor and a sense of grace. The Dalai
Lama was taken away from the warmth of his mother and family
when he was three years old. He was ensconced in the Potala Palace, an immense place full of silence, serious study and brutal winter cold. He was held hostage by his future. He was deprived of his
childhood, the place where play is born, yet he is as playful as a man
can be and still be a man. His laugh is booming and infectious and
it exists alongside his profound awareness of tragedy and loss.

To be the Dalai Lama, he lost his life as he knew it. As the Dalai
Lama, he lost, and is still losing his people. It is "either, or, and holy
both;" life as both the biggest gift and the biggest loss. Over the
years, as I fought my way out of my own tunnel, the one I couldn't
see, moments of the Dalai Lama—in print, on television, once even
in person, beckoned me to a place where both life and death were
possible at the very same time. It was the only hope I had. For sure
healing would never mean membership in the "have a nice day"
club; it had to mean something else, something that could recognize the language of love and loss in the same breath.

"Compassion," it is called in Tibetan Buddhism. But it is not
compassion as we know it, it is compassion first of all as self-under-
standing, and then as a wide and loving world view. One thing for

sure, it is not pity. And it is pity that our Western minds often resort to when we hear the word "compassion." Pity is easy. Compassion takes a little doing; most of all it takes a lifetime.

In *Transforming the Mind—Teachings on Generating Compassion*, the Dalai Lama writes: *"The way to examine how thoughts and emotions rise in us is through introspection. It is quite natural for many different thoughts and emotions to arise. Why this should be is, of course, a philosophical question. According to Buddhist philosophy, many of them arise from past habits and karma, which give rise to an individual's propensity for thinking and feeling. However that may be, the fact is that various thoughts and emotions do arise in us, and when we leave them unexamined and untamed this leads to untold problems, crises, suffering and misery."*

It's the word "untamed" that rings rampant through my body when I think of how I unleashed myself upon my world throughout much of my life. I caused nonstop problems, crises, suffering and misery. Not on a large scale like an earthquake or a plague but up close and personal like a poke in the psyche with a sharp stick, or a cutting remark to the heart. My friends would not attest to this; my lovers would; and so would my son.

It was the Vigilant One who tended the gates of our inner kingdom and determined who was safe. This turned out to be nobody. She wouldn't even find the Dalai Lama safe. "He's too intelligent," she would have pronounced. "It's not natural. Besides, he laughs too much. That's not natural either." Children were natural, if they were under ten. So were some old people. Dogs were always natural; it was the owners who made them mean Vigilant One figured. Even Brian, our knight in bright and shining armor, was a suspect for at least part of every session we had.

His weapon was patience. In his quiet, persistent way, Brian saw through to and attended to, the Little Ones, the ones suspended in grief who cried rivers of inarticulate anguish. They had no idea that Vigilant One was trying to help; she had no idea they were trying to get out. It was a psychic impasse of paralyzing disorder. Holding firmly to her position of protection, Vigilant One locked everyone out. Unbeknownst to her, she also locked everyone in.

I still sometimes see through her eyes; but somewhere along our healing path, all the others inside got a peek, too. And she finally got some company; she found out she wasn't alone. She discovered that there was a lot of other insight inside. She got to rest. The shift from the insulation and isolation of my parts to the beginnings of their relatedness as an inner system was the real beginning of healing, it was also a shift a very long time in the making. My mind of denial had no time for competition. After all, she was the reason I was still alive.

When I think about the landscape of the mind, it is where the "I" tromps through the fields of perception that distinguishes my experience from those who are "normal." Our Vigilant One didn't realize she wasn't alone, neither did anyone else inside our body know they weren't alone. This is where the normal "I" is most useful. It gets to see through everyone's eyes. My "I" was in hiding. There was no-one to guide all the different parts through either the landscape of the mind or the landscape of the body. This is a serious existential problem. We were all running on confusion; we needed a babysitter, a social coordinator, a ground traffic monitor and a horde of air traffic controllers to keep the internal clamor for recognition on the right path, whatever that might be.

Instead we had Brian. When we first started to work together, he was new to the therapy game, but I wasn't. My first bout with a therapist was way back when I was in the process of breaking the rules and getting a divorce from the dentist, way before my descent into reality. My mother insisted that I go to see that shrink. Actually, he was a psychiatrist. I explained to him about how the death of my infant son, Thomas, at Fort Dix, New Jersey, brought me to feeling and gave me the strength to leave my abusive marriage. I talked about my family and how the rage between my parents set us kids off into one camp of survival and them into another. I analyzed the family dynamics with philosophical understanding. I presented my big sister role with insight and equanimity. I talked non-stop for an hour and when I was finished he asked me if I thought I was "unusual." Absolutely not, I said. And never went back. Mostly because he wanted me to take some tests. Unbeknownst to me, the Vigilant One knew there was no good test on the planet. No way in hell was she going to let us go back.

Living in Maui in 1970 was itself a year-long, group-encounter therapy session. I taught in an alternative school with alternative teachers. We had nude group breakfasts on Sundays and stayed current with all the waves of attraction, distraction, repulsion and self-absorption that washed up on our naked shores. I started reading Fritz Perls and doing gestalt therapy on my dreams. I went to "intensive" weekends where we sat in pairs and learned to listen. I took "awareness through movement" classes and learned that the body held its own story whether we listened or not. I took Tai Chi classes, did weekend Buddhist retreats and threw the I Ching several times a day. I also camped out at Makena Beach with other naked hippies where we got dashed about by the waves and one another. The only thing I didn't do was drugs. Maui wowie was always somebody else's version of a good time.

In the seventies it was fashionable to be introspective, often at one another's expense. But even though self-indulgence often prevailed, it was possible to develop a few inroads to self-analysis. Back then, I was riding the wave of grief from losing my son and it was landing me on my own shores for the first time. When I returned to Seattle after that year in Maui, it was because I felt too young to be so seduced by the natural beauty, the kind climate and the convivial community. Somehow or another, it seemed that life should not be so easy. Back in the Northwest, it wasn't. I ended up in therapy with a woman who was Jungian-inclined and, I would recognize years later, stunningly narcissistic. I disengaged from that "therapeutic" relationship when I began to feel exploited. This for me meant I was being psychologically abused and flagrantly manipulated. Her version of "compassion" translated into pity for my poor pathetic self.

Her lack of boundaries had no boundaries. When I went to her in despair because of an abortion I had, she ended up being the therapist of the man who was the father of the aborted child. She got him back on track and one day she told me she would be going to his wedding and hoped I didn't mind.

So when I met Brian, I was ready for some straightforward therapy. But I started crying and didn't stop for a year. It was a convulsive, consuming grief and I hid it completely from everyone I knew. When I wasn't "on" with playwriting commissions, writing assignments or marketing jobs, I was almost comatose. It was an insane time in which fear and grief propelled me in opposite directions at the same time. I was cracking up and I had no idea why.

It wasn't that I didn't have things to be grief-stricken about because I did. I'd had the abortion a few years earlier and it had devastated me. I'd had so many failed relationships and so many of my hearts had been broken that it felt as though I had none left. My son had graduated from high school and moved to California to go to college. I was no longer a "mom." I went into shutdown when that happened and had no feelings at all. I didn't even miss my son. Inside there was nothing but wreckage, outside I was more efficient than ever. The splitting that had ended me up in Brian's office escalated into greater and greater grief and greater and greater competency. I was scrambling after sanity and the only sanity I knew was a kind of non-stop chaotic control.

It was a year in which I never stopped moving and never got anywhere. I lived in too many places to count, did too many things that didn't matter and felt too many things without meaning. When I wasn't in overdrive in Oakland writing marketing crap for Wells Fargo, I was either in a plane to or from seeing Brian in Seattle, or out on the coast hiding out at the old Coast Guard youth hostel at the Montara lighthouse just south of San Francisco. Perhaps it was those moments at the Pacific Ocean that kept me alive. For sure all my inner parts were getting fed up, overloaded, and very, very tired. To them, dying would be easy.

What I remember about Brian that first year was his presence. The one thing I knew about him without having to ask was that he had a spiritual base for his work. I knew because someone in me recognized someone in him. It was a spiritual recognition. Brian was not a "know-it-all" therapist. He had no advice and expressed no words of wisdom. He was a quiet and respectful witness to my inexplicable grief. He didn't hide behind pity nor did he make any attempt to fix me. From him I learned that the only useful therapist is one who knows that grief is good and that there is spiritual meaning in everything.

The Dalai Lama wrote in *Transforming the Mind* that in Tibetan Buddhism, feelings arise out of past habits and karma. Interestingly enough, I'd explored my karma long before I started to explore my suffering. Sometime in the early seventies, a brother I felt close to called me about a psychic he was seeing. Her name was Helen and she was half Indian (from India) and half longshoreman. She was hefty and had a deep and gravelly voice that defied the lightweight wispiness of the psychic stereotype-at-large in those days. Even then I knew spiritual charlatanism when I saw it and ran for cover. But Helen was different.

She lived in a cluttered house on Queen Anne Hill in Seattle. These days it's a high-end and trendy neighborhood complete with lattés and landscaping; back then it was working class, unruly and unkempt. So was Helen's house. Her husband was a blue collar worker of some sort—perhaps a fireman or a bus driver. She was large and gave any semblance of fashion no shrift whatsoever. She was startlingly direct. Her specialty was psychic journeys, which took place in an upstairs room in her messy house.

There was a small bed, a chair, a small altar and a couple of candles. Helen's presence was so dense, solid and uncompromising that I trusted her even as she scared me to death. The sessions were simple. I would lie down on the bed and she would sit on the chair in the corner of the darkened room. First of all she asked me what I wanted to explore. At that time, I wanted to know the spiritual reasons for my incapacitated left arm and hand and my incapacitating fear of eternity. She suggested a session for each and they started out in the same way.

Helen told me to close my eyes and begin deep breathing. From across the room she entered a kind of trance state. After many minutes of deeper and deeper breathing with a longer and longer pause between the exhale and the inhale, she would start to ask questions. Where are you? What do you see? Who is there? What do they have to tell you? Back then, my arm was a spiritual mystery but not a corporeal one. I had fallen through a window. Precisely why had to do with some karmic story. In those days, everything did.

In my psychic journey through the damage in my left arm, I found myself on a horse with a spear held high in my left hand. I was a man and I was killing Christians. We weren't in battle. They were helpless and on foot. I was savage and self-righteous. This image shocked the hell out of me. It was visceral in my body, the feeling of strength in a left arm and hand that was literally powerless, the feeling of being a man in my woman's body, a man full of disdainful hatred and a clever and vicious cruelty. I came out of it shaken and confused.

The next week we attacked eternity. It was the phrase, "Forever and ever, amen," that echoed in my head before the fear took over. It would become total terror in which I seemed to actually enter eternity, time passing without end and my frightened consciousness along with it. It was a bodiless mind, me and not me at the same time. Sometimes it would happen without warning and I'd have to do something drastic to shift my focus. I'd leave the room I was in and go outside and run, or I'd pinch myself hard to bring myself back to the present. Sometimes I'd scream in terror.

This session with Helen started out with the same deep breathing. This time she told me to stay with the fear, to enter it. Her gravelly reassuring voice kept me in the world as the hysteria rose in my mind.

"Stay with it, Janet," she said to me.

And I did. It was a horrific experience, a suspended and timeless terror that took captive my mind and choked it with fear. I still don't know how it happened, how I stayed with it, but suddenly the fear seemed to physically explode and as it did a brilliant white light burst through my mind and a great and blissful sense of peace flooded my entire being. I floated there with it for a long time until I heard Helen's voice urging me to open my eyes. But I didn't want to.

"Not right now," I said.

"Yes, right now," she responded, and starting counting backwards from ten in her loud, longshoreman voice.

Reluctantly, I returned. And in our subsequent sessions, Helen never let me go there again. It was years later that I recognized it as a near death experience.

I worked with Helen for about six months and during that time went out to the retreat place she was creating in the hills of northeastern Washington. She was building a pyramid structure and a friend and I went out to help. We slept on an open platform beneath the apex of the pyramid triangle and one night I had two dreams that went beyond dreams.

In the first I was being tested and sent through time. I had to go further and further out from the present until I was returning to the present by completing a circle through the past. It was during this trip through time that I got lost and woke up in a panic, my consciousness hovering high in the trees around us, my body dead on the platform below. Entering a dead body didn't have much appeal and so I forced my tree-flying self to go back to sleep and I prayed for a dream to get us back together in one piece. The dream ensued. It involved the removal of my head and in its place was put the head of an ancient wizened woman. "Great," I thought in the dream. "How will I know who I am?" So with a tremendously focused will I invested my new head with the knowledge of myself. Then I realized my friends wouldn't recognize me, and that could be a problem. So with my own two hands I molded my ancient face until it resembled the memory of my physical self.

When I woke up, I was back in my body, but something had changed in me. Something had come to life. I worked with Helen for about six months and then the psychic stress became too intense. All my life I'd had premonitions, senses of things, awareness of thoughts and feelings beneath the masks of daily life. Through Helen, I was being offered a path that heightened these experiences and gave them names. But I backed away from Helen and her psychic journeys. I backed away from my own journey into psychic space. What good could it do to know things beyond space, time and the body? But—unbeknownst to me at the time—I'd perhaps seen the karma behind my left arm of darkness. If there are past lives, and if I'd killed Christians in one of them, it would explain why this lifetime is so complicated. It would be many years before any of this got connected and even now, years afterwards, I'm reluctant to fully know it. Yet it is the only sense any of it makes. Why else would I have been tortured beyond measure as a child?

A year after I stopped my work with Helen, there was a forest fire and the pyramid retreat center was burned down. It seemed right somehow. I had trusted Helen because she didn't hide behind false love and light. But real love and light was missing, too. That's always the problem with power.

As the Dalai Lama says, precisely why our feelings arise is "a philosophical question." In Tibetan Buddhist philosophy, they arise out of habits and karma. Sometimes karma bites us back almost instantly. Sometimes it takes a lifetime.

NINE

It's my first wake-up in Dharamsala and even the Howard Johnson lampshade doesn't dampen my enthusiasm for the hint of dawn in the sky. I scramble out of bed in excitement. Thrinley is still sleeping as I dress quickly and get ready to go out and look around. We were only given one key and I realize I'll either have to lock my friend in from the outside or leave her vulnerable to invaders. I decide to lock her in and not be long. It's quiet in the hallway. As I go towards the front door, I notice somebody fast asleep on the floor in a sleeping bag tucked behind the check-in desk. I'm relieved to find the door unlocked and I step out into the early morning air. I am finally in Dharamsala. Within fifty yards of the lodge I am in tears, some of then in relief at finally being here—on purpose and by accident, some because maybe the Dalai Lama's here, too, and some because I am filled with a profound feeling of familiarity.

The awkward truth is that all of India has felt this way. The streets of Delhi, the hours driving across the plains, the rise into the mountains—they are all ripe with recognition. Not the "oh this looks just like…. (Fill in the blank)" recognition but the kind that knows the place up close and personal. It's a feeling I've been fighting ever since arriving; I haven't even confessed it to Thrinley, who of all people would understand. Because no matter how much divine intervention informs my life day in and day out, on some level, I resist it because on some other level I am always fighting to feel real. I want to know I have lived before I die. And that means to be fully earth-bound, not on just another plane of reincarnation.

In his last poem on earth, Raymond Carver wrote:

And did you get what
you wanted from this life, even so?
I did.
And what did you want?
To call myself beloved, to feel myself
beloved on the earth.

I know he wrote these words for his beloved Tess Gallagher, but he also wrote them for me. And it is not the lover I am yearning for, it is "to feel myself beloved on the earth." To be loved is to belong. To walk, run, play and crawl through life as part of life, not apart from it. It is this feeling that I want to stock up on before it is all over.

I walk slowly down the small street outside the lodge. I pass several modern looking hotels, one called the Him Queen, complete with a big lobby and glass doors. Small shops along the way are still locked up and one or two vendors are slowly unpacking for their day at their roadside tables. At the end of the road, where it meets up with three other small streets, I meet a cow browsing through life's leftovers. And then I discover a bookstore, *The Bookworm*. There are poets on display in the window, but more importantly at the moment, I see a stack of mysteries on the shelf at the back of the store. I've almost finished the one I'm reading and it's my last.

I want to keep on walking but I remember Thrinley who is locked up back in the hotel room so I turn and retrace my steps. Looming up to my left are the Dhauladhar Mountains, the "foothills" of the Himalayas. The sun rises pink on their snow-covered peaks. The air is chilly in the still-shaded street but it is clear and fresh. We have finally risen above the smog.

There's no room number on the key and I didn't pay attention on the way out so I have to guess my way back in, hoping that the key doesn't fit more than one lock. After one aborted attempt I get the right door open and discover that Thrinley, thankfully, is still asleep.

Now I just have to tell her that this lodge is too nice, too Western, and too expensive. I want her to wake up; I want out of here.

These weird reactions to innocuous, benign details of daily life are embarrassing but at least I've begun to recognize them. Not, however, always in time to avoid embarrassment. A lot of times it's just easier to negotiate my way out of situations sideways instead of explaining that which cannot really be explained. Sometimes it's really nice places. Sometimes it's really, really nice people. Really, really nice was one of the worst traps of all. As a child, I'd think I was safe with the nice people and then zap, down the hell hole. Tricked again. It left me with a lifelong mistrust of nice people. Not exactly useful in social situations where nice is the password to a successful evening, a pleasant lunch or a hot date. I don't even like myself when I'm being nice.

I'm aware of this pending crisis about our immediate and nice environment but when Thrinley wakes up I keep my panic to myself. I simply emphasize the expense. Now that we know how inexpensive lodging can be, the twenty-two dollars a night for this room seems exorbitant. With very little discussion we agree to go in search of where we really belong.

It's nearly nine o'clock when we head out. At the little intersection, now bustling with activity, there is a small hand-lettered sign pointing to "the temple." The sun is warm in the streets; shops are open and we are almost immediately approached by beggars. There were no beggars in Rajpur and I actually find myself startled to see them here in Dharamsala. I feel anger rising at being approached so aggressively and with such a sense of entitlement. I say "no" before I can get the word out of my mouth. I will not be exploited just because I am here.

As we follow the sign and walk down the road towards the Dalai Lama's temple, the beggars become more, and also more disabled. They have their places marked out on the ground like the vendors setting up shop for the day. Two fellows share a small fire built against the low stone wall along the edge of the narrow road. One looks to be in his twenties, his legs bent and shriveled behind him. He has a pair of slippers on his hands, which are also used as his feet. The other fellow is indeterminately old. His feet are worn away by leprosy, part of his hands, too. They are both too caught up in the early morning warmth of their fire to notice us. So I go over and drop a 20 rupee note on the blanket. The young man smiles in surprise and gratitude. He is very handsome.

McLeod Ganj, this small town where His Holiness the Dalai Lama set up his government-in-exile more than forty years ago, is known to those around the world as Dharamsala. It's built across the tops and along the edges of two ridges. Valleys of varying depths surround the town and are also part of the town. It feels as though we are on top of the world and out on the edge of it, too. Across the way we can see the road of the night before winding its way up the steep mountainside to McLeod Ganj. It's precarious with switchbacks and I realize it's a good thing the final leg of our journey ended up in the dark.

We have to find lodging; but both Thrinley and I want, first of all, to go to the Dalai Lama's temple. It's about a quarter of a mile down this road to the temple gate. We pass shops, a cyber-café and several small restaurants; there's a place to buy film, a travel agent, some small hotels and a whole lot of STD's—which are public phones. (Thrinley told me that throughout her first trip to India she thought they were Sexually Transmitted Disease clinics and commented to someone about the extent of such diseases in India.) Pine trees and bushes cover the hillsides dropping into valleys below, and snow-covered peaks rise into the clear blue sky.

As we get closer to the temple, the beggars get younger and more aggressive. "Miluk, miluk," is the request. "No money, miluk." A small disheveled girl grabs hold of me and drags me towards the food stall across from the entrance to the Dalai Lama's temple. She wants me to buy her a package of powdered milk. I shake her away and say, "No." And then wonder precisely how I am going to have a spiritual pilgrimage in the midst of beggardom. I am not immune to the irony but I am not amused by it either.

We go through the gates to the temple compound and walk along a narrow alley, past the Namgyal Book Shop, up an incline and some steps to a wide open courtyard. All the buildings are painted a light warm yellow offset by deep saffron on window frames and doors. It feels spacious and open and welcoming. The gate to the Dalai Lama's personal office and quarters is closed but the entire temple area and courtyard is open to all—from resident monks to curious tourists. We climb the stairs and gaze through the open front doors; a very large golden Buddha gazes back.

It's an extremely modest temple, particularly when compared to the Potala in Lhasa, where thousands of monks lived and studied, timeless treasured art was housed, and the Dalai Lama reigned as the temporal and religious leader of his people. The Potala was started in the 7th century and completed a thousand years later by the Fifth Dalai Lama. In photographs, it looks both elegant and imposing, as though it emerged organically out of the hilltop. It was an extraordinary accomplishment of both construction and design and it was almost completely destroyed by the Chinese after their invasion of Tibet.

Now the Potala is being restored by the Chinese in order to add to the tourist draw of Lhasa which is becoming a 24/7 city of bright lights, night life, prostitution, and token displays of Tibetan Buddhism in-action. The Chinese are as determined to preserve Tibetan Buddhism for tourists as they are to destroy the Tibetan people. They want to destroy their cake and eat it, too. It's a weird world. We never know what's around the karmic corner and I have learned that as blatant as cause and effect can be, it can also be exquisitely subtle. Many years ago, when I heard the Dalai Lama speak in Seattle, he was asked "why is this happening?" The first thing he did was laugh. Then he became dense and intense, his concentrated gaze warrior-like and piercing. Tibet was isolated, he said. We were happy to be isolated. Perhaps if we'd gone out to the world with our culture and our religion we would not have lost our country.

These are paraphrased words but what stayed with me was that brief moment of profound spiritual irony. That every tragedy has a cause and every cause has an effect is a lesson that even has to be learned by the Dalai Lama. Does he hold his head in anguish at all the things he did and didn't do that resulted in more and more violation against his people? Does he question all his steps along the path? Does he question and let go, question and let go, over and over as he moves through this lifetime? To us he has become a symbol of strength and gentleness, of persistence and patience, of acceptance and expectation. He expects transformation; he also accepts things as they are. And often they are very ugly. Through it all, he knows joy.

Thrinley and I decide to circumambulate the temple three times as is the custom. We join in with the Tibetan monks and lay people who are already in transit with this morning ritual. Most of them have their prayer beads running through the fingers of their left hand. Om Mani Padme Hum is muttered in varying degrees of whisper—some are so soft as to be unintelligible, others run the syllables together as though they have been spilling out of the mouth for a lifetime.

I am moved most of all by the elders. Their faith is worn on their faces; it moves with their very beings as their feet, some of them trembling in age and effort, take each step as a holy step, each bead a prayer, each breath an invocation, a call to spirit by spirit. They are living in exile, their escape over the Himalayas a long, arduous and often deadly trek to freedom. They are the survivors. Most of all they wanted to be where the Dalai Lama is; they wanted to be able to hold his photograph and not be afraid.

Tibetan Buddhism translates into sophisticated maps of the mind; it has helped me grapple with the most challenging psychological and philosophical questions about myself and my life. And here are the Tibetan elders, walking in simple faith, steeped in simple kindness, exuding a gentle direct love that, when I dare a glance, beams right through me. I feel awkward and self-conscious, as though I am riding their wave of grace, trying to slip into the fold like a hungry fox.

As we circumambulate the temple, the view from the walkway changes from snow-covered mountains and mist-layered hills and valleys to cows, merchants, monks, beggars and brightly colored signs all mingling in the street below. It's like walking around the heart of prayer and through all the realms of earthly reality at the same time. I can tell there will be no spiritual escape into delusion in this town. Nothing sends me running for beer and potato chips faster than spiritual elitism, in which devotees rise above it all into some pure land of prayer and meditation from which earthly mortals and their earthly ways are deemed beneath it all. The truth is we are all beneath it all; otherwise we wouldn't be here. And beneath everything and everyone is the spiritual authority of creation without end. Put that in your pipe of eternity, I tell myself as my mind wanders off into spheres of judgment and vile elitism of its own.

I must be hungry.

Last night, when our driver had stopped to ask directions to our lodge, I'd glimpsed through the door of a café, some weighty looking wooden chairs; I want to sit on them for breakfast. I don't tell Thrinley this because I have no idea if I can find the place. But as we go off to reconnoiter the town for signs of pancakes, the heavy wooden chairs are also on my menu.

We do find the café with the wooden chairs. "How in the hell did they get them up here?" was the question that flew into my mind when I saw them last night. Our fifteen hours of winding and climbing had seared itself into my perspective and I realized that everything had to come that way—from toothpicks and toilet paper to cement temple steps and heavy wooden chairs.

Blame it on the Brits. The Hill Stations in India—and McLeod Ganj is one of them—were established as relief centers for the British, whose affinity for hot weather was below zero. When they colonized India, they established these town and military outposts on accessible high spots all over the country's seven mountain ranges. The Himalayas, which stretch more than a thousand miles across the northern border of India, were a favorite destination. Although these places were isolated and difficult to reach, the Brits found a way and established little home-away-from-home towns complete with cream cakes and heavy chairs. Now I'm about on sit on one.

We are in the Shangri La restaurant and it is run by monks from the Gyumed Tantric Monastery in South India, which is where, it turns out, the Dalai Lama is right now. His whereabouts has been on my mind since I arrived in India but I decided not to make a big deal of it because I'm on a trip that is pretty much on a schedule of its own. Besides, he's a very busy man. I'm just happy that we're both in the same country. And anyways, who knows? We only just got here; he's got to come home sometime. In the meantime, we order pancakes.

There are lots of monks in here and one of them is learning English from a German fellow whose spoken English I can barely decipher. Everyone appears animated; perhaps it's the power of the chairs. They really are as heavy as they look, solid wood varnished and carved, with padded seats covered by some kind of brocade.

Only the pancakes can compete. They too, are solid and heavy. They're also very, very yellow. In fact, they are the same saffron color as the doors and window frames at the Dalai Lama's temple. With all the maroon robes in the room I can imagine the pancakes operating as hats. It's the perfect match of Dalai Lama colors. I know because at home I have a Dalai Lama room. It's a tiny space that started out as my office and is now an office without me. It stores everything that belongs in an office but I work in a corner of my little living room where there are windows at eye level. When I first decided to paint the small room I took a photograph of His Holiness to the hardware store and matched up the paint to the colors of his maroon and saffron robes. Sometimes, when my spiritual inclinations have taken a nosedive, I call it the Dr. Seuss room.

Although we give it our best Buddhist shot, we can't eat the Shangri La pancakes. Like any good teacher, they are dense and impenetrable. I wrap mine up and put it in my pack. As we are paying our miniscule bill, I notice a sign that says there are rooms available in the guest house here. We ask if we can look at them and we're led up narrow stairs to see the darkest, dampest, and most desolate rooms imaginable. At less than two dollars a night, it's probably a decent deal. And if you're a monk perhaps it can be transformed in the mind, but suddenly I'm flying back down those steps really fast. The last thing I need is a meltdown about where we are going to sleep.

After twenty years of therapy, forty years of consciously knowing grief, and a lifetime inside my ever expanding and contracting mind, I have learned most of all to pay attention to fear. No matter how irrational it appears to my grown-up mind, fear always has a truth of its own. It's physiological. It ripples through the body with great authority; it sends all the juices of adrenaline on a wild ride of flight preparedness that demolishes reason, judgment and understanding. Fear always comes first and even though I know I've simply been triggered by a couple of innocuous empty rooms, it makes no difference; I'm almost in its grip. Finding a safe place to sleep has suddenly become a matter of life and death. There is no way I can explain this to Thrinley.

When we get outside, almost next door is an official bookstore of the Tibetan government-in-exile and it is open. Stretched out on the small bit of cement beneath the window is another sound asleep dog. This one's blond. We hike up two very high steps to get over the threshold into a small space full of books about Buddhism, Tibet and the politics of Tibetan survival. I pick up *Impoverishing Tibetans* which explores the ways in which Chinese policy has pushed Tibetans not only out of their country but also outside the workings of the economy inside Tibet. There are pamphlets about the degradation of the Tibetan people, landscape and natural resources of Tibet as the Chinese government exploits every level of life in the country. I find myself hating the Chinese, even as I know the Dalai Lama does no such thing.

I know, in fact, that the policies of China hurt the Chinese people themselves beyond measure. The so-called "Cultural Revolution" meant first of all the extinction of culture. Writers, educators, intellectuals and religious leaders were the first to be eliminated. The freedom of the mind is considered the most dangerous freedom of all.

I remember Felix and Bing, the two Chinese men I met in Maui in 1970. They were both philosophy professors who had escaped from the Cultural Revolution in China and set up a Hawaiian trinket shop in Lahaina. They introduced me to the Tao Te Ching, and in-between serving tourists they gave me lessons in Taoist philosophy. "If you do not revolt when you are young, you have not the right to grow old," said Bing.

One of the things that happen when I get afraid is that shortly after, I get mad. Being in this particular bookstore, while I'm still reeling from being reminded of a fucking lifetime of dealing with fear, means that I feel like blowing up every mother-fucking oppressor on the planet. It is moments like this that make me realize how far I really have to go to meet the Dalai Lama.

I buy two books and am aware that the man behind the table who collects the money could care less about customers. He is intent on reading something and taking notes, his concentration complete. As I get to the door, however, a thought stops me and I interrupt him. "Can you recommend a place to stay that's run by Tibetans?" I ask him, rather bluntly.

He's not happy to be disturbed but I don't care. Something tells me he is precisely the person to ask. He's a serious man and I'm looking for a serious answer. Besides, I just bought a couple of serious books. "The Om," he says, seeming to surprise himself. "And the Loseling Guest House," he adds. He says something else, too, but it's too Tibetan for me to understand. When we get outside, the dog has not moved an inch. And there twenty feet down the road in the midst of a sea of signs, I see one in red and white that reads "Loseling."

"We're going there," I say to Thrinley. "Let's check it out."

The sign to the Loseling Guest House sends us down a dark alley and into a dark room where there's a registration desk and a tall Tibetan man in attendance. He's wearing a turtleneck sweater and a leather jacket, glasses, too. His hair is cropped short and he looks rather stylish. In the small lobby area there are a few single chairs in a row and along one wall is a bench-like couch covered in movie theatre maroon velour. Above it stretch three long shelves with rows of pop, bottled water, and toilet paper. The TV is on and on the screen is the BBC news. There's more toilet paper in a glass case under the TV as well as on the shelves behind the registration desk. All the toilet paper is colored pink, green or yellow. The thin carpet on the floor is a dark forest green; the curtains on the windows that look out into the dark alley are white and lacy. It's my kind of place: lace curtains and lots of toilet paper.

We ask about a room and the fellow behind the desk peers at us intently. After a moment of either hesitation or consideration, he says in a confident but nearly unrecognizable English, something that might translate as, "I'll show you my best room." He grabs a key from the basket on the counter and off we go up three flights of stairs. This is when I become aware of being at seven thousand feet. By the time we get to the third floor I'm nearly dead from trying not to appear old. Then we turn the last corner and I really lose my breath. We are suddenly out onto a roof patio with a vast and wonderful view of sky and mountains. Prayer flags are flapping from rooftops all around us as well as across the valley to the ridge where the rest of McLeod Ganj clings to the hillsides. There are tables and chairs up here and the ornate wrought iron balconies are painted a playful red, green, white and blue. The view drops to valleys, across the town below, and over to the ridge where the Dalai Lama's temple is located. It seems as if all Dharamsala can be seen from here, as well as all the small hamlets and distant temples scattered across the lower realms of the Himalayas.

There are three rooms that open on to this wide and wonderful rooftop and our man in Dharamsala takes us to the one on the furthest corner. My heart is starting to pound. The room he shows us is very tiny with two small beds, a dresser, a small table, a chair, and most miraculous of all, windows on three sides of the room. It's a penthouse closet and I couldn't feel happier.

"Ahhh," I'm blubbering. "It's wonderful."

"And then there's this," says our man with a proud flourish. He swings open a door and proudly presents us with our own bathroom, complete with a Western toilet. I'd been so overwhelmed with the view that I had completely neglected to consider our sanitary well-being.

Thrinley and I are instantly of one mind and one voice. "We'll take it," we say.

Back down at the desk we discover our penthouse room costs 250 rupees a night, about six dollars, total, for both of us. We immediately want to pay for ten days but he says, "No, stay one night and then you can pay tomorrow." He hands us our key on a big brass rectangle. We're in number 301. My fear evaporates into the skies and a great happiness arises. Day one in Dharamsala, lodging accomplished.

By the time we schlep our luggage to our few square feet of fancy penthouse, it is mid-afternoon. The small streets are crowded with colorful and opinionated diversity. Monkeys swing from the electric wires overhead; cows nuzzle the garbage scattered across the small intersection; motorcycles, silenced as usual for the downhill gas-saving advantage, find their way around us in alarming proximity. Cabs and vans with horns are less subversive. I do what the locals do—never look back. It is something I know how to do all too well.

Not looking back is the hallmark of survivor strategy; yet it is in looking back that we know we were here. For me, this is becoming a journey about looking back, about getting a glimpse through spiritual time and finding the through-line of my existence. It is also about being here, completely. Perhaps it is this that enables me, finally, to turn, to look back and see.

TEN

For more than twenty years I have wrestled with, and been wrestled by, the truth. When I collapsed between Christmas and New Year's in 1984, I had no idea that I was falling off the edge of my world, that the inner framework of my life was imploding, and that the rest of my life would become a psychological reconstruction zone. The moment was visceral. I could no longer make my self up. But it would be years before I could begin to describe what happened to me. And the way to the truth was through lies.

The issues of mind control and medical experimentation, ritual abuse, Satanism, Nazi science, occult practice, child pornography— they all exist within a world of denial, and sometimes ridicule. Some of it is rooted in societal denial, some of it is professional denial from within the therapeutic community, and some of the denial, and the ridicule, is promulgated on purpose to protect the dark reality. The truth is—*mind control, illegal medical experimentation, ritual abuse, Satanism, Nazi science, occult practice, and child pornography* all exist. And they all exist within a world of lies. In many ways, the words themselves are lies because they are not experience. And this is a book about experience and those words have nothing to do with my experience, even as they were my experience. Because I was a child. A child to whom those words had no meaning.

As I recovered my memories, I began to recover my core self, the self that knew its own inherent being. I learned the truth because I began to recognize lies. And the biggest lie of all was that I did not have a self. It was a lie I was raised inside, a lie that left me without control, and a lie that was my truth. It was also a lie that saved my life. Because underneath the lie of my non-existent self, was another lie—that my self, should I choose to discover it, was bad. It was easier to live with a created good self that didn't believe in the existence of hatred, abuse or evil than to face a self that was defiled. It was the lies I was told and the lies I told myself that became my truth.

Our minds are miraculous. We are all told how little of our brain we use, how much of it is a mystery, how much we don't know about what we know. Our mind is perceived by us to be separate from our brain. Our mind uses our brain to create our reality. And along the way our senses come into play, giving us contact with the reality we can experience. The sight, sound, smell, touch and taste of things are what we know most intimately. They are experience; and we don't have to make up our minds about what we experience.

But it is only in less evident ways that we "know" what we are told. We "make up our minds" about things we hear and read based upon what we think and believe. But there is a Buddhist bumper sticker that reads: "You don't have to believe everything you think." And its corollary is true: "You don't have to think everything you believe." My thoughts have fought to lay claim to my life, but it is what exists underneath my thoughts that saved my life. It was my faith that believed in me when I was unable to do so. A faith I had no words for. Just as I had no words for what happened to me.

"What happened to you, Janet? You used to be such a good girl."

These are my mother's words. And their significance became evident only 20 years after they were spoken. She said them to me out of the blue when I was somewhere in the midst of expressing enthusiasm for a play I was writing for the Empty Space Theater in Seattle. I was having some success, beginning a career. Her question startled me. But I did not ask "Why do you say that?" or "What do you mean?" Questions, I have come to realize, that are most normal. Instead, I let it slide by with a shrug of acceptance. I didn't even know if she expected an answer. It seemed as though she was expressing a thought out loud and could not help herself. She looked at me curiously, as though she'd never seen me before. Perhaps it was then that I began to win the war I didn't know I was waging.

It was during the year before my implosion. A year in which experiences with my father, too, took on an altered hue. During a massive ice and snow storm in the Northwest, he had successful heart surgery. I tromped through thick snow to visit him in the hospital. During one visit, a doctor came into his room and asked him if he was allergic to a certain medication. "I don't know," my father said. "I've never had any." It turned out that he was.

An hour after I left, after receiving the medication to help him heal, he went into allergic shock and cardiac arrest. But he was in a hospital and the resuscitation team saved his life. And it changed his life. He had a near-death experience and the details of his journey out of his body, his experience looking down upon himself, watching himself be saved, and the nurse who comforted him as the shock paddles were administered, became the story of the rest of his life. He knew spring. He noticed flowers budding for the first time. He could smell the changing seasons and feel the new light returning. He was a changed man. A human man.

Throughout my life, I felt so much fear of my father that it was all I knew. And I knew nothing about him. He was formal, completely emotionally contained, and, from what I have observed in the lives of others, he knew no fatherly ways of being. He told us he was a Mason and that what he did was secret. He went out alone a lot in the evenings and never said where. He was a profoundly mysterious man whose only show of emotion was an agitated wringing of his hands, sometimes around the steering wheel of the car when he was driving. He had an eminent sense of himself. He was the authority in the family and he ruled through psychological intimidation. There were no bloody noses, just irreparable damage to heart, mind and soul. After his near-death experience, came signs of the human being; the father that never was suddenly had a second chance. It was his epiphany. But I was too far gone to take any comfort. It meant I would have to face that which was unknowable, unspeakable and un-faceable.

When I look back at this time from the vantage point of healing, I see the ways in which I was plunged into a profound psychological crisis. I suddenly had a father. Like my mother, but for different reasons, he, too, was seeing me for the first time—through the eyes of life. But there was no way for me to feel perceived through the eyes of life. I really was still "the good girl"—obedient, obliging, obligated—my servile role in the family intact. To be seen through the eyes of life meant to be seen *in* life, as alive, as free, as me. I had no reference point for this experience, no way to feel it, no way to know that it was even a feeling that could be had. It was an existential dilemma that I can write about now; but at the time I was a sitting existential duck. All of my life had been a lie. And that was the truth.

My parents had divorced years earlier in a frenzy of hatred and recrimination. I rallied to my mother's side even as I understood the ways in which they should never be together. My father never spoke ill of my mother to me but he controlled her life in cruel ways by withholding financial support and treating her with dismissive disdain. My mother's rage took on a wrath that would be impressive if it were not so destructive. We were not allowed to speak my father's name nor even imply his existence. I slipped up in this regard at Thanksgiving when I asked one of my brothers if his new girlfriend had met our father; we were summarily tossed out and our stuff unceremoniously tossed out behind us. Months of rage and recrimination followed. But I remained at her beck and call. And I remained my father's ally, too. Yes, he's vile, I told her. Yes, she's crazy, I told him. Their divorce didn't change the ways they had never loved one another, or the ways in which neither I nor my brothers had ever been loved.

More than twenty years later, from both friends and acquaintances, I have learned what love looks like between parent and child. Even my own profound love for my son didn't have the unconditional loyalty and dependability and safety that I see in familial relationships. Colin has forgiven me. Forgiving myself is far more complicated.

Satanism is a word that cannot be written without the corresponding language of urban myth, science fiction, Salem witch trials and false memory syndrome co-opting its reality. But Satanism is a real thing. It's considered a religion—allowed in prisons, disallowed on the tax rolls, taught in colleges, and given legitimate standing in courts of law. When I speak the word, I hear its artifice. Yet I fight against its nihilism, its degradation, its sour derision about all that carries grace in this world. It is a battle I win, and lose, every day.

The weaving together of cult-trained children, medical experimentation, and criminal activity is nothing new. And it's very easy to hide. A child, whose mind has been extracted, manipulated and de-personalized through drugs, electric shocks, sensory deprivation, and other forms of manipulation, can be trained to forget. And then trained to forget that she has forgotten. For me, this meant that having no memory was a natural state. And because we moved so much and I was continually isolated from having friends, or knowing even geographic constancy, I was unmoored even from the physical links of continuity that give ready reference to a life.

"What happened to you, Janet?" It is a question I am asked and, often pointedly, not asked. It is a question I answer and don't answer. In theatre there is the phrase, "suspension of disbelief." It invites us to enter an unreal world and experience it as reality. It is what I am listening for when, "What happened to you?" is asked, or not asked. Because answering it requires words to come out of my mouth. And when they do, I, too, have to face the truth. I have to face the fear, the disbelief, and that strange stone self inside me who can neither speak nor know she is alive. To remember what happened to me is to remember dying.

It is what I know and don't *have* to remember that gives foundation to all that I have remembered. Electric shocks were always part of my vocabulary. I had shocks often because I heard those words when I was very small and I knew that's where I was going. They said it was because of my arm. I had my photograph taken often. I know because I know I went there. Knowing things and remembering things are different. I know I had electric shocks; I didn't remember having them. I know I had my picture taken without my clothes on and I felt the painful intrusion into my body; I just didn't remember the actual sexual acts of my five-year-old self. Forgetting them was part of the shock treatment. Electric shocks eliminate the memory of electric shocks. They also eliminate the memory of self and experience. But trauma rests in the body and in the psyche. It neither forgets nor does it get forgotten. It plays out its truth as though suspended timelessly inside the body—still happening. Trauma, hidden from memory, must be remembered by the body and acknowledged with the greatest of respect by the mind and tenderness by the emotional self; or it runs roughshod over a life. Its causes are either uncovered or trauma goes about perpetrating itself even more upon others as well as upon the suffering self. It took the Vietnam War to put post-traumatic stress disorder into everyday vocabulary, but it was already a reality to untold millions of victims of violence throughout history.

The professionals only get it right after the fact. From the vantage point of healing I know how it feels to have a self and I can compare it to no-self. The feeling of no-self is a disarray of disconnected moments. Self is connection, continuity and commonplace. It is, therefore it will be. And it is everywhere all at once and forever a web of both pleasure and pain. No-self has no connections to anything but a precarious and unsettling fear.

The weirdness about healing is that the self who went into hiding, the core of me, did not have these experiences of life. It meant, also, that I did not have her. In healing, she has a place to come to. In her, I have a place to go. The journey between these two places is convoluted and complex. It will always make me a liar to someone.

But in the realm of *mind control, illegal medical experimentation, ritual abuse, Satanism, Nazi science, occult practice, and child pornography* there's plenty enough to believe and not-believe—for everyone. The facts are in: Nazi scientists were brought to Great Britain, the U.S. and Canada after the war and their work with human experimentation as well as nuclear science was utilized. Mind-control experimentation is well documented. In 1988, the CIA settled the lawsuit filed by Canadian victims after years of mind-control experimentation by CIA-funded programs run by Ewen Cameron in Montreal. He was a Scottish psychiatrist who lived in the U.S. but ran his mind-control research through the Allan Memorial Institute, which was, and is, part of McGill University. There is enough evidence of online child-pornography to satisfy the most skeptical of Pollyanna's. And those children are real. They are not photographs. They are innocent victims, stolen and sold, sometimes by their parents. They are subjected to sex in vile and painful ways. They are photographed. They make millions, perhaps billions, of dollars for their perpetrators. As children, their bodies and faces change and grow. They are not easily identified. They live next door to you. And so do their perpetrators.

Satanism exists. Googling the word brings up more than a million links. Some of them are simply Goth-like sites dedicated to adolescent rebellion. Others link to the Church of Satan established in the U.S. by Anton LeVey and celebrated by the likes of Colonel Michael Aquino who used to run daycare centers throughout the U.S. Army. Other links take you to the occult and the history of the metaphysics of Satanism. Hitler was an occultist and a Satanist. He believed in controlling the human mind and overpowering the human spirit. And he was successful. And his legacy is still at work. It is our denial that will do us in. Believing in that which does not believe in us is essential to our survival as human beings. We have to know what we are up against.

In her thoroughly researched and award-winning book, *In the Sleep Room—The Story of the CIA Brainwashing Experiments in Canada*, journalist Anne Collins maps out the landscape of Cold War paranoia that led to the expansion of official mind-control experimentation. She writes about Allen Dulles, who was to become director of the CIA in the fifties and "was in Switzerland and Germany recruiting fascist intelligence agents for the new war against communism before the old war was over."

I am often in denial as much as the person I tell my story to who thinks all this mind control business is the stuff of science fiction. But it's not. And there are heroes to prove it.

If you go to the official Presidential Medal of Freedom website you can find recipient Joseph L. Rauh Jr., who was awarded the Medal of Freedom on November 30, 1993, by President Bill Clinton. The letter recommending Joe Rauh Jr., was signed by such notables as: Justice William Brennan, Vernon Jordan, Eleanor Holmes Norton, Frank Coffin, Judith Lichtman, Arthur Miller, Thomas Eagleton, Marian Wright Edelman, John Kenneth Galbraith, Katherine Graham, Senator Edward Kennedy, Benjamin L. Hooks, Ralph Neas, Arthur Schlessinger, Jr., Senator Paul Simon, William Taylor, Roger Wilkins and Coretta Scott King. The letter of recommendation is important for two reasons: for what it includes and for what it doesn't include.

"We are writing this letter to recommend that the Medal of Freedom be awarded posthumously to Joseph L. Rauh, Jr., the foremost civil rights and civil liberties lawyer of our time. Joe Rauh died on September 3, 1992, at the age of 81. For more than half a

*century, he devoted his life to the fulfillment of the Constitution's
great promise of equal justice and freedom for all. No one has ever
fought harder or longer for the rights of minorities, the disadvan-
taged and the underdog."*

The letter continues in pages of laudatory prose about Joseph
Rauh's lifetime of work in the public interest. What it leaves out is
Joseph Rauh's last great public interest case—a lawsuit against the
CIA on behalf of a group of unsuspecting Canadians who were used
as guinea pigs in CIA-funded brainwashing experiments at a Mon-
treal psychiatric hospital.

It was an eight year-long lawsuit on behalf of nine plaintiffs that
was settled out-of-court in 1988. They each received $100,000, and
later, 76 other people received $100,000 each from the Canadian
government, which, along with the CIA, had funded Cameron's
work. It all happened behind the looming grey walls of Ravenscrag,
the mansion that once belonged to shipping magnate Sir Hugh
Allan and eventually became the Allan Memorial Institute. Ewen
Cameron eventually became president of the Quebec Psychiatric
Association, the Canadian Psychiatric Association, the American
Psychiatric Association, the World Psychiatric Association and the
Association for Biological Psychiatry.

Under Cameron and his colleagues' experiments, patients were
subjected to an onslaught of drug cocktails and injections—including LSD—that left them in states of terror, disoriented in mind and
body and amnesic regarding who they were, where they belonged,
and who belonged there with them. Add to the mix electroshock
therapy that far exceeded the normal voltage and frequency, and
drug-induced brainwashing comas for days at a time. The results are
easy, and horrifying, to imagine. That apparently was not of concern
to researchers who more than anything wanted to break the code of
the human mind. They wanted to know how to erase memory and
rebuild the psyche. They wanted to learn what the mind could be
made to do, and not do. It was, and still is, the ultimate challenge in
some circles. When it comes to power, prestige, money, or all of the
above, being a human-being sometimes doesn't matter much.

But it mattered to Joseph L. Rauh, Jr. He is a hero to those of us
who cannot speak out for ourselves, cannot fight for ourselves, and

cannot even name our fears for ourselves. Drugs and electric shock wipes out memory of life and memory of self. It does this thoroughly and it did it to me. But the self has a memory deeper than we can remember. It is a self that remembers us. It is that place in us that can neither be created nor destroyed. It goes into hiding but it does not die. Even though it sometimes feels like it.

As is often the case when things are claimed true by so-called "experts" who make money from them, the effects of electroshock treatments have been historically minimized. But in January, 2007, the nation's top electro-shock researcher, Harold Sackheim of Columbia University, who had long claimed that the electroshock treatment doesn't cause damage, repudiated his own 25 year-long claim. The man who taught a generation of electro-shock practitioners that permanent amnesia from ECT is so rare that it could not be studied announced that it "causes permanent amnesia and permanent deficits in cognitive abilities, which affect individuals' ability to function."

What also came to light was Sackheim's role for more than 20 years as a consultant to the electro-shock device manufacturer Mecta Corp. After Sackheim repudiated his own life's work, Linda Andre, head of the Committee for Truth in Psychiatry, a national organization of electro-shock recipients, said, "Those patients who reported permanent adverse effects on cognition have now had their experiences validated." Amen. The National Institute of Mental Health estimates that more than 3 million people have received electro-shock over the past generation.

This stuff fuels my rage. Expert information is too often attached to somebody's massive ego or revered bank account—usually both. It's why Joseph Rauh, Jr. deserves to be known, revered and remembered for his last case—the one overlooked by history.

Rauh's partner in the lawsuit against the CIA, James C. Turner, spoke about Rauh at the inauguration of the District of Columbia's public law school, along with a showing of the Canadian Broadcasting Company film based on "The Sleep Room." Here's an excerpt from Turner's talk:

No one knows how many hundreds of patients were abused in these CIA experiments, but the people we represented had their health devastated and their lives shattered by these bizarre experiments – all conducted without any patient knowledge or consent in violation of the code for medical ethics our country enforced at the Nuremburg War Crime Trials.

Joe was outraged at this story of how the CIA abused its power to conduct secret operations, and believed that accountability for this misconduct was critical. In a word, this was a public interest fight for the principle that no part of our government is above the law. We also believed that reasserting this principle was especially important in the 1980s with the emergence of an increasingly out-of-control CIA led by its then Director, William Casey.

'The Sleep Room' captures the essence of a public interest fight, as well as Joe Rauh's personal humanity to all those who knew and worked with him. It also documents Joe's incredible determination and fortitude – for those of us who knew and worked with him have no doubt that the CIA's decade long strategy of litigation by attrition cost Joe his health and ultimately shortened his life.

You won't find any of this information about Joseph Rauh, Jr. on "The Official Site of the Presidential Medal of Freedom." Nor are you likely to find much in any mainstream media. *But mind control, illegal medical experimentation, ritual abuse, Satanism, Nazi science, occult practice, and child pornography* – all these things exist. And in my personal experience, they are all related.

I was born in Wales at the end of the Second World War. I was born into a family in which my father—and his wealthy English father—prevailed within the throes of Nazi sympathizing and admiration. This was not uncommon in England. Years later I would recognize it in the tone of my father who spoke about Winston Churchill with derisive respect. It was as though the victory over Nazism was an accident, a mistake.

During the war, my father was a munitions inspector who traveled throughout England and Wales. He was from a wealthy English family. He met my mother, the oldest of six children in a working-class Welsh family, in the course of his work. "Your mother got us into something she shouldn't have," was a refrain of my father's. For many years I heard this as a lie. He was far too powerful and frightening to be coerced by my mother into anything. But as the course of my separation from my parents unwound its way through my life, my mother took on greater and darker shadow. And over the course of years, as the pieces of my past fit inexorably into place, I found out that she had a cold manipulative mind long before she met my father. Perhaps she did lead the way into their secret life. But perhaps they met through it, each of them already vowing allegiance to the unnatural, the place where love is mocked and the power of mockery worshipped. The bond between me and my mother has no echo in my memory.

I was a bright and beautiful expendable little girl. It was easy to exploit me in child pornography and prostitution. I have remembered this in ways that are far too graphic to write about. Then, when I was five years old, and already psychologically fragmented—both on purpose and for the sake of my own survival—I was used in medical experimentation. I was told I had polio. I was whisked away in an ambulance with dark windows. It seemed as though I was more often in clinical environments than I was at home. I don't, in fact, ever remember being at home in England. I remember clinics, hospitals, ether and fear. And there was some kind of a school where we slept in rows and weren't allowed to use more than one square of toilet paper. There were terrible smells. And there was a photo studio. And once I remember falling off a swing on purpose and asking a young boy to walk me home. Why was I alone in the park? Why did I fall off the swing on purpose? What happened to the little boy after I took him home? Where was home?

When I was five years old, my arm was cut open and the nerve serving my left hand was severed. I was taken from the school "three times a week for a year" (these words echo from my childhood memory) to receive electric shock treatment, perhaps to see if the nerve would grow. Perhaps to eliminate the memory of my sexual exploitation. Perhaps to have personalities implanted through intimidation and terror and "the good girl" put in the place of the self that might remember. My thumb and forefinger are half the size of those on my right hand. My thumb doesn't bend. There's very little feeling in my left hand and it does not grasp. All my writing is done by two fingers on my right hand. Throughout my life I adjusted to my numb and helpless five-year-old fingers the way I adjusted to my numb and helpless five-year-old self—by pretending they weren't there.

I was seven years old when we moved to Montreal, where we lived in four different places over the next five years. I remember where they were. I just don't remember being inside them. In Montreal, I was "sent places" to "see people." I was "special." Sometimes people came to see me in the large closet up in the attic, where there was a mattress. I was sent to drama classes in the basement of an old church, where I wore a lot of make-up and pleased people. I was sent into the city by myself on the train to see a "mind doctor;" and next door to one of the houses in which we lived there was a couple who were "mind doctors." It is the clinical places that are familiar to memory—and the clinical people. I don't remember where I slept, where I played, where I ate, or where anything was in my world.

Was I subjected to the drug induced sleep and de-patterning programs perpetrated by Dr. Ewen Cameron? I don't know where it was I was sent for my "treatments". I do know that the Allan Memorial Institute has resonance in my past. And that in Montreal, I was subjected to massive electric shock treatments and ongoing exploitation. I do know that "doctors and nurses" were involved—scary people wearing white coats, in my child memory. As I look back with the language of my adulthood, I recognize that I was more of an experiment than somebody's child. There were mirrors that were windows, always appointments to keep, and extended times when I was sent away. I recognize a child in shock, a child trained to perform sexually and otherwise, a child arousing continual clinical curiosity and observation, a child who could see through it all and could do nothing about it.

After five years in Montreal, we took a ship back to England for the summer. I was twelve years old and I remember a yellow cardigan "twin-set" that my grandfather bought me. He was my father's father, the one who owned both a toy store and a brass factory. Once, when we were in Montreal, he came to visit us and had my father take a photo of him in front of somebody else's fancy mansion so he could show it to his friends as the house his son bought. He was jovial and frightening. His own house, grand and formal, had rooms that were rarely entered. Like everything else in my life, the trip that summer is lost to a fugue in which there is no memory of place or of people. Only the fresh air of being on the high seas and the freedom of being outside tells me I went.

When we came back from that summer visit to England, instead of going home to Montreal, we moved straight to Vancouver where my father had yet another new job as an engineer. This was a shock. It was also where my life as I know it began. Not in the first Vancouver neighborhood, where I know we lived because I went to school there and remember its name. It was in the second house, the one in North Vancouver, where I remember where I slept. It is there where the first experience of being takes shape in my memory. I was thirteen. This is not unusual in survivors; we are saved by puberty partly because our exploitation could make us pregnant, and partly because our lives grow more external and less controllable. I remember friends and parties and boyfriends and hikes and French fries after school. I had my own room. I looked after my brothers and was a surrogate mom to a new baby brother, who thought later in his life that perhaps I was his mother. Because I loved him.

What little I knew of human love was as a big sister. When, at the age of 41, I made a decision to suspend relationship with my parents, I lost my brothers. This was the real loss. That my parents didn't or couldn't love me I had experienced my whole life. But I had counted on my four brothers. After years of healing, I understand how the family system abandoned them, too. As well as how it replicated itself.

The "training" I experienced was to eliminate "the self" and replace it with artificially created parts, or personalities that could perform accordingly in sexual ways, and always obediently in other ways. Electric shock was the primary tool. But there were other states, too, that leaked through in to my later life. Lying for hours, dead-still, staring at the ceiling, knowing neither time nor space is a life-long experience resulting from sensory deprivation and drug treatments. I didn't recognize this as unusual until it stopped happening as much. It is still a place I can slip into too easily. Not being able to talk, to say what I mean, think, or feel was my life for nearly fifty years. The great irony here is that although I was not allowed to speak for myself, to ask for anything, or to name myself in any way, nobody ever told me I couldn't write. In one way or another I leaked out in my writing and I claimed my life through my writing. Books were miracles because they were written. The writer did not have to exist.

The writing part of my life must have been an immense shock to my family. At the time I didn't recognize this because I was long used to being invisible and did not know how to expect recognition from within the family. My ability to give language to the characters in my plays was an immense irony when I could not give language to myself—or as it would turn out—my selves. Perhaps it was the first sign that all had not gone as planned.

This mind-control business is not big news. Getting control over the mind has been, and still is, a juicy goal for everyone from neuroscientists to military experts to dictators to marketing consultants. They are all out there, and in the back of this book there are many legitimate resources listed for those interested in educating themselves about these issues. Kids indoctrinated into cults and their perverted money-making schemes are great resources for mind-control experimentation because they have already been trained not to exist. Kids in general are great resources because they are helpless, available, and malleable. In less hidden ways, the flagrant international child sex-slave and sex-trade business—an epidemic of it—is thriving barely underground. Incest and child sexual abuse are words that have only become acceptable over the past 20 years, but their reality is part of age-old abuse. It might take another 20 years for the survivors of mind-control experimentation and its attendant abuses to become household words, but we will. And I do not stand alone.

There are thousands of us scattered throughout North America, tens of thousands of us around the world. Some of us are lucky enough to find one another. Within my very small island community I personally know three other survivors of mind control and sexual abuse who struggle every day to find their way into being. They are accomplished, respected people who keep private the circumstances of their past and their struggle.

The culture of denial does not welcome disclosure, does not welcome the grief, the isolation, the need to be seen and to be recognized that is at the very core of our experience. So we reinforce our insularity through our competence, our skillful means of dissociating, and our need to somehow in some way appear "normal." Some of our stories begin in our families when we are born, some of them happen later at the hands of outsiders. Some are part of "official" programs; others stay beholden to illegal greed and exploitation.

There are many stories in my life that defy belief. The man I married, who, from a later perspective, appeared to have been placed in my life on purpose. My infant son who died suddenly and mysteriously, giving rise years later to the possibility that he did not die but was taken. The people who seemed to come into my life by accident but didn't; my continual self-sabotaging; the sabotaging by others; the extent and depth of what I don't remember about my life; the way memories surfaced without context of time and place; the way fear defined my very existence. It was only when fear was not my basic frame of reference that I began to realize it had been my entire life. By then I was in my fifties. All the ways in which I had no choice in my life are also difficult to comprehend as well as difficult to believe. They are as difficult to believe as the ways in which I was continually saved from death and despair by circumstances of divine intervention and protection, by grace.

Grace has always intervened in decisive ways, introducing me to painters and poets, to books that call to me from a shelf, to places and jobs, to my therapist, to my spiritual teachers and to people who became my friends and helped love me into being. My inability to plan a life for myself left nothing but grace in its wake. Everything—from Buddhism to Christianity to where I live and to how I got here to India—is evidence of grace. It's with me even when I am unable to be with it.

Every day I doubt the experiences of my childhood. And every day I know they were true. And every day here in Dharamsala is a massive confirmation. Because everywhere I go I am surrounded and encountered by self. No matter how limited and challenged are the lives of those around me, their expression of self-ness is loudly and visibly apparent. It is an innocent, unconscious and unquestioned self-ness. Back home, in the world in which I live, deep self-ness is masked by the cultural self, the accomplishing self, the social self, the self that shows up for special occasions. They are masks that call out my own. But here, in India, it is the unencumbered self that calls out my own and tells me I am home.

Free will is an extraordinarily subtle experience. It is an experience I continue to learn to have and I expect to be doing so for the rest of my life. Most of all, it is a feeling that rests in the body. To want something—whether it is to take a nap, a vacation or a bike ride—is simple, and seems to rise easily in people. Whether they get what it is they want doesn't get in the way of the wanting. But I was trained not to want. Wanting something automatically and immediately put it out of the realm of possibility. And when I was actually offered something I wanted, like an ice cream cone, if I expressed wanting a certain flavor, like chocolate, I was not allowed to have any ice cream at all. I was punished for wanting, which meant that the feeling of wanting was the very thing that destroyed the possibility of having. The convolutions around this predicament continue to be a challenge, even all these years into healing. To want something still carries with it the knowledge that I can't have it—whether it's a love affair or a stick of licorice. I was trained to be obedient to the will of others and to never, ever want something. How this played out in my life, from my servitude within my family to the ways in which I capitulated to the needs of others in my adult life—particularly when it came to sex—is a realm of shame and humiliation.

It is profoundly ironic, that at the age of forty, when love took me down, it wasn't a broken heart that first got me into therapy with Brian. It was the real and present promise of my own passion that I could not face. When my passion surfaced for its first pure view of the world it presented me with the perversion in my life. I didn't know these words back then. I knew racking, irreconcilable grieving. Falling in love and being loved back with passion and pleasure derailed me completely. The conditioning of my mind had completely kept my past at bay; but when, through layers of denial and amnesia, passionate love surfaced in my body, it plunged me into complete breakdown.

In therapy I came to memory in odd and unaccountable ways, many of them through abiding grief. It was the way I "knew" things. And I knew them through my child's body, through people being around me watching me in fascination, through circumstances of sex and exposure that made no sense. It all felt so organized, so purposeful. I could not understand it. There was a context missing and it was driving me crazy. I was a year and a half into therapy and over my head in unending grief and paralyzing fear when I was driven in frustration to the Seattle Public Library one day. I looked up organized child abuse in England in the card catalog. There was no Google in those days, no way to make it easy. When I saw the words "ritual abuse" my whole body went cold with recognition. What I had remembered was not crazy. I was not crazy.

When I got to Brian's office that afternoon in the spring of 1986, I sat on the couch and I said those two words. "Ritual abuse." He was very quiet and tears came into his eyes. He opened his appointment book and showed me a small yellow square sticky note. "Suspect cult abuse with Janet. Should I tell her?" I was the topic of his discussion with peers. What to do about me?

Years unfolded. Therapy, body work, retreat, isolation, greater and greater grief, shame, belief and disbelief—it was a slow and inexorable facing up to the truth. Brian learned along with me. He never, ever, put words in my mouth. Even now, all these years later, it is only when I ask him for information that he offers any. His commitment is always to my healing. To helping me unfold into the mystery of the life that is rightfully mine.

He told me how people reveal their truth. "It's like a puzzle," he said. "Different pieces are turned over, and at first they are connected in unidentifiable clumps. Soon parts of the picture begin to make sense, and then, finally, the big picture. Some people put the whole puzzle together face down. Only when they decide to turn it over and look at it does it makes sense." It's this last description that resonates. I had to reconnect to and rebuild my self before I could face the facts of my life. I could not name my past until I had named myself.

"How will I recognize my core self?" I asked Brian. He laughed. "Because it's so comfortable there's no question about it." He said it feels comfortable precisely because there's nothing to feel. It simply is. And he is right.

The road to recovery is a complicated trek but the destination is simple: to simply be. When we get there, it is heaven. The most normal moments are transcendent. Waking up and getting out of bed without thinking about it is a miraculous moment. So is looking into the eyes of another without feeling shame, or playing spontaneously with a child without feeling a blight of self-consciousness, or walking down a crowded sidewalk without feeling alien. It is the place inside us that cannot be named that is targeted by those who think it can be destroyed. They, however, are wrong. The spirit has an invincible vocabulary of its own. All these methods of abuse, no matter how brutal or "scientific," can not kill the human spirit.

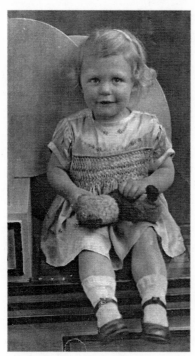

I am two-years-old in the photo above left, and five in the one taken at the beach with my brother. As a five year-old, my arm had already been cut; the nerve damage is evident in the awkward angle of my left thumb and forefinger.

In this family photo with my parents and two of my brothers, I am seven. It was taken just before we moved from England to Montreal, Canada. My two youngest brothers were later born in Canada.

With Colin At Fort Dix, New Jersey, in 1966.

With poet, Kenneth Rexroth, in 1978.

My first play, *Heads and Tails*, was produced at the Empty Space Theatre in Seattle in 1979. The occasion of this photograph was a production of *Ten Minutes for Twenty-Five Cents* at the Northwest Playwrights Conference in 1981.

In a eucalyptus grove in Berkeley, California, at the first conference on ritual abuse that I attended in 1988.

With Colin on a Green Tortoise commute between San Francisco and Seattle sometime in the mid-1980s. My favorite jaunt with Green Tortoise was to the Southwest for ten days where we camped out under the stars and hiked the desert and canyon beauty every day.

As editor of SPA Magazine. I went on assignment to Hawaii with Fabio (left), and to Wales (right), where I hiked along the Pembrokeshire Coastal Path.

"The Battle in Seattle" was published in time for the first anniversary of the 1999 WTO protests in Seattle. If the mainstream media had done their journalistic job during WTO Seattle and informed their audience about the issues, we might not be in the mess that now defines our world.

Buck was my faithful companion during many years of healing..

(NY17-April 20) FUGITIVE GOD-KING--The Dalai Lama, Tibet's fugitive god-king, smiles on arriving in Tezpur,India, Saturday, en route to Mussoorie, his home-in-exile north of New Delhi.This photo was made by AP photographer Dennis Royle.(AP Wirephoto)(pr21301cm)1959

I lived with a woodstove most of my years on the island, along with a great community of friends and the unending inspiration and solace of the nature.

This AP photograph of His Holiness was taken in April 1959, just after his escape from Tibet through the Himalayas to India.

(Above) The vista from the patio of our penthouse digs in Dharamsala encompassed the life of the family next door as well as the grandeur of the Dhualadhar Mountains.

(Left) Our five-dollar-a night room is the one with the door open.

ELEVEN

A s we settle into our new room in Dharamsala with its windows,
mountains and hefty comforters, I feel buoyant and joyful.
We've been in India less than a week and already I've experienced
lifetimes of familiarity—with the landscape, the people, the colors,
the smells, and most of all, the spirit. None of it is defined by language; there are no words deflecting meaning, distorting experience, manipulating the mind. It is a language of body and soul; it is
spoken in reality, in the ways in which life is lived out loud, above
and beyond whatever it is that can be uttered. I feel right at home.
Until I realize that we don't have any electricity in our room.

I go downstairs to find out what's up. In the guest house lobby,
the electricity is working, but our English-speaking monk in the
leather jacket is nowhere to be seen. A lovely young woman tells me
he'll be back soon so I sit down beside her to wait. She introduces
herself as Amy from Australia. She's here to give Nawang, the guest
house manager, his English lesson. Within a few minutes I discover
that she came to Dharamsala for a visit two years ago and simply
stayed on. She teaches English to several monks each day and she is
passionately in love with the place and the people.

"There's a celebration at the temple tonight," she tells me. "You
must go. All the monks will be there."

I find out a bit more and tell her that I, too, would like to teach English. Even if I have no idea how. What I do know is that there is no way I can be here and not be of use. Just then, a monk in robes comes in; he sits down as though he lives here and smiles at us. I attempt to enlist help with the power problem. It's quickly obvious that he neither speaks, nor attempts to speak, English. With some inventive gestures of switch-flipping and bewilderment, I attempt some form of useful communication.

"Ahhh." He suddenly gets it and off we go. In spite of his flowing robes, he races up the stairs like an athlete. When we get to the landing on the third floor he stops at a complex of fuse boxes high up on the wall. After flipping a few switches and grunting a few grunts, he is satisfied and we round the corner to our quarters. He flips a switch on the wall outside our door and gestures for us to try our lights. Neon suddenly lights up our life. So does the small light between our beds. We are all happy and with a brisk flourish our monk is gone.

Thrinley and I lay claim to the shelves and surfaces in our room. I've noticed that this happens without any decision-making whatsoever. We'd already laid claim to our beds without talking about it and now the rest of our small space is divvied up accordingly. My bed is furthest from the door and is tucked along a wall with a window I can touch from a reclining position. The window sill is broad and I stash everything—books, bathroom bag, Clif Bars and camera—on it. There's one small wardrobe with a few shelves and a few hangers for our clothes. And we each have a chair. The curtains are a crisp white with blue flowers, the walls are white and the ceiling is a bright sky blue, just like the color on the ceiling of the gonpa on San Juan Island. The room is clean in all its corners and as I gaze out the windows at the majestic mountains I cannot begin to imagine a better place anywhere in the entire universe.

Just as we start to think about dinner and the celebration, Amy arrives breathlessly at our door.

"I met a monk," she says. "Come and meet him. He wants to learn English."

Well, ask and ye shall receive. I trundle downstairs with my useful intent and out on the street I meet Dakpa. He is tall and thin, young and shy, and he completely disarms me with his smile and his gratitude. We make an appointment to meet the following day.

Back in the room I feel a bit self-conscious about it all. Perhaps I should have found a monk for Thrinley, too.

"I know there are more of them," I tell her. "You'll be teaching soon, too."

As we get ready to go to the Dalai Lama's temple, I notice an Indian man leaning over the balcony and looking along the outside of our room. Weird, I think. When we leave I notice he is adjusting colored lights all along the balconies and testing to see if they light up. Like Christmas, I think, as we head off to the mysterious celebration about which we know nothing.

When we get to the Dalai Lama's temple, there is indeed something auspicious underway. Wave after wave of Tibetan Buddhist monks are streaming into the courtyard, up the steps and circumambulating the temple. There is a chant rippling through the ranks. It starts somewhere within the throng, then swells in echoes and refrains as the hundreds of monks sweep around the temple. Thrinley and I join in and the sound carries us around and around. It is not the familiar "O Mani Padme Hum" but something more lyrical. It's a singing sound with a rise of joy in it, a sound of celebration growing larger and larger as the crowd expands.

We decide to sit and watch the throng go by. I see Dakpa circling by and he comes over in greeting. Amy goes by with a handsome young Tibetan man with long hair and a contemporary look. By now the walkway around the temple is packed deep with monks. There is a playful call and response in the singing as well as bursts of laughter and mischievous moments when monks tug at one another's robes or push one another in fun.

We join back in the crimson tide of celebration and circumambulation until the monks pour into the temple and sit down in rows. The singing abruptly becomes a deep and reverent chanting; a solemn feeling descends. I am caught off guard by the sudden transition and I feel tears rising for something I cannot name. Thrinley and I choose not to join the Westerners crowded in at the back of the temple and instead go back to our new digs for a good sleep. High all around us, next door and on boxy buildings across all ridges above and below us, flashing colored lights light up the sky. Our days in Dharamsala have begun.

All night the pulsing lights outside my window burst rhythmically under my eyelids. Each bright pulse gives me a start and I know I am being triggered. Electric shocks, the buzzing in the body, fear rippling under my skin, the way it jolts and shatters. Then the knowing that it is coming and the forgetting that comes before it happens. The way there is no control over anything. The old familiar paralysis sets in. I can't even reach over to the sill to grab the flashlight, to take refuge with my cozy mystery under the covers. This is a state I understand, but even that does not liberate me. Like in the goofy mirrors at the carnival, I see echoes of myself knowing all there is to know, yet I am utterly unable to connect my knowing to the simple movement of my body.

I had carefully prepared my psychic tool kit on the window sill—the book, the light, the munchies—and I cannot reach for them. I never in my life thought this state was weird until years after I started therapy and brief bursts of fearlessness made me giddy with a feeling that can only be called freedom. Now, with as much as I know and have learned and practiced, this immobility is still my most loyal friend: if I am frozen in time, nothing will happen. It is also my most loyal enemy: if I am frozen in time, nothing does happen.

The alternative is to find time and place for the frozen ones to thaw so they, too, can be part of life. This is a pretty delicate state of affairs. "I contain multitudes," is a poetic exclamation of Walt Whitman. Well, I contain multitudes, too, and there is nothing poetic about it. My multitudes are young, many are naked and cold, most can't speak, some don't dare open their eyes, others are invaded by body-snatchers who have entered the places that were once special, secret and private. Some are locked in dark places where toilets overflow with filth and the stink sends them even deeper away from time. Many are locked in the sterility of "doctors'" offices where their small minds were manipulated, electric shocks were administered, and all hope was lost. Staying frozen is staying numb, non-existent and not a nuisance. Opening my heart to them and allowing them to enter rooms with my friends has been, and is, impossible.

Thrinley is sleeping deeply, her steady soft breathing only two feet away in the next bed. It brings me a moment of comfort and I think about the time. I think about my watch on the sill, how cold my nose is, the price of electricity, and these flashing lights. I think about dawn. If it's close to dawn, I can get up. I can go outside.

At some point in my healing journey I realized that I never felt safe at home. I knew this was true about my many childhood homes—we moved around constantly—but I didn't realize that the very concept of home had been fouled by my abuse and my fear. As an adult I was never able to settle at home, to celebrate being "home," to feel safe and secure—even when I was. It was an affliction all too easily passed on to Colin. I moved us around constantly. It's only in recent years that this connection became clear. As I finally learned how to cozy into my small home zone, most of all I realized that I had deprived my son of this birthright, too, his home security. In one way or another, we pass on everything. All I can hope is that I also passed on my wild and unadulterated love affair with the outdoors.

It is this that rouses me to get the flashlight and my watch. It is just after 4:00 a.m. A couple of hours until sunrise. But this movement breaks my paralysis so I grab my book and stick my head under the covers to read. The lights from outside still flash through the comforter but now they are just lights, just another nuisance. I settle in and finish another book.

At six, I quietly bundle up all the parts of me—frightened, frozen and otherwise—into all the warm clothes I have and slip quietly outside onto the patio. The mountains loom in shadows against the bright stars; the air is crisp and quiet; the colored lights flash from across the valley as well as all around me. In the sky, there is no indication of morning. I take a chair over to the corner closest to sunrise and sit and wait; what I don't do is meditate.

Once upon a time I was pretty proud of my meditating ability; then I realized that I was simply perfecting my ability to dissociate. This all came about when I was at Cloud Mountain Retreat Center cooking for a small group of people who were in silent meditation for a year. I had gone there because I had to get away from the noise of it all, including the sound of my own voice. It was 1986, early into my descent and the tools of my trade and the props of my life were toppling like dominoes. I want to be of service, I thought. And I had to be quiet, to feel quiet. Cooking in silence sounded just about right.

There were workshops a couple of times a month at Cloud Mountain; those in the year-long retreat would stay in private meditation when outside teachers and participants arrived on the weekends for different forms of Buddhist meditation practice. Tom, my cooking partner and comic side-kick who nicknamed me Basil because he said he couldn't call me Sage, and I would trade off on our duties so we could each participate in teachings. Two teachers got my attention in a big way: Alan Clements and Julie Wester.

Alan popped every presumptuous Buddhist bubble of pretension that anyone could muster. He rattled our peaceful minds with his self-righteous wrath about our self-indulgent spiritual ways. He was ruthless and funny. He was also in active rebellion from his years as a Buddhist monk in Burma. He'd learned a few things and he had no reservations whatsoever about telling us all just a bit more than we wanted to know. My own inner rebel, silenced by inside tides, whooped and hollered in recognition.

Alan spoke up to spiritual hypocrisy. He was crazy and contradictory himself, but he never tried to hide it. We are our emotions, too, he let us know through his own ranting and raving; and we'd damn well better wake-up to them or they would sink us in ignorance. He was outraged and outrageous. From Alan I learned how easy it is to be just as full of spiritual materialism as it is to be full of material crap.

From Julie Wester I learned that Buddhism was in my body as well as my mind. We did walking meditation and a kind of sensory exploration of who we were physically in the time and space we inhabited. She taught an "embodied" Buddhism and I got the first clue that my meditation practice was perhaps just a bit too easy to be true. Julie was also my first Buddhist woman teacher and I gleaned practicality as well as tenderness from her work. Unlike the heady stuff of a Buddhism that could be named and analyzed, she brought a more sensual awareness to the practice. It made me cry. It felt good.

During my stint at Cloud Mountain I'd been regularly going up the hill to the small and beautiful meditation hall which was available when there was no public event underway. I would sit dutifully, disembodied for a long and barely breathing time. As a child, I was trying to die. As an adult, I was a good meditation practitioner.

This partnering up of my abilities and disabilities was an existential conundrum. I was scared witless as a kid; my mind grew wings and transported us to safer ground. It became facile and heady with its own abilities. It left my body in the lurch. It had no time for pain and pleasure—both of which are rooted in the senses. Instead it had its own sharp shortcuts to perception. It could read other minds; most of all it could read its own as it split off into mind patrols scanning the surface of things and people for signs of threat and danger. It was a kaleidoscopic mind, shifting with every breath into a new mosaic of perception. Its job was to keep us out of the body; yet it was only through the body that we could be saved. The problem was: the body was a war zone.

Re-entering the body was like astronaut John Glenn re-entering the atmosphere in his hurtling one-man cone of imminent destruction. It was a rough ride through searing heat, volcanic turbulence, and a hell-realm of unknown and unthinkable possibilities. Through all the years of therapy it became clear that this was the final frontier: to enter the body and stay there.

As I sit here in the dark corner of the patio, waiting for morning to arrive in Dharamsala, I suddenly smell the earthy sweetness of incense. Then I hear footsteps in the stairwell and somebody passes behind me and climbs the stairs to the roof. I turn my head and catch a glimpse of a monk's robes. Then a boy comes up to the rooftop of the guest house next to ours. He turns a tap and starts filling the huge water tanks on his building from some community source I cannot see. Then he, too, waits without moving, leaning against the balcony, gazing out over the rooftops of this small town. From above I hear the monk's soft chant as he circumambulates the roof in a morning prayer. The monk, the boy, and I, are so close, yet I don't know if either of them knows I am here. But I do. I really am here. I am an occupant in my own body.

And it's that awareness that rises with the imperceptibly rising dawn. The clear mountain air, the soft sound of crows' wings flapping by, a dog's good-morning bark from across the valley, the slight smell of smoke from an early warming fire, the sound of a cough clearing the throat of someone in the street below, the glow brightening in the east, my whereabouts becoming evident to the monk on the roof above and the boy on the roof next door; they all conspire in this moment of being here now, fully, without reservation. I feel the inexplicable happiness, the sense of being completely at home, in this body and in this place called Dharamsala. So this is why I am here, I am thinking, as the sun rises in small increments on the mountainside and the light begins to fill out the surrounding day. I am here to celebrate my life.

For too long I have measured my life in losses. Lost loves, lost children, lost family, lost career, lost potential, lost possibilities; they have claimed my attention and my life. But I am not lost. This awareness is articulating itself to me here on this rooftop. It is unexpected and foreign. In the night I had been possessed by fear and I am too experienced with it to think it will ever completely disappear from my life. But just as I have had to make friends with fear, I realize that I have to make friends with faith. This, too, takes practice. And right now practicing faith means I am feeling the simple satisfaction of being myself.

In her poem, *Wild Geese*, Mary Oliver writes:

You do not have to be good.
You do not have to walk on your knees
for a hundred miles through the desert, repenting.
You only have to let the soft animal of your body
love what it loves.

As the activities of morning, the daily rituals of life on streets and rooftops of Dharamsala get livelier and louder around me, I sit here letting the soft animal of my body love what it loves. And it is loving this moment and being in this moment and being part of everything that is alive. And there is nothing that is not alive.

It's only minutes before the sun is fully up and my bundled up body is too warm. I come out from under my blanket and peel off a few layers. The monk still circumambulates above me and I notice his outer robe, his shawl, is draped over the railing. Without looking, I see his pace is quick and determined. I imagine his fingers turning his prayer beads as he counts his mantras and how this routine of faith has become his second nature. Perhaps even his first nature. I stretch up towards the sun in a ritual of my own and start to do the tai chi arm-swinging exercise that I learned so long ago when Colin and I lived in Hawaii. The arms are relaxed and the turn is from the waist, the weight shifting fully from one leg to the other as the arms flop loosely from side to side. It's an exercise that loosens the spine, softens the shoulders and warms up the hands. I do it a hundred times, and then another hundred.

Thrinley is sitting up in bed doing her morning practice when I go back into our room. I quietly grab my small spiral notebook and go back to the patio to catch up on my notes. By now the birds are whistling, croaking, chirping and singing their way across the sky. More dogs are barking in the streets. I hear sweeping on the steps, and on the rooftop below a Tibetan woman is hanging out laundry and a man is brushing his teeth. There's the sound of buckets of water being splashed on the dusty walks and the honks of taxis as they begin their daily conversation. The day is underway.

We search around the neighborhood and find breakfast through a small door, up a narrow staircase, and across a cement floor still smelling dank from its morning wash. A young man greets us with a warm smile and as we seem to be the only customers it seems only right to stay. Another narrow staircase goes up to another floor and we gesture for permission to ascend. He gestures us onward and so we climb to the top floor. It's a Spartan arrangement with just the basics – white plastic chairs and wooden tables with brown and white checkered plastic tablecloths. But all is tidy and clean. And there's a lovely view stretching out the window and across the small valley to the other side of town. The morning sky is brilliant blue and all the colors of daily life are in full bloom.

On one wall is a large photograph of the Potala, along with a formal triptych portrait of His Holiness the Dalai Lama. A white prayer scarf is draped over the frame of the photograph and underneath it a small table with a plastic white lace tablecloth is home to a small vase of plastic yellow flowers. This display of reverence in this shabby, well-meaning room is a tender gesture of love and respect, a rising above poverty in a time of poverty. A holding to what is precious, the embodiment of compassion and kindness, the Dalai Lama. In Tibet, it is illegal to have a photograph of the Dalai Lama. In Dharamsala, his image is everywhere.

My first awareness of His Holiness the Dalai Lama was in 1959, the year he escaped from Tibet. I remember hearing about his journey, his youth, and his burden. I remember because it was early in the birth of my remembering self. My life in space and time started the year the Dalai Lama made a break for freedom and went into exile. It is a fitting description for the survivors of abuse, too. Our break into freedom sends us into exile from our former selves, from our families, and from the societies in which we live. The world moves on. Nobody likes to look back, to see the damage to the Tibetan people, to their country, to their culture. Nobody likes to know about suffering. Yet it is only through suffering that healing happens. I know His Holiness the Dalai Lama suffers when he remembers his people left behind in 1959, just as he suffers when he sees the constantly newly arriving Tibetan refugees who make the treacherous trip through the Himalayas to freedom. But his suffering doesn't impair his great capacity for joy. It is this that has always given me hope. It is this that has allowed me to keep my grief and lose it, too.

The great paradox of healing is that we have to suffer to get there. And when we do, the healing takes on new dimensions and new suffering. It is a great spiral of suffering that leads to a great spiral of liberation from suffering. Realizing that I would never wake-up one day "recovered" was shattering. But only then was I able to turn to the parts of me that had always been healed. To begin to know my suffering selves as noble, to come out from under the shame. Only when I realized that I would never be "recovered" did I truly begin to recover.

There is a phrase in the lexicon of psychotherapy, "recovered memory." It implies that a memory returns; it comes back after a long time away. But recovered memory is limited in scope to that which can be perceived and uttered. It is limited to facts of description, events that can be articulated. It is limited to a shared consensus of what precisely is truth. Is there truth before language? Was the red wheelbarrow in William Carlos Williams' famous poem still red before he knew the word red? Was there life before it could be named? Was there rape before it could be named? Was there torture before it was a word? Was there mind control before it could be described?

Just because I didn't know the word "rape" when I was five years-old, it doesn't mean that I didn't know how it felt. This was one of those paths I traveled with Brian upon which I had to redefine memory and bring it into a personal vocabulary that made sense to me. And it only made sense through my body and my feelings. Whenever I began to utter a word of description, of literal understanding that was beyond my young mind, the truth was twisted into a lie by language itself. I was five years old; I didn't know the words. And on top of this predicament of innocence, through electro-shock, sensory deprivation and drugs, I was trained to believe that everything I said, believed, felt, knew was a lie. I am a lie. And if I am a lie, all I know are lies.

Recovering my memories meant recovering my experiences. Even now, years into my life and the uncovering of my history, when I say I was raped there is an odd disconnect because I did not know that word when it was happening to me. What I know is that I was very small, I could not breathe, that someone was very heavy on my body, and that it hurt, it hurt a lot. And that most of all I could not breathe. And it is this that tells me I was raped.

It is the physiological fear rippling through my body and the suspension of my self outside my body that tells me of electric-shock. It is the immense amount of my life spent immobilized in a silent, paralyzed mind and stiffened body that tells me of the drugs and the artificial means used to separate me from my self. To name it, to know it, to face it, means to die. Creeping up on memory means creeping up on panic. And who in their right mind wants to uncover a perpetual panic, a suspended state of terror, a psychic shattering in which all the anchors of time, space and self are unmoored and there is nothing but the eternal facing of imminent death?

When I do "remember" things, like the time I was sold to customers on a bus, I remember the curiosity of it all. How some people went up to the bus driver and asked him if they knew anyone by the name of so-and-so, who might live in the neighborhood. My mother quickly spoke up from her seat beside, "Oh, yes, by the way, I do." Voila. They identify one another; I am identified and off I go to have sex with strangers.

Or the time we were going to the "doctor" and I had forgotten to put on panties under my dress. We were still in England so I was younger than seven. My mother was shocked, "Oh, how could you!" But I was unperturbed. The privacy of me there, the tender innocent parts of me, no longer existed. Why should I wear panties when there was nothing there anymore? How curious.

Or when they told me I had polio and whisked me away in a car with dark windows. "You can see out but no-one can see in," someone said. I remembered thinking how interesting this was. But I didn't remember what happened to my body when it became research property. When my arm was sliced open to see what nerves would do. When electric shocks became the whole and defining nature of my experience. I simply chose not to live in my body anymore. I lived elsewhere. But where? This is the real mystery to me. Not why people can be so stupid and exploitative, so twisted and greedy, so pathetically enamored of what they think is power in this world, but where did I go and what did I do when I went there? And who was there with me? Because I know I wasn't alone.

I first became aware of my spiritual guide and protector when I was four years into therapy with Brian. The complexities of my therapeutic process during the decade of my descent into healing are beyond description, only Brian can bear witness; but only I can bear witness to the Wise One. He (Yes, Virginia, he is a "he") lay claim to my mind before I knew I had one. He held the space around my childhood suffering; he knew where my mind began and ended, where it could not bear to go, and why. He never stopped paying attention. I once asked him if he was God? He laughed. "Of God," he told me. "Maybe."

It is my friend, the Wise One, who keeps on keeping on, who holds out grace to me all the time, even when most of the time I am so propelled by fear that I can't even turn my head to see. And he's always been there. When I was a child, he was my safe place. Throughout the forty years of my life in which my self and my selves were in hiding, he brought me to people and places and books. When I was married and captive on a small island, there was the yearning for knowledge. Philosophy books followed me home from the library. I was 19, my mind was not my own but his led the way. He is a learned man. He knows that knowledge and the struggle for deep truth is the path to salvation. And I needed to feel salvation in life before I would be able to claim it in death. I needed to get to the truth.

Right now, the truth is that I'm drinking the best cup of tea I've had in years. It is a perfect blending of creaminess and tea-ness. It is strong but not bitter. It is hot, but not too hot. And it is the Dalai Lama in the photograph on the wall across the room who holds witness to my secret pleasure: the perfect cup of perfect tea. My happiness at this moment is as strong and perfect as this cup of tea. It runneth over, spilling out of heart and mind with an inarticulate vengeance. And all I can do is grin at Thrinley as we order the safest thing on the menu, boiled eggs and bread.

It was only hours ago when I woke up in deathly fear with all the echoes of my childhood rattling my bones and my being. Now I can barely contain my gleeful self. This set of extremes is not lost on me. Neither is my awareness. I have delivered my dueling opposites to India, where opposites reign. My struggle, to make sense of it all, to integrate all the life and death of me into some coherent "self," suddenly seems absurd. India simply holds it all, with neither judgment nor censure. So why can't I?

I am delirious at the thought that there is no resolution. That my life can simply be complicated with its array of pains and pleasures, and that maybe I don't have to be "fixed" into some acceptable state of being that in turn fits into some acceptable state of normalcy. So far, I have seen no sign whatsoever of normalcy in India. My inner landscape, with all its unpredictable twists and turns, its sublime reaches and defiled descents, its secrets and shames, is a landscape of constant contradiction. And so is India. I have finally come home. And it is here.

Our eggs are good, cooked hard and tasty. The pot of perfect milk tea lasts for four cups. Thrinley basks in her perfect pot of lemon ginger tea. We chat about the days ahead. She has people to see and search out. For years she has been sending money to help a young Tibetan boy go to school; and a friend back home sent art supplies to go with her search. I have to get ready to teach English to Dakpa, a bookstore to search out, and an entirely new universe to explore. I thank the Wise One who has always led me to the Dalai Lama, from that very first inkling when I was fifteen years old to just a few months ago when the urge to come to his home in India rose in mystery inside me.

TWELVE

As a child I wasn't allowed to speak. But somewhere I had learned to read. I dove into books as though drowning in the written word would save my life. When I do the math it is curious. I was only seven years old when we moved from England to Montreal, Canada, but I recall that by then I'd read every Enid Blyton book I could find. *The Wishing Chair* series, the *Famous Five*, the *Secret Seven* offered a world in which children triumphed over wickedness and evil, even as they nattered on at one another and loved sweets and cakes.

The books, I recall, all came from libraries, one big one in particular that was close to the home of my father's parents in England, where it seemed I went a lot. And another somewhere else, maybe in Wales, with dark and dusty rooms of books and a smell that I cannot remember that I will never forget. In St. Eustache, on the outskirts of Montreal, the library was in a small house where the smell really was the smell of library: paper, bindings and ink all pressed together in a way that I still recognize in every library I enter. Bookstores are different. The smell is more chemical, vaguely reminiscent of a science lab. Perhaps it's the fresh ink.

But no matter where I am, the bookstore and the library are the first things I look for and here in Dharamsala it's no different. Somewhere on my early morning ramble the day before, I passed a bookstore with politics and poetry in the window. I drag Thrinley off in a rambling search to find it and we do. The Bookworm is open. There's a Tibetan man behind the desk reading and he glances at us only briefly as we enter. After reassuring myself about the selection of mysteries, I turn to the display of poetry books in the middle of the room. One of them catches my eye. On its cover is an image of a river running through a lush valley edged with mountains. Its perspective is from the mouth of a high cave and I am reminded of that long ago meditation in which Alan Wallace guided us up the slopes and into the dark recesses where our stream of collective consciousness poured forth.

How much is this book, I ask the man. He's startled for a moment and then tells me, 195 rupees. My shortcut estimate is that it's less than four dollars for this hardcover book of poetry by Lhasang Tsering. The cover tells me he is a freedom fighter for Tibet, as well as a poet. The dedication reads: "This book is dedicated to the idea of Freedom and Democracy and, therefore, to all those in every land and through every age who have lived and worked; suffered and died for Freedom and Democracy. Above all, it is dedicated to the people of Tibet who continue to suffer under China's colonial occupation of their country."

As I stand there reading, the man says, "It is mine."

I'm startled. "Yours?" I ask him.

"Yes," he says.

His gaze is a wave of grief, dense and overwhelming.

"You're a poet," I say.

"I wrote that," he says, looking at the book in my hand.

Then he removes his glasses and we talk about the politics of rebellion and resistance. I try to tell him about being in Columbus, Ohio, where everything went wrong on Election Day. Somehow, from this place of exile, it all feels insignificant and my passion dwindles. He signs his book: *To Janet, in friendship*. It is this that brings tears to my eyes as I re-enter the streets. The language of poetry is so much sweeter, so much superior to the language of politics.

Thrinley and I go on another search, this time to find the path around the Dalai Lama's home and temple. The entrance to the Lingkhor, as the path is called in Tibetan, is a simple right turn off the dusty road. There are a few prayer flags blowing in the wind and an old man squatting by the path, a rusty tin can beside him inviting a contribution. He is Tibetan, a beggar in a culture that does not beg. He beams a smile at us, even as neither of us drops anything into the tin. Just inside the entrance, a whole community of Indian beggar families is camped in haphazard tents and lean-tos. As soon as we are noticed, they swarm around us. Neither Thrinley nor I have quite figured out our relationship with those who live beyond the edge of everything we understand. Small silent children shadow us as we walk along the path. My voice gets harsh and I am aware that I am walking this sacred path hating the poor people around me.

Real life is once again usurping my spiritual inclinations. Damn it, I don't want to be distracted by beggars. My adolescent Western notion of spirituality, a spirituality split off from any of the complications of responsibility, of real life, wants to bask quietly, reverently, in its own juices. I know enough to see what is happening. But I don't know enough to know what to do or how to be. "No," I say again. By now it is simply a matter of some hollowed out principle that I am stubbornly adhering to. "No, no, no." And I am swamped by my own swirling arrogance. Welcome to the sacred path around the Dalai Lama's home and garden.

Inside, I start to laugh. To make an even bigger deal of things by basking in guilt and remorse seems even stupider than my oh-so-holy "no-ness." Why do we think we are so important? Why does what we do, or don't do, matter to us so much? Who cares if we do the right thing or the wrong thing, spiritually speaking, when it is always so much about us, whoever we are?

In front of me, two elder Tibetan women are walking, muttering "O Mani Padme Hum" and deftly moving their prayer beads between the fingers of their left hand. They are shuffling, hampered by aging bodies and a lameness most likely long-endured. The old women are so deeply in prayer that our presence on their heels startles them, but their mantra continues without a pause, even as their eyes sparkle at us in pleasure. Suddenly, I am a beggar, too. Holding out my soul for some spiritual sustenance, something for nothing.

On this walk, Thrinley, too, has been repeating her prayers and twirling through her beads. So we haven't said much to one another. My own prayer beads, a special gift from a special friend, are around my neck, hiding under my clothes. I'd like to put them in my hand and run them through my fingers, but I don't. My left hand doesn't work well. It can't feel the beads and the fingers are too weak to move them smoothly, even when I'm looking at them. At home in meditation I use my right hand, the one that does everything. But I don't know if the right hand is the right hand to use on this sacred path. I make a note to ask Thrinley about this later.

We eat lunch at the Namgyal Café in the temple compound. A chocolate cake is in prominent view on the counter when we walk in. On the wall behind it is a photograph of Richard Gere, posed with someone in the café. On the shelf is a bottle of blue Windex-like cleaner with a label reading Colin. Colin Cleanser. My son's name as a brand.

The café is high-ceilinged and the tables are clustered in cozy conjunction, one tucked into a kind of bay window area. A woman sits there reading and I realize how much I love to see someone, all alone, delved deeply into a book. It's reassuring, like seeing some-one loving their dog. We sit down at a corner table and I notice the young English teacher, Amy, and a friend at a table by the door. We smile and wave.

Nobody comes to ask us what we want so I get up and ask Amy how things work.

"Oh," she says. "Just write down what you want and what it costs on the piece of paper."

We notice the small basket on our table with its cut up pieces of paper and a pencil. There are exotic pizza specials listed on a board as well as a menu. We can't imagine ordering pizza in a monastery café in the Dalai Lama's temple so we decide on big bowls of vegeta-ble soup with fried tofu. When the waiter, who is also the cashier and the busboy, comes to our table I tell him how good the cake looks.

"You want some?" he asks.

"Yes," I say.

"Now?" he asks.

Why not, I think and nod my head.

He brings us two big pieces of chocolate cake and tea; when we're finished with our cake we get our two big bowls of soup. It is all astoundingly good.

During lunch I read the book of Lhasang Tsering's poems. In the foreword he writes about his love of poetry as well as his politics. He is not a deep pacifist like the Dalai Lama. In 1972, as a student leader, Lhasang Tsering joined the armed Tibetan resistance movement operating from Mustang in western Nepal. For years he was the editor of the *Tibetan Review,* the English language edition of *Rangzen,* the official magazine of the Tibetan Youth Congress. As a scholar and an activist he has traveled the world speaking up for Tibet. Unlike the Dalai Lama, who wants Tibetans to be part of the governing body with the Chinese, he wants fully restored independence for his people and his country.

As I read, I discover that in 1983 Lhasang Tsering suffered a complete memory loss. He could no longer remember all the words in Shakespeare's *Julius Caesar,* the play he memorized as a student. He could no longer remember the poems he loved. He writes: "This damage to my memory has adversely affected not only my personal enjoyment of poetry but greatly diminished my ability to share with others the joy I find in poetry."

Our Tibetan restaurateur sees me reading the book, looks slightly surprised, and then smiles in approval. Poetry, too, breaks down barriers and renders us human.

As we leave, Amy and her friend, Damchoe, are still there. They too are engossed in reading. I ask Amy about the festivities of the evening before.

"Tsongkhapa's birthday," she says.

Tsongkhapa was a revered teacher who, in the fourteenth century, brought a spiritual renaissance to Tibet in which Buddhist education in philosophy was synthesized with spiritual realization. In 1409, he founded the Great Prayer Festival in Lhasa. For more than five hundred years it was an annual celebration uniting all Tibetans—until the Chinese ended it, forcefully, in 1960.

After lunch we find our way to the small town square, where buses unload and Western Union offices prevail. There are restaurants and cabs and shops and people bustling about. In a large tent on the edge of the square about twenty people sit in meditation protesting the death sentence of Tenzin Delek, a revered Tibetan monk and scholar who's been imprisoned in China since 2002. He's scheduled for execution at any moment.

At four-thirty I meet Amy back at our Loseling guest house.

She's scheduled to teach Nawang English and I'm going to sit in and watch how it's done. We chat while we wait for him. Her bright eyes and youthful idealism spill over me like a balm. The freedom she emanates, to be where she loves and to do what she wants, inspires my own lost youth to sit up and take notice.

When Nawang arrives we retreat to his small room where he and Amy perch on either end of his small bed. A fluffy white dog is curled up on the pillow; he opens one eye halfway as we invade his territory then rolls it closed and goes back to sleep. I sit on a small chair only feet away from Amy. It's an intimate arrangement and my over-sexualized self can't help but project questions about this situation. The lovely young woman from Australia and the young handsome Tibetan monk in the leather jacket meeting in a small bedroom to explore English.

It's quickly apparent that exploring English is precisely what this is all about. He reads from the newspaper; she tells him about the sounds of letters and sometimes the meaning of certain words and phrases. They laugh a lot. In speaking to me he is confident and voluble. I nod as though I understand everything, but I don't. Perhaps it's because he's learning English with Amy's Australian accent.

Watching them both, the trust and openness they share, I am reminded of the innocence of innocence. It is a real thing. And when it's lost before its time, nothing can ever restore it.

 I meet Thrinley afterwards, feeling a bit guilty that I'm preparing to work with Dakpa tomorrow and she is not yet so engaged. But when we go to the Green Hotel for supper, two young Tibetan men at the next table, one a monk, join us in conversation. The monk, whose English-speaking skills are good, tells us his friend would like to learn the language. By the time we leave, Thrinley is scheduled to meet Dorje for an English lesson.

When we get to our small room, the lights work and there is hot water. I crawl into bed thinking about Lhasang Tsering and his poems and lost memory. Can you be fully human if you don't have a memory? If someone's experience of us is built upon a series of shared moments, what does it mean if we don't remember them?

I think of a dear and trusted friend of mine whom I first met on the soccer field when we were thirty years old. We shared many years of child-raising, professional struggles and personal travails throughout our long friendship. She once reminded me, with affection, about a trip we had taken together. I smiled in recognition. But the truth was I didn't remember a thing; not one image of it came to my mind. It is an experienced repeated with too many friends and in too many circumstances. Every time I am shocked and shaken.

Over the years of unreeling and healing from my past, I have asked my son about our life together. He, too, tells me things that have no shred of resonance in my memory. My grief about this has no bounds. I want to remember every moment of being his mother.

I think of fights with lovers, how I devastated relationships because I could not remember the foundation of experiences we had shared. How only betrayal, large or small, imagined or otherwise, had meaning. It destroyed every kindness, every fondness, every trust.

I think about this as I think about the end of my life looming at any moment or in many years. If I don't remember my life, has it been real? I know that Alzheimer's claims memory as well as the recognition of memory. But I recognize that I don't have one. My survival depended upon it. By forgetting, I was able to live. Now it feels as though only by remembering will I be able to die.

I curl up under the covers and notice that it's dark. All the lights that blinked their way through last night have been taken down. It was a one-time Tsongkhapa celebration that adorned the homes and hillsides and activated my fears of electrocution. Will I ever learn? Will the whole of my life be spent reacting to right things in the wrong way? If I'd known we were celebrating Tsongkhapa would my night have been peaceful? Would I have woken up without fear?

But if I hadn't woken up in fear, would I have ventured out into the night and into the deep peaceful rising of the sun, the monk's prayers, the bird's song, the water filling the tanks and the sociable smoke rising into the air? I needed everything about this day. Perhaps I need my lost memory, too. Perhaps it has linked me more strongly to the present. After all, isn't that where a Buddhist is supposed to be?

It starts to occur to me that perhaps these years of recovery have blurred into what it means to be healed. And that out of habit, I have failed to recognize my healed self. Could this trip be a pilgrimage into my strength, into the terrain that I have learned how to carve out of the present? That's what seems to be rattling at my cage, the cage that appears to have the lock on the inside.

All the work I've done to heal, all the time and money devoted to the task of simply feeling alive from one moment to the next and still the door is so often locked from within. The experimentation upon me—in which I was denied existence—has been immensely successful. I have internalized it and it has internalized me. The assault on my body was nothing compared to the assault on my mind. Even now, when I know I have won, I also know I will never know normal; even as I know normal doesn't exist. But something exists—something simple and pure that links body, mind and spirit into a recognizable whole—something that isn't an ongoing fucking conundrum of consciousness. But undoing the damage puts me through a mind-field of time bombs, even as I wield my own array of weapons of mask-destruction.

I drift off to sleep thinking about a past I cannot remember, a past I can, and tomorrow, when I will try to teach English to a young monk from Tibet.

THIRTEEN

I am sitting out on our rooftop patio in the afternoon sun waiting for Dakpa. Earlier today I bought him a notebook, some pencils, and a kid's reading/coloring book that illustrates some of the details of daily life, like forms of transportation and what happens in the kitchen, and when it rains. When I was young I took training as a Montessori teacher in the tangible and physical stages of learning to read – from tracing the sandpaper letters of the alphabet to word-building sentences. How can I make learning English tangible and meaningful for Dakpa?

He arrives right on time, carrying a shoulder bag from which he brings out a notebook and a Tibetan-English dictionary. We settle down at the small table out on the patio. First of all, I focus on introductions. "Hello, my name is Dakpa." We introduce ourselves back and forth a few times. "What did you do today?" I ask him. He looks at me intently, staring at my face as though the words might suddenly translate into Tibetan across my forehead. He doesn't understand a word. Using the dictionary, we piece together the meaning of the question. Using the dictionary, he pieces together an answer.

"I study."

I get more specific. When do you get up? What do you eat for breakfast? What do you study? Slowly we get through the details of

Dakpa's day. But the dictionary interferes with our progress. Dakpa is extraordinarily competent looking things up. He is more comfortable inside the pages of the dictionary than inside the messy process of communication.

After an hour-and-a-half, both our attention spans are wavering. Dakpa has dutifully written new words in his little book and we have repeated them back and forth. He can say bus, train, car and taxi. He can say "Where do I eat?" for the next time he is on a busy street in London or New York or San Francisco, even though he has no money, no passport, and no country. The ironies of teaching him something that will inform him of the limits of his freedom and the scarcity in his life is not lost on me.

Dakpa leaves as the sun goes down. I crawl under the covers on my bed, shivering from a kind of psychic chill as well as from the dropping temperatures. His great earnestness in wanting to learn, along with his great exile and his great need, all conspire to leave me empty and sad and helpless. Just being useful to this one sweet struggling person feels as though it will swamp me. He carries with him the loss of millions of his people, along with the loss of his family, his country, his past, and perhaps even his future. I gaze around this small room and realize that the cost of my ticket to India would support him for years.

The price of pilgrimage is pretty steep I'm thinking when Thrinley comes in complete with happy stories about her day. She found the young student she sponsors and distributed gifts at his school. It took her hours to walk there and back and she is tired. We rest awhile and then head off to find equilibrium at the Chocolate Log, which is closed. The neighboring bookstore is open, though, so we get grammar books and learning-English tapes for our new students. Then we head to the Namgyal Monastery Café for supper where we eat walnut, goat cheese and dried tomato pizza. It's the best pizza either of us has ever eaten.

Back in our room the day catches up with me and in absent-minded obliviousness I brush my teeth with the blasphemous tap water. As I drift off to sleep, thoughts of life-threatening diarrhea and the artifices of language dance in my head. I'm coming in out of exile in a town full of exiles. Pilgrimage is nothing if not a study in opposites.

Dharamsala, which means a shelter for pilgrims, is on the edge of the Himalayan Range and the great reach of the Tibetan Plateau which averages 15,000 feet. At 7500 feet, Dharamsala is as close to home as the Tibetans can get. It is why the Dalai Lama finally decided to settle here after his escape from the Chinese. It was 1960. The town, which came close to being completely destroyed in an earthquake in 1905, was nearly deserted when he arrived.

In *Dharamsala – Tibetan Refuge* by Jeremy Russell, the Dalai Lama writes in the foreword: "I still remember well my first arrival here in the spring of 1960. We drove up by road from Pathankot station, through beautiful countryside, the lush green fields filled with trees and colorful flowers. After about an hour we caught our first glimpse of the gleaming white mountains of the Dhauladhar range towering in the distance. These peaks were also the first sight to greet my eyes when I awoke for the first time in my new home the following morning, and of course their presence remains the dominating feature of the landscape."

Every refugee who survives the month-long escape through the mountains between Tibet and India is welcomed by the Dalai Lama in Dharamsala. It is home to Tibetan monasteries, libraries, hospitals, schools, temples, craft and performing arts centers as well as shops, restaurants, guest houses and the government-in-exile. As the Tibetans settled here and the Dalai Lama gained in stature throughout the world, pilgrims of varying persuasions poured in; scholars came to study; Indian merchants re-established themselves in the marketplace; and a uniquely cosmopolitan town took hold. In the streets of Dharamsala it appears there are no strangers, even as the make-up of the crowd ranges from wealthy Westerners to destitute Indians, from Tibetan monks to Chinese tourists. Dharamsala and the Dalai Lama are of one breath and somehow the spirit of this place is infused with a kind of equanimity and multi-cultural authenticity. "The Little Lhasa of India" is how some of the guide books describe Dharamsala. Yet I'm sure very few exiled Tibetans are of this inclination.

We are all in exile from something—innocence, perhaps, or our family home, our ancestral grounds, our yearning hearts. They all conspire to hold us hostage to things we cannot name. For the Tibetan people, however, it's simple. They are in exile from their homeland. They are Tibetans in name only. Their country is now the plundering ground of the Chinese. Our Western imagination could not imagine saving the country about which the whole world once dreamed as Shangri La. We fight only for things we think we should own, like oil and gold and capitalism.

Someone once said, "Capitalism destroyed communism and now it's destroying democracy." Capitalism is all about making, buying, selling and owning stuff. Democracy is all about preserving freedom. And freedom begins and ends with our minds. How free are our Western minds from the burden of capitalism? By the looks of things—our addiction to huge malls, small gadgets, newer vehicles, other people's reality shows, computer unconsciousness, and all things youthful—we are slaves to capitalism. We betray democracy with every buying breath.

A meditating monk preserves democracy with every contemplative exhale. The mind revels in its freedom to soar through the power and beauty of its own reality as well as the exquisite ever-expanding creative brilliance inherent in all life. There is a great reverberating song of celebration that inhabits the free mind. It soars beneath and beyond any "thing" that can be owned, any pleasure that can be named, any theory that can be thought, and everything that can be bought. This is what the sages of Tibetan Buddhism know, the monks meditating in huts on the hillside above Dharamsala, Kenneth Rexroth's single monk meditating in silence and solitude on the top of a mountain. They are defending the freedom of our minds. And we did not even begin to help them defend themselves, their people, and their country.

It's all perfect, of course. The Tibetans got expelled into our world where they are needed the most, into our suffering minds, and into the hell-realm of run amok capitalism where spirituality, too, is spit out and consumed like a Big Mac. I am, of course, romanticizing their feudal history, their elitist religious practices, and the hardship of daily life at fifteen thousand feet. But I know, from the faces of the Tibetan elders as they circumambulate the temple, from Tibetan Buddhist teachings, from the monks and nuns I have met, from Dakpa who is an orphan in the world, and from His Holiness the Dalai Lama who is a citizen of the world, that there is an inner life of grace and wisdom that even capitalism cannot destroy.

In the morning I meet Matt, our next door neighbor at the Loseling Guest House. He's a Brit beginning a round-the-world year-long journey. He's young, hung-over and smoking non-stop. His long reddish blond hair is pulled into a ponytail. With his tall slender body, pale skin and metal-frame glasses he looks like a poet-in-practice. Turns out he's a recovering technophile on the run from the modern world. India is his first stop. He's just finished a retreat at Tushita where he encountered formal Buddhism for the first time and is heading off to the Tibetan library for ongoing classes. We sit and eat breakfast together on the patio. His daily special is an omelet. I stick with the banana pancake. We both guzzle tea and proclaim its brilliance.

Matt is in the first throes of falling in love with Buddhism. Through a haze of smoke and gulps of tea, he pours out questions about meditation, the mind, attachment, non-attachment, and who was the Buddha anyways? I stumble through responses that aren't quite answers. Thrinley comes out and we all share a few minutes of Buddhist bonhomie before he dashes off to become enlightened. I envy his beginner's mind, even though his trembling hands belie his bright cheerfulness and indicate turmoil too deep for one so young.

Today is yet another holiday, International Human Rights Day, the anniversary of the day His Holiness the Dalai Lama received the Nobel Peace Prize. Once again flags are flying and throngs are thronging. Once again we head back to the temple where thousands of Tibetans have manifested themselves into an array of brilliant color and good cheer. Traditional dancing and singing is underway in the courtyard and every bit of temple real estate is taken up by Tibetans of every age and inclination. We squeeze into the crowd. I lose sight of Thrinley and shout to her that I'm going to look around.

On the balcony, where dancers and musicians are getting ready to go onstage, there is great playfulness at-large. The children, all dressed in ceremonial gear, chase each other around in glee. A group of older women practice their dance movements, stopping to grin as I take their photographs. Two girls run in front of the camera and flash a peace sign. I show them their image in my digital camera and they squeal at their friends to come see. Soon I fear that I'm too much of a distraction from the song-and-dance at-hand so I tuck the camera away and begin to circumambulate the temple, a slow path through the great wave of delight that marks the beginning of this day.

Through a small opening in the crowd I look down upon row after row of monks, some laughing and smiling, others serious and somber, all wrapped in crimson robes and rapt in deep attention. It is as though they are seeing in the singing and dancing all that has been gained and lost through the thousands of years of Tibetan history. This celebration, so vivid and vital, is visible proof of something that no longer exists—the freedom of Tibetans to ever be at home in their own country ever again.

A film crew, dressed with careless chic in New York black, focuses large cameras and balances lighting equipment with professional concentration. I suddenly don't know how to look at anything. All the layers of parallel reality are playing themselves out and none of it is for me, a stranger here, an observer. I envy the film crew and their immediate mission in life. I envy the monks, their grief and their carefully defined lives. I envy the elders with their prayer beads, the playful children, Thrinley and her place in things, all the swirling versions of life. I get out my camera again and furiously take photographs, trying to capture everything I am missing and have always missed.

This has been the most devastating part of healing—facing everything that's been missed. It's a big paradox alert loaded with its own versions of shame and grief. Riding the wild minds of my selves came with an intoxicating immediacy, a self-righteous sense of existence, and a compelling presence of intellectual authority and emotional intensity. Taking a ride with my deep being, where mind is but a modest event, is a ride into deepest relationship, not only with self but with other. That I screwed up with men is minor. That I screwed up with my son haunts me non-stop. I know I did the best I could. But the moving target of my selves, the inconstancy of who was his mother, the very recklessness with which my parts prevailed left us both lost and abandoned. And I never knew how to play.

As I look around at the Tibetan families, the palpable nature of their connection to spirit and to one another is infused with love and playfulness. It is a naturally occurring event, as though bred in the bones. It is a spontaneity I could never feel until all too recently and much too late. This is what age sixty holds, the ability to finally play in the world. But I can't turn back the clock. Nor can I turn back my denial. The ways in which Colin was left vulnerable to others, and to my family, is shocking to me now. My parts skimmed across the surface of the present, my amnesia so profound, my consciousness so buried, that my protectiveness was but skin deep. From this distance I can hardly comprehend who I was and what I didn't, couldn't, and wouldn't do to protect him. For me, the bond with my mother was broken when I was very young. How could I know what it felt like? I do now because I have finally learned how to connect with my most helpless self.

These words are in this book because I have Colin's permission. He tells me that my journey has helped him and that he is grateful for the spiritual understanding that my road to recovery has brought into his life. And I accept this as true. This inarticulate faith of mine helped him even when I couldn't. Now it's his articulate faith that helps me. Grace happens whether we recognize it or not.

All around me is celebration and there are no colors missing. The Dalai Lama received the Nobel Peace Prize in 1989. He symbolizes peace in the world and he cannot bring it to his people. Yet it is here in this moment of great joy and clarity that the loss becomes meaningful. We cannot hold joy without also holding grief. These two most human feelings need one another in order to be fully realized. Yet our have-a-nice-day culture diminishes them both and us along with them. In the long run, we end up losing our lives.

So far, emotional exuberance has been the staple on this trip. It's everywhere. From the streets of Delhi to the path around the Dalai Lama's temple, the air is full of unabashed, unencumbered, unfettered feeling. All of it fresh and fleeting as a high mountain stream, rippling through the lives of the people and then going on its way, trapping nobody. I am in awe and in love with this landscape of emotional freedom. If I'd lived here, all my parts might have found a place in the world. Perhaps healing would not have seemed so lonely, so isolated.

I take refuge from my thoughts and find my way back to the temple where, in the midst of festivity, there is the silence and privacy of prayer. This time I take out my prayer beads and run them through the five-year-old fingers of my left hand. The limited feeling and movement means they pass slowly through my hand. It slows me down and I enter that wordless place of prayer that is simply presence: one foot after the other, eyes half closed, mind spiraling down into gravity and the body, the feeling of being right here right now and all of life present. This prayer doesn't feel reverent or religious; it feels exquisitely physical and formless. I am here at the Dalai Lama's temple in Dharamsala. The Tibetan people are here in celebration. The sky, the mountains, the colors, the people, the perfection, the imperfection, it's all here and I'm walking in my own small circle of celebration. Tears find their joyful way down my cheeks. All I can feel is gratitude.

When Thrinley and I find one another again we leave the festivities and go to the Green Store on Bhagsu Road to refill our water bottles. The old gent is there, beaming as usual. The sign on the wall says "Tourist Problem" and tells of the damage done to the environment by all the plastic bottles discarded by travelers who can't drink the tap water. They now have a way of purifying the water many times and the Green Store offers refills for a few rupees. They make paper, too. Beautiful books are stacked on shelves and brightly colored sheets drape over racks. I buy face creams untested by animals and some handmade incense.

Across the rooftop from our guest house, we've noticed a restaurant but haven't been able to figure out how to get there. Today's the day, we decide, and go in search of an entrance. It's hidden, of course. There's no sign indicating the place, just a steep staircase that lands in a hallway where the restaurant begins. We gesture that we want to eat up on the roof and are led to an even steeper set of stairs. Plastic tables and chairs are filled with an assortment of Tibetans—from sedate monks to boisterous fellows playing some kind of card game. One of them is in charge of a beaming baby girl in a stroller.

We write down our order for the friendly Tibetan man who knows no English and sit back in a reverie of appreciation for the day. Over the roof edge we look into the street that leads from the town center to the temple. Monkeys are swinging their way across the electric wires between buildings. Commerce of all acquaintance is going on below. Up here we have a wide blue sky, the mountains, and prayer flags flying in the breeze. Across the way, the Geshe in residence at our guest house is circumambulating the roof, his burgundy robes billowing in the breeze. Off another end of the roof, there's a big cluster of satellite dishes, radio towers and an astonishing array of antennae.

Our food is superb. Momos steamed to perfection with excellent sharp cheddar grated and melted across the top. Vegetable-filled spring rolls, crisp with flavor, and eggplant sautéed in garlic sauce. Each bite is a surprise. There's no pretense at atmosphere in this place but the food is the best we've had. All of it delivered from the kitchen up the steep, precarious staircase.

Then the baby spills out of the stroller. Thrinley and I jump with concern but the father is there before we exhale, scooping up the child and cooing and comforting her with maternal tenderness. Soon she's back in her seat and the card game goes on.

It's nearly three o'clock, time to go and teach English to Dakpa.

Dakpa's late arriving. There's still sun on the patio so we start outside. As in our last session, he insists on looking up every word in his English/Tibetan dictionary. He surprises me with knowledge of the grammatical terms for words, stumbling out "past participle" and "conjunctive." Phrases I have not heard since high school. Dakpa has made good use of books about English words; he simply hasn't spoken them. He watches me intently as I say them, how they shape the lips and where they come from in the mouth. Then he's almost too shy to say them back. His attention keeps going to his dictionaries; my attention goes to getting him back out loud, in language. With no translator, we have no way of easing things by saying who we are. So we stumble through the first hour caught up in nouns and pronouns, adjectives and verbs. None of which have anything to do with, "Hello. Who are you?"

Then I ask him to tell me his story.

It spills out slowly, irrevocably, between the pages of the dictionary: his birth in an isolated region of Tibet; his mother's early death; his father's imprisonment by the Chinese and his subsequent ill-health; Dakpa's escape from Tibet when he was 16. It took him nearly a year and included a stay in Lhasa where he worked to raise the money to get himself an under-the-radar ride to the foothills of the Himalayas where he began his journey through the mountains to Nepal. He tells me of the old monk on the trip who had to be carried much of the way, and the continual hunger. Dakpa then spent three years in a monastery in Nepal before getting permission to come to Dharamsala. Here, he's studying the history of Tibet and learning the more common Tibetan language because his own dialect was unique to his region. He's studying philosophy and folklore and will soon begin his studies of Buddhism. This stops me short. Dakpa is a Buddhist monk who has yet to study Buddhism.

I write the first part of his story down in my English school-girl printing, putting it in Dakpa's first-person voice, and have him read it aloud. He goes to open his dictionary and I say, "No. No dictionary. Just read." He stumbles through pronunciation, forced by circumstances to experience the sound of his own life in English. I know he'll go home and translate it all into Tibetan.

Two hours goes by and soon Darje, Thrinley's student, will be here for his lesson. We finish up. As he gets ready to leave, Dakpa dives into his dictionary and tells me about the peace festivities for the Dalai Lama. His face lights up and I see a hint of his inner life. The Dakpa who escaped through the Himalayas with great strength and courage is the same slight young man so shyly learning English. *Nothing is as it appears to be; nor is it otherwise.* I want to hug him but I don't know how. Instead, I give him my ten-year-old down jacket. He seems to have nothing extra to wear as winter descends from the mountains and my other warm clothes are serving me well.

Thrinley starts her session with Darjee and I head out for a walk, full of feelings I don't know how to feel. Back at the temple the peace festivities are still in full swing. It's been at least seven hours since the first dance group took to the courtyard and still there are dancers and still the crowd is thick and jubilant. I watch for a bit and then head down to the Lingkhor. It's close to sunset and all the colors are edged with brilliance. The path, once I get past the beggars, is not crowded. So I take out my prayer beads and run them slowly through the small fingers of my left hand as I walk. Two very elderly women are straining to push the big prayer wheel in a circle. I try to make it easier and one of them giggles at me in appreciation while the other is lost inside her prayers. The world is full of beggars and Dakpas, of costumes, color and joyful celebration. I know that but I have not felt it all at once as I am feeling it now. As if the world is happening all at once in my mind.

When I come around the last corner of the Lingkhor I bump into a large gathering of young people with lit candles and an impassioned speaker addressing the crowd. It's Students for a Free Tibet and they are getting ready to do a peace march through the streets of McLeod Ganj. Some are holding signs in support of Tenzin Delek Rinpoche whose execution by the Chinese is imminent. It's why there's a hunger strike going on in the town square. Every day since we arrived there have been an increasing number of monks, nuns and lay people in the tent. Some just go for shifts. Others are there for the duration. Tenzin Delek was arrested in Lhasa in 2002 for alleged involvement in bomb blasts and for inciting "separatism." Along with a relative, Lobsang Dondup, he was sentenced to death with no evidence of guilt or any legal representation. In Tibet he was revered for helping Tibetans build schools, orphanages and monasteries as well as roads and bridges. He is an intellectual and an accomplished academic who fought tirelessly to preserve Tibet's culture, religion, language and traditions.

Both men were sentenced to death in early 2002. Lobsang Dondup was executed right after a secret summary trial confirmed his guilt in January, 2003. Tenzin Delek Rinpoche's two-year suspended death sentence was also confirmed, which means his execution could be at any moment. There is a world-wide push underway to save his life. The hope is that the Chinese, because of Olympics in Beijing, will be sensitive to world opinion and withdraw the death penalty.

The feeling in the crowd is much different than the celebratory goings-on inside the temple grounds. There's a determined edge to the voice of the speaker and the crowd is serious and intent on the issues: Freedom, not only for Tenzin Delek Rinpoche, but for the Tibetan people, too. They want their country back and it is the youth who are leading this campaign. To some, the Dalai Lama is too passive, too patient with the Chinese. I am reminded of the college students who showed up on the streets of WTO Seattle and ended the ministerial meetings. They manacled themselves together, sat down, and blocked the intersections. I remember seeing the Free Tibet contingent on the streets and how I was reminded of all the Tibetan teachers who had influenced me and the long-standing inspiration of the Dalai Lama. Yes, I understand the power of his patience. Just as I understand the power of these young people's impatience. I race back to our penthouse to get Thrinley. I know she'll want to be here.

We bundle up against the cold night and track down the peace and freedom march as it's winding its way back to the temple, joining up with our flashlights as flames until two young monks give us their candles. Along the way through the streets of McLeod, we see Dakpa walking by with another young monk. He gives me a big shy smile of approval. I am out on the street and it matters. There is no sign of the down jacket. Dakpa just has his candle to keep him warm. When Thrinley and I get to the temple, all the singers and dancers have gone home and the candlelight peace marchers fill the courtyard to hear various speeches, some translated into English. We bump into Thrinley's young friend, Tsering, and as we leave we pass on our candles to her and her friend.

We don't talk too much on the way to our room. There's too much to think about. After crawling into bed I open the curtain to let in the night, the stars, the barking dogs, this whole crazy country in which all the world is a stage and everyone a star. "The play's the thing," wrote our friend Will Shakespeare. But even he might have been rendered speechless by India.

Above: The Geshe, "honored teacher," taking in the view from the Loseling Guest House roof .

Left: Thrinley with the Loseling monks. The Geshe is wearing robes. The other monks are wearing regular clothes out of respect for their Tibetan guests who are uncomfortable when monks do service work for lay people.

A wrong turn on the long road to Dharamsala landed us in the presence of poet, K.V.S. Thapar, who kindly gave us copies of his book, *Cries of Anguish*. He and his gracious wife served us tea and cookies, even though we were utterly foreign and unexpected strangers on their doorstep.

Lhasang Tsering owns the Bookworm in Upper Dharamsala. I was in his shop, browsing through a book, *Tomorrow & Other Poems*, when he said quietly, "That's mine." I bought it; and later discovered I had met a legend as well as a poet.

The Dhauladhar Mountains as seen from the Lingkhor, the sacred path around the grounds of temple and monastery of His Holiness the Dalai Lama.

At a cafe above Dharamsala, where "The Morning Freshener" features cornflakes as well as excellent Indian fare.

From left: Thrinley, Dakpa, Matt the Brit, and Thrinley's student, Darjee, on an outing at the Norbulingka Institute in Lower Dharamsala, where the art and culture of Tibet is preserved and taught.

Thrinley and Norbu on the patio outside our room. It was Norbu who guided me up the mountain in search of Gen Lamrimpa.

Om Mani Padme Hum
The Jewel at the Heart of the Lotus

Above: Young Tibetans walking the sacred path of the Lingkhor.

Left: An elderly woman spinning a prayer wheel as she turns her mala beads.;

Praying and meditating on behalf of all sentient beings is second nature to Tibetans..

Left: Women doing their prostrations in the courtyard of the Dalai Lama's temple in Upper Dharamsala.

Young Tibetan girls ready to dance at the anniversary celebration of the Dalai Lama's 1989 Nobel Peace Prize award. Tibetans make use of every opportunity to celebrate their customs, culture and community.

The manager and his grandson in the Green Store, where we refilled our bottles with purified water. A sign in the store reads, "Tourist Problem;" it describes the destructive extent of the discarded plastic bottles spilling out in the wake of travelers to the area.

I was sitting on a bench writing in my journal when this Tibetan mom and her three children came up to me with their laughter and questions. The children were learning English and their mom was very proud of them.

These are photos taken of two photographs on exhibit in the Tibet Museum, which is located on the grounds of the Dalai Lama's monastery and temple. Taken in 1959, they portray the first Tibetans to escape over the great high Himalayan pass that brought them into Nepal on their way to India. A dangerous trek of several weeks, it is a route still used today.

Above: Dakpa, my English student, preparing "thukpa," a Tibetan soup made with vegetables and home-made noodles.

Left: High on a mountainside above Dharamsala are clustered mud and stone huts where Tibetan Buddhist monks enter into life-long retreat. Their basic needs are provided for by the local community.

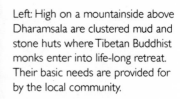

Lower left: This giant prayer wheel is on the Lingkhor, the path around the temple grounds. It is filled with many prayers, all carefully written on small pieces of parchment by Tibetan nuns. The more prayers inside, the more blessings go out to all sentient beings with each turn of the wheel.

The middle-of-the-night fire in Upper Dharamsala took a terrible toll on Tibetan businesses—more than 15 were destroyed along with a busy hotel. Fortunately, no-one was hurt. There was a great outpouring of support from the Indian community; many merchants donated money and necessities to their Tibetan friends and neighbors.

Left: Fighting the fire brought out the local fire department and the Indian Army.

When India welcomed His Holiness the Dalai Lama and the Tibetan people into exile in 1959, it made a serious commitment to their well-being. Now, 50 years later, Tibetan communities are flourishing throughout India. Because China is an uneasy neighbor, India's balancing act between politics and generosity is sometimes a moving target of controversy. But India has held the course. Throughout 2009, the 50-year anniversary was honored by a year-long celebration of India by the Tibetan government-in-exile.

Saint John's in the Wilderness is just outside Dharamsala; it was built by the Brits in 1852 and was one of the few buildings in the area to survive the earthquake of 1905.

Christmas in Dharamsala, 2004

A Tibetan monk at Saint John's in the Wilderness;

Matt and his friends in front of the thanka (wall hanging) we gave to the Loseling monks for Christmas.

Monkeys grooming on the water tank.

May peace prevail.
May all sentient beings be free.

FOURTEEN

My first play, *Heads and Tails,* was produced at Seattle's Empty Space Theatre in 1979. It was inspired by an upcoming contest deadline and upcoming visitor. My friend, Roberta, a brash East Coast intellectual who was obsessed with her writing, had three children, a wild mind, and a reckless disregard for order in her environment. When another friend and I discovered she was about to be visited by an old East Coast boyfriend, a philosophy professor, we conspired to get her house cleaned so she could make a semi-respectable first impression as a laid-back, liberated West Coast woman. The play opens in an ironic frenzy of cleaning and proceeds through the psychological landscape between men and women in which the intellect never has tits big enough to make an intellectual man happy.

I lost my friend Roberta because of that play. She said she felt betrayed, that in our friendship I had not shared with her as much about myself and what I thought as my play did with the world. Our friendship had been based on writing—how it was done, how as soon as the words were on paper they became beholden to a truth all their own. She wrote non-stop "fiction" that was based on her own carefully examined life as well as the lives of her friends. Only the names were changed. I thought she afforded me the same writing freedom and she said she did. But no matter what the reason, I lost my best friend from whom I learned that writing was a spiritual practice. It was all about faith, all about trusting the writing to lay claim to its inevitable story.

What I experienced writing that first play was the way in which the characters created themselves, laying claim to language and personalities over which I had no control. Although the writing started inside a kernel of reality, the evolution of character and circumstance quickly took on a life beyond anything that I knew as the "truth." Years later, after another dozen plays had been produced under various circumstances and I had begun my slide down the slippery slope of my selves, I became terrified that my plays were a manifestation of my parts. What I'd interpreted as a near-religious experience became a manifestation of my multiplicity, my disorder. I packed up all the plays into boxes and put them away; I boxed up my faith and banished it into storage.

I hated what I was learning about my self and my selves in those early years of therapy. I hated the phrase "multiple personality disorder." I hated the ways in which the depth of my psychological and emotional distress had taken over what I had assumed was my life. My recovery from one kind of shame was deepening into another: the shame of being a name in the textbooks of mental health. The only self I knew was the one who'd been getting us through our daily life with stubborn fortitude. She had no use for this therapeutic journey. She had no use for all the suffering ones, or even the wise ones. She got out of the way of the writer because the writer was harmless. And besides, when I was fixed to a chair and a desk for hours at a time, the heroic self of our survival got to take a break. But mostly she hated the surfacing parts of me because they implied that perhaps she had not done her job. I wish I could have told her otherwise.

I am haunted by that hatred. What I see now is a brilliant array of shining selves, all valiant and triumphant, even the debased ones. They rallied forth, carrying the weight of all the fear, the childhood shame, the guilt, the grief. They took all the ugly experiences and transformed them into life—my life. I am so grateful to them, and to her, too, the one who prevailed and also hated. I love her and am slowly teaching the others to love her, too. What haunts me are the years lost to embarrassment, my adult shame. I shunned my lifeline and my most direct link to my inner selves—my writing—because I couldn't face not being "normal." It cost me a career in something I loved, the theatre. The irony is not lost on me—after all, what better place for a "multiple" to hang out?—but neither is the reality. In healing, I had to find my way *in*, to where my birthright self was hidden. But why was it such a shameful journey? Fear, is one answer. Society, is another.

Brian worked so hard to get me beyond this immobilizing hatred of my selves. His patience was insurmountable, as was his gentle prodding to see myself beyond the label of mental dysfunction. It was a tough sell. All I knew were the narrow limitations of my survival self; even my imagination was held hostage by the deep terror of my own existence. What I knew of my self was not who I was; what could be crazier? I resisted the conversations with my inner selves; I refused to give them personal names; I dismissed them as quickly as Brian coaxed them forward.

When I feel my life now, sitting here on a rooftop in India, able to see and feel the immensity of this experience and the sheer unadulterated beauty of life in all its complexity, I know I should have gone easier on myself and my selves. Yet it is such a typical reaction of survivors. We take on the shame of the abuser. Instead of feeling pain, we feel shame. Instead of allowing comfort and healing to enter our lives, our insulated selves insist upon isolation. Loneliness may be lonely, but it's safe. Breaking through this veil of fear and self-hatred means trusting another human being. Yet our survival-self has protected our lives through mistrust. The conundrum continues, until exhaustion or insanity or death intervenes.

For me, it was the intervention of writing that kept me alive before I began to remember. I know I wrote stories before I could write. Perhaps I was making them up in my mind; perhaps it was the Storyteller spiriting us away from the terror. I don't know. I do know that writing has always been a way in, and a way out. I wrote to find out what I thought, what I felt, what I knew and what I wondered about. I kept journals non-stop. I'd write a poem for eight hours without stopping in order to capture a moment's existence. I wrote plays to understand life. Out of them came characters, uninvited and opinionated. Life happened in my plays and I got to go along for the ride. That it was a ride through the inner landscape of my lives did not even begin to occur to me. I just remember surprise. My characters were so much more interesting than I was, and so much pushier, too.

When I first envisioned *Ten Minutes for Twenty-Five Cents,* set in a local laundromat where artists and other misfits gathered to wash their clothes as well as their dirty laundry, I remember a moment when I knew there was another character trying to push her way in to the play. The characters were just too full of themselves, she figured, and they needed her wisdom and guidance to get over their important selves. Lottie Roberts landed on the scene with compelling authority, surprising the hell out of me and taking the entire cast to task. Lee, the black poet Vietnam vet with his voice of rage and outrage did not surprise me. It was easy in those days to turn my inner rage outward towards the warmongers and oppressors. They were an easy target. But Lottie, "Mrs. R." as she was called, was full of insight, compassion and ironic get-over-yourself humor.

The Longest Walk explores Native American, Christian and Jewish faith in the face of holocaust—nuclear and otherwise. It was based on a real experience—a religious gathering at Chief Sealth's grave to welcome Japanese Buddhist monks to the Northwest where Bangor Nuclear Submarine base was getting ready for operation. It was the Cold War and fear ruled the day. The voices of the faith-filled came onto the page, autonomously and in spite of my inability to know faith. What I knew was something inarticulate; in those days I would meditate with the monks before dawn, chanting in a language I could not understand. But what I could understand is that they walked and drummed the world for peace.

This play was produced at the American Place Theatre in New York City. I was there for rehearsals and opening. Julia Miles took me to an awards ceremony and I sat in the back seat of a car with Meryl Streep, who is more beautiful in life than in the movies. She was anxious to get home to her baby. Claudia Weil directed the play; the cast, with whom I fell in love, included my friend Kevin Tighe who was more aware than I of my retreating behavior. He counseled me not to forget to belong to my theatre community. "You need it," he urged me. "We all need each other to keep going." But I had never belonged anywhere and there was no way I could imagine what I was missing. All I knew was an unadulterated physical terror of dependence and connection; and I knew how to hide it. Here was a dream come true: I was in New York, my work was appearing onstage, and I could not feel myself there.

Another constricting part of my experience as a playwright was the excruciating personal exposure. My plays began to be produced in cities across the country and with each production process my psychic distress mounted. Who wrote these plays? I didn't know. And when actors, directors and audiences had questions about the characters, their circumstances and their behaviors, the Playwright had to answer out loud, but she did not exist out loud. None of us did. The disorientation was immobilizing. I'd go home from being a talking-head of authority at rehearsals and performances and fall into shattering states of confusion and fear. I had no idea why. Somehow, when the next appearance was required, someone showed up to get us there. But whoever it was, was always a newcomer on the scene, quickly manifested by Mind to keep us going. What little access the inner family had to the occasional comfort of the body was denied by a disembodied streak of intellect. It took days for me to recover from even the most gratifying time with my theatre experience.

I had no idea I was shape-shifting psychologically, emotionally and even physically. I was in effect, through writing, speaking out from behind the façade of a moving target of a self. And speaking out, I later realized, meant I would die. It was imminent fear of death that prescribed those years. In writing, I was breaking the code of silence that had been tortured into me as a child. These days I know that fear still, but it teaches me that I'm on to something good, something that represents me.

Writing saved my life because it gave voices to life and to being. It existed when I did not. It breathed life into me. It inspired me. It was spirited, of the spirit, mysterious and profound. The writing leaked out around my edges, saving us all. It had an authority that I could not begin to claim, but it did insist upon itself, and in my amnesiac ignorance about my own life I let it have its place, even as I didn't. Then, when my conscious search for the embodiment of spirit, for being-ness, began to emerge, writing had to take a back seat. It couldn't take my place anymore. When the unraveling of my selves started me on my healing journey, playwriting was no longer my friend. It became simply a form of dissociation. This was not something I could think and reason about.

Writers of all ages and circumstances have honored the autonomy of the writing voice—these days I teach about it in my memoir classes—but as *I* started to emerge, a combination of fear and shame rendered me voiceless on the page. Entering grief was entering a state of being so profound—physically, emotionally and spiritually—that there was neither thought nor reason. As my life returned to me, I thought about this a lot. Does creativity rise from inarticulate subterranean grief and take shape in art, music, and writing? If grief is entered and named, does it lose its numinous power and illuminating form? I still don't know. I do know I lost my freedom to write for a long time and I can't imagine otherwise. It was the only way back.

Whether or not I lost a career, I don't know. Whether or not I've honored the mysterious gift of writing, I don't know. Whether or not I've "realized" my creative self fully, I don't know. I do know that I am alive, that joy has never reached me so often, that I can love and that perhaps, in ways barely decipherable, I am learning how to *feel* loved. Could I have written myself here? No way. I've needed every moment of therapy, of bodywork, of spiritual search, of confusion, of grief, of mental anguish, emotional suffering and emerging truth to get me to this moment. And these moments have never been so sweet.

There is blissfulness in being present in the body. It fills time and meaning in a way that nothing else does. And curiously, it goes beyond the body, connecting us to a universe of meaning, an eternal state of grace. It rises above the self, but it has to have a healthy self to rise above. I had to find a healthy sense of self from which to explore and connect to that which extends beyond the self. I can write about all of this now, but for many years there were no words that worked.

Now my life is playing out before my eyes on this stage that is India and all the languages around me that I don't understand are delivering me to a realization of healing. If this world can be so complex in such living color, why can't I? What use is normal in a country so full of complexity and contradiction that no one truth has the upper hand? I have lived within a shattered mind. All of

India shows signs of shattered mind and I am in love with it all. Why not fall in love with my own shattered self? Why not liberate my selves from the bondage of normalcy and introduce them to one another. All I have to do is insist upon respect. And that is what I'm learning in India: respect for the sublime catastrophe of being human.

FIFTEEN

I didn't sleep well last night so I get up with the first rays of sunlight and go to walk the Lingkhor. Yesterday at the bank I loaded
up with five rupee notes so I have a pocket-full of give-away. I twirl
my beads through my five-year-old fingers, and practically without
looking hand out money with my right hand to every beggar who approaches. I can tell it's not enough for some. Others, particularly the
two men immobilized by twisted, useless legs, beam in appreciation.

The walk is crowded this morning. When I get to the courtyard,
halfway around, there is a morning ceremony underway. About fifty
people are gathered on rugs and blankets in the early morning chill.
A monk leads the chanting and prayer pages are turned. I sit on the
bench behind the crowd and think about peace and sanity, morning cow shit in the streets and piles of garbage in the corners. And
everywhere prayer.

I am the only white person here. To avoid invading the privacy
of the morning, I keep my head down. I don't want to be an observer. I, too, want to be in prayer. To be open to whatever it is that
enters us when we stop and let it all in. Everything. All at once. The
whole enchilada of life rising with the sun, of the sun, because of
the sun. Who are we? Why are we? Where did the sun come from?
This planet hanging by a heartbeat within timeless space, populated

with hope and hunger, love and longing, an endless question hovering just out of reach. It all swells up in the voices of these gentle old people whose lives are etched in tragedy, resilience and reverence.

The prayers go on a long time and I watch as the sun rises in warmth over the gathered crowd. When the morning ceremony is over, some put money into a big bowl sitting beside the monk leader. It is always the poorest people in the world who give easily and without thinking. Learning how little we need is the beginning of generosity. Humbled yet again, I put something in the bowl and move with the crowd along the path. Along the way I see dogs stretched out sleeping peacefully in patches of early morning sunlight.

Acceptance in this country is palpable. No matter what religion, race or status, there is blatant acceptance, even if there is also criticism, distaste and frustration. Acceptance doesn't mean affection. It just means acceptance. India is the biggest democracy on the planet and it's in full-swing in every direction.

This is real democracy, I'm thinking as I remember my experience in the polls in Columbus, the growing paranoia in the country, the fear-breeding Patriot Act, and the growing class-divide throughout the U.S. Yes, there are class divides in India, but they are not hidden from view, or from the psyche. People live with them, struggling in some way every day with the complexity of it all instead of hiding away in their insular lives.

Thrinley's finished with her own prayers when I get back and we eat a late breakfast on the patio and plan our day. She'll be teaching Darje English. I'll go for a stroll, send a few emails, take a few photographs, and go drink tea and read at the Namgyal Café.

I'm on my way to the email joint when this idyllic plan goes astray. A young boy, scrawny as straw, asks me for money. I give him a five rupee note which satisfies him not in the least. "More, more," he shouts, grasping out with his hand. "No, no," I say to him. His voice gets louder and louder and before I know what's happening he's scrambling up the front of my body like a monkey. I'm revolted, frightened and afraid of hurting him if I push him off me. His ferocity is feral and I despise his wretchedness, his grasping and his very existence. He holds on to me fiercely. "More. More." And I begin to panic. Suddenly an Indian merchant shouts at him and with a cheeky smile the boy drops to the ground and jauntily goes on his way.

I am shaken and tears start down my cheeks. My body is all hot with shame at my whiteness, my privilege, my hatred and rage. And I feel so terribly violated. I'm trying my best to understand, to be generous, and nothing I can do is enough. This, too, is real. I walk into the cyber stall upset and trembling, surprised at the depth of my reaction. That boy is part of me, too. The desperation, the relentless grasping after some sense of entitlement that I deserve but will never come my way of its own accord. The computer fellow writes down the time on a piece of paper and smiles at me as he gestures to an available keyboard. In visceral relief I take a seat amongst the cyber-spaced-out monks and tourists and check my email.

This time I feel no impatience with this technological imperative. The emails from friends remind me of civility and all the things that I at times deride. My adventurousness has turned to timidity and I want nothing more than to hear of hearth and home. One email is particularly comforting. Peggy Sue, who is gonpa-sitting while Thrinley is in India, writes of the red berries scattered on the ground by the white stupa. It is a quick winter image of the island, a moment of nature from a friend who once chained herself to a tree and was jailed for trying to save its life.

I walk briskly all the way to the café, avoiding eye contact as well as any interest in the goings-on around me. Over a hot cup of strong tea I read *The Times of India* where I learn that Delhi has the most polluted air in Asia and that 1.39 billion people live on less than two dollars a day and 550 million on less than one dollar a day. There is an editorial about language: "Those who know nothing of a foreign language know nothing of their own... The politics of language is an endless process of negotiation."

The politics of language is the politics of life. My own inner languages, of the small ones, the wise ones, the raging ones, are an endless process of negotiation. I have learned through my work with Brian that my inner reality must be negotiated as needs and fears arise, so why not the outer reality, too? If I treat my inner selves with disdain I get brittle and isolated. If I treat this small boy climbing up my body with disdain, I get brittle and isolated. Life is an endless process of negotiation. If we stop negotiating, if our worldview becomes static, we become brittle and isolated. If we are invested in being separate, in being better than, or luckier than, or smarter than, or more wounded than the other, we close life out. We are spared both pain and pleasure. This world, this life, is erupting in all-encompassing reality. That's the gift—if we dare to look at it fully and fearlessly. All we have to do is dull the edges of our opinions and sharpen our skills of negotiation.

In Celtic Christianity there is a kind of consciousness called the "Thin Place." It is where the veil between the material and spiritual gets less and less opaque and the two worlds become more and more partnered. It is a tender place, a fleeting moment in which everything is seen again for the first time. Perhaps it is not a moment for mere mortals. Perhaps it is where we become part of all that is eternal, immortal. I had the opportunity to see beyond my mortal being when that small boy grasped on to me for dear life. I could have thrust untold riches in his direction. Instead I wanted to shake him to the ground and out of my sight.

I know it was a game to him. His smug little grin as he was being told to go away made that clear. But he was also as skinny as a child can be and still be alive. He definitely needed something to eat. Even so, his scrawny strength was astonishing, as was his persistence and audacity. His cocksure attitude belied poverty of any description. He was a rascal, a starving, homeless rascal who knew a good score when he saw it walking towards him in a well-nourished daze of naiveté. Some part of me starts to laugh and wish I had the moment to live over.

We all know we are supposed to give to the poor; it is a basic tenet of Christianity. But what if we are supposed to take from the poor, too? What if I was supposed to take this child's reality in to my heart and be changed? Who would I be? What would I do with my life? These are all hypothetical questions but they take me to the essence of my struggle. If I take the defiled, degraded and defiant part of myself into my heart, who do I become?

"Suffer the little children to come unto me," said Jesus.

One of my friends asked me honestly and sincerely why I was going to church after being involved with Buddhism for so long. I gave my usual answer: "Because the Dalai Lama says we should know our own religions." Like so many ready answers this was not entirely true. Most of all, I needed to know only one simple thing: that Jesus loved me.

I didn't realize this for a long time. Going to Saint David's Episcopal Church on the island where I live was most of all an intellectual decision. In my healing I had discovered my hatred for the hypocrisy of Christianity, for the smug self-righteousness that so often accompanies religiosity. As a child, I was conditioned to despise organized goodness and to be an outsider. And because of the trickery of "nice" people, I also learned to mistrust for good reason. Getting my self into church was an immense and complicated challenge.

It started with Larry Tuller, a gay man I met when I was manager of the San Juan County Fair. He'd moved to the island to be near his family as he journeyed through dying of AIDS. Larry was intelligent, funny and wise as well as an extremely talented artist. At his memorial service, the Episcopal minister, West Davis, used the opportunity to berate us about our un-Christ-like fear and intolerance of the disease and those afflicted. It was 1994. The message was searing and I was astonished to hear it within the confines of this small island church. Over the next two years, I slowly worked up the courage to actually attend.

West Davis was a very human, human-being who just happened to be an Episcopalian minister. He was a religious scholar but he was not a religious man, at least not in the way that had always made me nervous. West and his wife, Sue, had experienced great tragedy, hardship, and struggle and it was never far from his ministry. Sometimes he was an emotional wreck. His scholarly approach to the Bible always put things in the context of the times. We learned what things meant back then instead of having Biblical hyperbole layered upon what was happening here and now. West Davis always distinguished between the actions of Jesus and the interpretations of those throughout history who had social, cultural and political agendas. He made Jesus human. It turned out that a small child inside me, perhaps the newly growing up part of my real self, wanted to know that Jesus loved her.

This realization was slow in coming. For a few years I was forced by some guiding spirit to go to church on Sundays. Some part of me knew how critical it was and kept making sure we showed up. My adult observer self was suspicious and reluctant. I resisted every Sunday and I was always glad I went. I was doing something that I desperately needed: to feel as though I actually deserved to go to church and be part of the spiritual community I had been trained to despise. And underneath it all, I wanted to be a little girl safe in the lap of Jesus.

This is where the search for spiritual grace gets so very complicated and time-warped. My intellectual self had long been active in studying various religions and philosophies of life. My connection to Buddhism, long-established, was a connection to the ways of the mind and the disciplines of self-knowledge, compassion and selflessness. It took many years before the small child in me felt safe enough to lay claim to a love of Jesus and her need to know that Jesus loved her back. Spiritual healing happens backwards. The skills of the intellectual self are much more easily accessed than the vulnerable self living in shame and isolation.

So I started to go to St. David's where West Davis wrestled with all the challenges of being spiritual beings in a material world. I met people who had as many doubts as I and who were there every Sunday precisely because of their doubts. I found my self part of a community of searching, questioning and loving people. In the local paper every week was a classified advertisement from Saint David's: "Skeptics, Doubters, Searchers and Believers Are All Welcome." But my search for spiritual worth was long underway by then and it had taken a variety of twists and turns.

One conference I attended was *Sexual Assault: Emerging Issues – A Two Day Training Seminar for Criminal Justice, Mental Health and Spiritual Health Service Providers.* It was the words *Spiritual Health* that commanded my attention and got me to sign up. The two-day conference was at the regal Claremont Hotel on the border between Berkeley and Oakland.

I stayed with my friend, Karen, in Walnut Creek. She not only gave me a place to stay but she sent Tom to the airport to meet me. He was a survivor, too, and was excruciatingly anxious to meet someone else who had a similar history. We made plans to meet in the morning and go to the conference together.

The atmosphere at the Claremont conference was vastly different from that of the previous one at University of California at Berkeley. The general environment was elegant, inside and out. The attendees were predominantly professional and the tone was detached and formal. The earlier conference was designed with distinct support for survivors. This one was primarily for professionals. I felt like an outsider and was careful not to give myself away. I began to dissociate almost immediately.

Tom and I sat side-by-side at the panel discussion: Ritual Abuse: Spiritual Healing of Victims. We listened as James Ward, an Episcopal priest and a graduate of Yale College and Yale Divinity School, spoke about God, sin and guilt and the necessity of transforming the negative triggers of liturgy and ritual into an experience of blessing and love.

David Delaplane, an ordained minister of the United Church of Christ, spoke about the difficulty of ministering to ritually abused victims who desperately need and also desperately question theological thought and pastoral responses.

Walking the halls and gardens of the Claremont was like being in a dream. Flowers rich in color and smell, a sky warm and clear, everyone dressed in casual California chic. People chatted and smiled, comparing notes like idealistic students. My head spun with the incongruity of it all. Behind closed doors the horrors of abuse were exposed and explored. In the halls and gardens the air was ripe with normalcy. Tom and I wandered here and there like a couple of lost souls.

We got food from a local deli and ate lunch on a bench in the garden. Our chosen afternoon session was the criminal justice track: Ritual Abuse Indicators and Responses. Detective Jerry Simandl of the Chicago Police Department would be talking about the Identification and Investigation of Criminal Activity. His presentation partner was Patricia Hills who would be discussing Child Pornography and Prostitution in Ritual Abuse. I'd heard Patricia at the earlier conference. It was Jerry who would be the surprise.

He started his seminar with a compassionate and passionate understanding of the issues with which a ritual abuse survivor struggles. He spoke knowledgeably about the different levels of satanic cults and the vast difference between teenage dabblers and organized inter-generational groups. He spoke of crime scene investigations: what to look for both inside and outside the crime scene that gives indication of ritualistic activity. He handed out a 47-page manual of information. He was emotional and factual. And the room was packed. Here was this detective, a 23-year veteran of the Chicago

Police Department, talking about the intricacies of ritual abuse. And people were listening.

Patricia Hills followed Jerry Simandl with her own authoritative presentation about child pornography and prostitution. Together they were a two and a half hour reality check that would throw another brick of belief at my unrelenting denial system.

As we said goodbye that afternoon, I made Tom promise to meet me at the conference the next day. I was afraid that, given the slightest excuse, I would not show up myself. I felt brittle and stiff, alienated and estranged. I needed encouragement, the obligation of a meeting time and place.

That night I stayed at a friend's apartment only a few blocks away from the Claremont, just over the border in Berkeley. She was gone for a few days and I sank into the relief of solitude and the anxiety of sleep. I wanted to call Brian but he was in the Soviet Union for a month. Deep in one of his pockets he was carrying a little ivory figure carved by an Alaska native. It was to remind him of me. To remind me of him, he had taped himself reading my favorite *Winnie the Pooh* story as well as a favorite of his own, *The Velveteen Rabbit*. He never abandoned my children.

Tom and I got espresso the next morning. Everyone around us looked so healthy, so full of belonging. I was filled with admiration, almost awe. How did they do it? Carry on the niceties of life, chat together, read their papers with such carefree charm? I knew their lives weren't easy but something was. They didn't have to make themselves up from second to second. That was it. They didn't have to pretend to exist. I watched them from out of all the corners of my eyes.

The morning session was with Esther Cancella, a nurse and a survivor of ritual abuse. She was an experienced presenter across the U.S. and was on the faculty of the Sixth International Conference on Multiple Personality. The title of her presentation at the Claremont conference was Sharing Hope for Healing. Tom and I squeezed into a packed room.

To a survivor there is no expert as expert as another survivor. No matter how accomplished, how understanding, or how effective, a non-survivor expert is always distanced by his/her normalcy and remains essentially a stranger. When a survivor takes to the podium and speaks from the hallowed halls of recovery there is a resonance of recognition in the soul. And the irony is that it is their very normalcy that gives a healing survivor such exquisite power.

"Here I am. Here are the things that happened to me. Here is my unbearable burden. Here is my shame. Here I am recovering. Here I am, recovered. Here I am, normal."

Esther Cancella did not say those words, she was those words. Bright, attractive, direct, articulate, she spoke the professional's language from the heart of the survivor. She had grabbed her demons by the throat and banished them from her life. She had done it herself, by herself, for herself. This woman, who had gone through it all and was standing there inside her own skin, being her own person, unabashed and unashamed, telling us that she took both responsibility for and credit for her own recovery, was a bombshell.

Cancella's ten-point survivor's guide was topped by a simple sentence, "I am responsible for my recovery." These six words are as complex as the universe yet they are the real, and only, key to recovery. But getting that first glimpse of possibility can take a long, long time. As Cancella said in her talk, "Recovery takes as long as it takes."

When I first heard those six words, "I am responsible for my recovery," they were not yet within the reach of meaning. All I knew was that I was hearing a ritual abuse survivor say them, so it must be true. The rest of her 10-point list of survival tactics was as resonant:

Get a good therapist. Interview. Be aggressively selective.

Build a support system.

Trust yourself as the expert.

Consciously build self-esteem.

Learn to diffuse the constant intensity of the pain.

Keep a journal.

Correct incorrect ideas. Put life in the middle.

Practice healthy boundaries.

Focus on a goal. Strive to be a thriver.

As I sat there listening to this warrior of a woman lay claim to her life, I had no idea how often her words would reach me during the next few years of recovery. Over and over there would be another baby-step of recognition, a new realization, but it was a long time before her list of survival tactics made sense from the inside out.

By the end of the day Tom and I were both exhausted but there was still one last event, a memorial service for those who had died as a result of abuse. It was to be held that evening at Herrick Hospital in Berkeley. I would not have gone alone, but Tom, who was a devout Christian, had both car and inclination. The service was sponsored by Bay Area Women Against Rape, The Center for Women and Religion, and St. Cuthbert's Episcopal Church.

I remember being awkwardly dressed. A funny, rebellious mixture of prints and weaves. My hair was messily pinned up. The earrings I wore were from an old Indian who sold jewelry out of the back of a truck on the edge of Canyon de Chelles in Arizona. They were round and silver; the outline of a small cactus was carved through like a shadow and there was a small circle of turquoise slightly off center.

I had no idea what I was doing there. Ritual abuse was a myth. These people were phantoms. This service was a bad play with lousy actors and a ludicrous script. I was there, and not there, simultaneously. I could feel the familiar stone throughout my body, the leaden heaviness anchoring my disbelief. I could also feel my abject gratitude, the sheer opaque yearning of someone inside who had led us here and knew why. Sitting beside Tom, I pretended I was real, breathing, human.

Down in front there was a row of chairs set off to the side and I was stunned to see a man in Zen Buddhist robes suddenly take a seat. The faith in me leaped in recognition. Here it was in this room of grief and pain—a Buddhist presence. The row of seats was soon filled with others who would participate in this interfaith service. There were several unfamiliar women and a familiar man— Reverend James Ward of St. Cuthbert's, who had been a conference presenter only the day before.

We were welcomed by Pamela Cooper-White, M.Div., Ph.D., director of the Center for Women and Religion of the Graduate Theological Union in Berkeley. She was touchingly pregnant. Her talk was large of heart, deeply gentle, and expansive. The essence of Christianity without the Christian rhetoric.

Rabbi Pamela Frydman-Baugh lit candles and spoke eloquently from within her own faith. Reverend James Ward read from the Scripture and there were shared prayers of justice, healing and peace. The Zen priest spoke about the light in the room, how it had brightened as we had entered. People in the audience gave testimony through tears and prayers. Candles were lit. The service had an ebb and flow of reality. If these faith-filled people could bear witness to this service and to the pain it represented, then perhaps my isolation could be lessened, my spiritual devastation relieved, my soul restored.

When I woke up the next morning I could feel the convulsions of grief even before I noticed it was morning and there was sunlight. My pillow was already damp from crying, my body wrapped around itself in anguish. All the unfelt feeling of the past few days flooded through me like a river. I cried in bone-deep relief. Years of yearning for spiritual witnessing, for the look that said, "Yes, you are hurt beyond life and you are whole. Your soul is there; your faith can live and breathe; your spiritual life has meaning. You have the right to pray." The interweaving of faiths, the unity of love, the generosity of spirit—all these things from the night before coursed through me. I cried myself back into the world.

I called the Zen priest to thank him for being there and for representing my beloved Buddhism from which I'd felt so isolated. I asked him if he'd consider speaking in my community about the impact of abuse upon the spirit and the soul. He invited me for tea. I went. He told me he was attracted to me and wanted to make love. I was shocked. This man wanted me, a woman tainted by the throes of satanic nihilism, by sexual abuse, by a lost soul. He wanted me. Through a rising resistance that knew better, I rationalized a relationship, a soul mate, a synchronicity in which sex was the beginning of a great and lasting love affair. And so began a year of ending a relationship that should never have started.

Of all the things that happened to me during twenty years of seeking healing, this experience was the hardest to accept. Because the partnership of spirituality and sexuality carried such weight, and because I so desperately needed to be seen as whole, I capitulated to a relationship that was hollow at its core. Underlying it, still almost impossible to acknowledge, was my conditioning to never disobey, to never say "no."

Even now, these many years later, I want to take the blame for that incident. I want to feel that I had a choice, that I made a choice. But I didn't. I didn't want to have sex with this man but there was no deep self to say "no." What was there was the part of me that was so well-trained to say "yes." I've often wondered how many years of healing I would have gained if the Zen priest had honored my spiritual recovery over his sexual interests. I will never know. What I do know is that the healing of spirit from the violations of abuse is an impossibly tender process, made possible only by impossibly tender care. It should be the fundamental awareness of every priest of any religious or spiritual persuasion.

Coming home to spiritual healing needs spiritual guidance, spiritual authority, spiritual integrity; it needs trust as spiritual ground. It needs trust in spiritual self. But what precisely does this mean? As this trip to India tightens its grip on me, an answer begins to take the shape of language: *The freedom to feel one's self, to know one's self, and to assert one's self is a spiritual birthright. Spiritual recovery means recovering relationship with life from the inside out.* That little boy who climbed up my body in the streets of Dharamsala this morning was definitely fearless from the inside out. He had a fierce relationship with life. In his determination to get what he wanted he reflected all that it meant to have a spiritual birthright. Jesus would love him a whole lot.

Sixteen

There's a museum in McLeod Ganj, Demton Khang, The Tibet Museum. I've walked past it daily on my trek to the temple grounds but it's never been open. Today we finally get the chance to visit. The exhibit honors the ordinary Tibetans who suffered extraordinary means to get to freedom; the plight of imprisoned monks and nuns who spoke up for freedom; and the Tibetan history, culture, spiritual treasure and environmental resources that are being destroyed by the Chinese. Tibet, the Shangri-La of our collective imagination, is being systematically destroyed and degraded. It has been going on for more than 50 years.

Sometimes I feel my racism to the core. And I am a racist. Back in the seventies I went to Unlearning Racism workshops where I discovered the depth of the cultural racism within which we are raised, and how hard we have to work to combat the effects of such cultural brainwashing. I know when I am not working hard and the truth is I haven't been, not for years. Cultural complacency is epidemic in the white world and no matter how estranged I might personally feel from the rest of civilization, I am still a white woman in a privileged white world.

The sixties might have been sandbagged by free love but the seventies actually reflected some serious soul-searching. We not only looked at our inherent racism, we also looked at our imminent extinction. The nuclear threat was not only at our doorstep, it was our doorstep. Trident nuclear submarines plied the waters of Puget Sound and Japanese Buddhist monks came to build Peace Pagodas and pray. The insanity of big boys with big toys that could wipe out civilization was part of daily life.

Back then, a friend of mine, a very bright, well-educated man of a certain ethnicity said that a nuclear war between Russia and the United States might not be so bad because it would reduce the white population on the planet. I was viscerally shocked by this remark. It also forced me to face a moment of visceral truth. No matter how the population stacks up on any given day in any given place, it is a white world, after all. The bottom line is that white people live better and expect to live better. I know this can be argued ad infinitum in any number of directions but the truth is, "So what?" It's still true.

When I'm faced with this I have no idea what to do. All I can do is face it back. And in the Tibet Museum, all these years later, once again, I do. The name of the exhibition is the "Long Look Homeward." It tells the stories of Tibetans who escaped from Chinese oppression, on foot and in fear, through long perilous months in the Himalayan Mountains. The museum describes the exhibit as ...*a collective consciousness of memory, commemoration and hope depicting the darkness of invasion, destruction and oppression, and shedding light on the magnificent past of Tibet, and expressing hopes for its future.*

Genocide. Torture. Rape. Darkness. Hope. Memory. An extinction of homeland, a brutal attack on a cultural landscape, and a violation of everything it means to be human. All of it happening as much right now as it did 50 years ago. The Tibetans are suffering through the loss of everything they have ever known, as individuals, as families, as communities, and as a people. Why don't we care? The only answer I can come up with is because we (white people "we") don't relate. And we don't relate because we are white and they aren't. We expect to live better. Obviously, they don't.

Obviously I've got a lot of rage about this and I wish someone would come along and put me right about this complicated issue. But I don't even think His Holiness the Dalai Lama could get me beyond this mess of useless white racist guilt and rage. Walking through the museum I am struck to the core by the pain and the hope of the Tibetan people. I am struck by the word "freedom" and how white a word it is. I am struck by how privileged is my poverty and how blind-sided has been my quest for healing. As is so true with so many people I know, I turn to the wisdom of ancient cultures for spiritual sustenance while turning a blind eye to the plight of the people.

I see it all around me. Native American teachers, South American shamans, gurus in India, Zen priests in Japan, we white people pack it up and spend thousands to soak up spiritual tradition without a heartbeat of recognition of the injustice served the indigenous world. I hate this in myself and I hate it in others. I also know it is necessary. It's a way to break the boundaries and begin the steep climb out of our own self-involvement. When I think about the years lost to regaining some spiritual enfranchisement, I see years lost to self-absorption. And it's affected those closest to me as well as the world at large.

My big dose of worldly responsibility came on the streets of WTO Seattle. My history as an activist was always issue-based—the Vietnam War, civil rights, nuclear weapons, environmental issues—but it never fully encompassed the human-being in humanity. When I found myself in the midst of an international euphoria at the WTO demonstrations, I was bewildered. Human spirit prevailed and we all recognized it in one another. Every one of those 60,000 reasons for being on the streets of Seattle had to do with our love for the earth and for one another. Sweat shops, global warming, healthy food, fair wages, fair profits, healthcare, an end to corporate greed and corruption, respect for indigenous peoples, well-being for children, environmental preservation, cultural preservation, the restoration of time in our lives, the restoration of freedom and deep democracy in societies co-opted by a culture of consumerism—all these things were on the minds and in the hearts of those in the streets of WTO Seattle. It was a bird's eye view of what we were up against as a civilization in the David and Goliath battle with corporate culture.

It was a bit like facing my personal past. In the mid-80s, when the immensity of my struggle started to sink in and the depth of my psychological distress became apparent, despair became my sidekick. Brian kept bringing me back to hope through the expression of my feelings. And if I thought my grief was interminable, my rage reduced it to a few measly tears. I call it the Year of Yellow Pages. Brian kept a stack of phone books in his office and when I was finally able to take the lid off my rage I pounded those weighty tomes against the brick wall in his office until they were shreds of their former selves and I was an exhausted heap on the floor. I'd leave his office in tatters only to discover the colors were back in the world and my energy restored.

Somebody once said, "The only way out is through." When I think about what is real, here in India, there in Tibet, in China, South America and the United States, I know we have to face our ignorance and complicity and it feels lousy. But it is the only way to restore the colors in the world so that everyone gets to see them.

Walking around the Tibet Museum brings it all flooding to the surface, the complexity and contradiction as well as the hope for a future that cannot be imagined. The Chinese will not give back Tibet. All I can imagine is that the Tibetans could get invited back into their own country to take their rightful place as custodians of their own culture. The Iron Curtain came down, the Cold War ended, apartheid was destroyed; something keeps moving us towards collective survival. Maybe something will happen in Tibet, too.

It is late afternoon when we leave the museum. Thrinley has to teach English back at the pad. I am beset by so many thoughts and feelings I decide to sit on a road-side bench and write a few things in my journal. Ten minutes later, a voice says to me, "English! English!" and I look up to a lovely Tibetan woman and her three shining children.

"English?" she says again, pointing to my writing.

"Yes," I nod.

"English," she says, proudly gesturing to her children.

They are smiling at me, too. Two boys and a girl, ages somewhere between ten and sixteen. They are meticulously groomed and all three are holding on to their mom. It is the daughter who practices her English on me.

"My mother is here to visit," she says. "She lives in Lhasa."

The boys wear blue jeans and the older one has on a Nike jacket. They wear new T-shirts sporting Tibetan symbols. The girl has her ears pierced and her hair parted traditionally down the middle. Her mom beams irrepressibly as her daughter speaks to me in English.

Through a half-hour of creative communication I learn that her mom comes once a year to visit her children, who attend school at the Tibetan Children's Village. This is their annual reunion and their love for one another and joy in being together is palpable.

Questions spill through my mind: How did they get here? How long have they been here? How does their mother get to McLeod Ganj each year? How did they become so full of life in the face of so much death? They hold on to their mom as though doing otherwise would make her disappear. Yet there is no anxiety or fear. Just joy and they are sharing it all with me.

As our shared verbal language runs out of articulation we are left with nothing but love and recognition. It is a moment I have had before with Tibetan people. They acknowledge the grace of being, and of being together, and isn't it grand? It's what the Dalai Lama exudes with his presence. It's what Gen Lamrimpa poured forth so many years ago at Cloud Mountain where I had gone to be silent. It's what I have felt from the very old people walking slowly and prayerfully on the Linkghor each morning. It speaks straight to the spirit and it stays there.

Then the mom says to me, "You come." She looks at me expectantly.

"Where?" I ask.

"To Lhasa," she says. "Come visit."

It is almost a command.

"I'd like to," I say.

"You come Lhasa," she says to me, woman to woman, mother to mother. Her children no longer mediate this situation and I am struck by her intensity. It is as though she knows something about me that is of some other place and lifetime.

"I'd like to," I say again.

And I can feel it coming: a moment I will fail. A moment that, years later, I will regret. I shift into being a tourist and gesture that I must be going. But first, I ask, may I take your photograph? The children cluster around their mom and I take a photo which I share with them in small digital scale. They are delighted.

We walk up Temple Road together and when we get to the divide in the road I say I must go this way. The mom gestures for me to keep going with them to where they are staying.

"No," I say. "I must meet my friend."

It's a lie.

I find out where they are staying and indicate I will visit. This, too, is a lie.

What I know is that I can't stand the love and the pain. That if I enter their lives, mine will never be the same.

I've felt these moments of soul connection before. They invite us to enter a place never before explored and not going there is a recipe for everlasting regret. Once I had it with a man I met. All day on an art jury together, evaluating and selecting projects to fund. Our sensibilities in synch to such a degree that it seemed we occupied the same body. He was a Taiko drummer, yet in this group of voluble, opinionated writers, artists and musicians he emanated a profoundly quiet presence, saving his words for his vote of preference.

Later, as we walked side-by-side out to our cars, he quietly asked me where I lived.

"In the north end," I said, without asking him back.

His gaze was penetrating and accepting. We got in our cars and were gone. I've missed him ever since.

It was 1985 and in those days there were never to be any more men in my life. I was spoiled goods, operating fraudulently in the world. Now I have no such excuse to avoid the connections of soul and spirit that draw me forward. As I turn away from this extraordinary family that entered my day, I know they will stay with me. And if I let them, so will I.

It's what memory is about, I'm thinking as I walk down the small alley leading to the Loseling Guest House. It binds us to others and to ourselves. It's where my brilliant forgetting fails so immensely. It forgets everything and everyone and me along with it all.

I have salvaged memory by diving into the wreck. Some of it leads me to a precipice I don't dare get close to. Some of it leads to sterile rooms, chairs with straps, and men and women rippling with self-righteous authority. That very first memory, of being strapped down and watched by a group of people, holds the key to my embodiment of memory. I "re-membered" how it felt to lay there, a small child terrified and abandoned. I didn't know what was happening because I was too young to understand. This is the way of remembering things that are impossible to the adult mind. Even as

I put all the pieces together: the scars, the terror, the multiplicity of selves, the lies I was told about my life, the body-memories of rape and sexual performance, the family I had that never had me, the way electricity rippled through my body, the way I rippled out of my body, the ripple effect of torture, still it challenges the mind of my daily life, this adult mind to whom it didn't happen. If I didn't have this mind, I would be dead.

When I climb the stairs to our penthouse digs, Thrinley's still teaching so I go to hang out in the small darkened lobby of the guest house. There are several monks lounging about watching Tibetan soap operas on television. Even though it's monks who are operating this place, because they don't wear their robes I forget that we're staying in religiously owned and operated accommodations. And I found out why our monks don't wear robes: Tibetans do not like to have their monks work. It makes them uncomfortable to stay at a place where their spiritual teachers sweep the floors and change their beds. So these monks forego their robes in order to keep their monk-ness invisible and their guesthouse clientele comfortable.

The Geshe in his flowing robes, the monk-in-evidence who circumambulates the roof each morning and lifts hand weights up there in the afternoons, does not sweep floors or do dishes. His one domestic specialty is getting the temperamental propane heater to work when the cold evenings penetrate the lobby. Now, he's sitting cross-legged, huddled over the thing which is laid out in pieces across the floor. Two other monks-in-lay-clothing are loudly gesturing their expertise to the problem-at-hand.

I find a bit of light and sit down to read the newspaper. I've lost track of the days so I don't even know if the paper is current. The monks on the couch start surfing between BBC news and soap operas. The floor debate regarding how the heater gets put back together is getting up its own head of steam. The phone rings behind the desk. But there's no-one who speaks English around to answer it, so it's ignored.

There is such a diversity of identity within these few square feet. Behind the monks on the burgundy brocade couch are the rows of supplies for Westerners: rolls of yellow and pink toilet paper, bottled water in plastic bottles, and soft drinks in prehistoric bottles. I'm reminded of the Coca Cola in Delhi and its derelict container, and all those bottling plants draining the water tables in parts of agricultural India. But right now all it looks is ludicrous. The woman on the TV soap opera, the Geshe wielding his screwdriver, the lace curtains, the vocal expertise, the pastel toilet paper and the Coca Cola all exuding their own particular brand of autonomy. Surreptitiously, I get out my camera and flash the small room with a shot.

The Geshe looks up, startled, not knowing that either I or my camera is in the room. I know that I'm invading privacy and am wide open for criticism but this moment is not to be missed. I just grin at him. The Geshe pushes his glasses more firmly in place, throws back his head and laughs. He has been caught unawares. His deep involvement with the puzzle of the propane heater surpassed his usual attentiveness to his surroundings. He catches my eye and laughs louder. It's as though we see together a moment of mischief in the universe. Then he goes firmly back to work with his screwdriver.

Fifteen minutes later there is a very loud bang and a very big flame. We all jump to attention and an outburst of hilarity bursts through the small room. The Geshe is congratulated, the flame is quickly tamed to safe proportions, and everyone gets back to whatever it is they are, or aren't, doing.

It's dark by the time I head up the stairs to meet up with Thrinley. We catch up on the day's events and crawl into our respective beds to read our respective books for the evening. It's cold in our little room so I'm wearing layers of fleece and a hat. I check the contents of my little shelf: flashlight, something tasty, my glasses and my bottle of water. Bedtime in India is taking on routine.

SEVENTEEN

Today we decide to spend money. This is not as simple as it sounds. First of all, we don't have much—even if it is more than most everybody in this town. Second of all, we want to spend it "right." This means we have decided to spend it where the women are. Walking to the temple and the Lingkhor takes us past two endeavors that set up every day along a small hillside. Two Tibetan women carry in tables each morning and fabric bags full of their jewelry. One of them comes with her mother, or auntie, or perhaps elder, who takes care of her small daughter while she works, constantly creating the next necklace or bracelet for sale. The other woman, who sets up just down the road a few feet, is always alone. Her table is smaller and she, too, focuses more on her creations than trying to catch the eye of the next buyer that passes by the stall.

When the Dalai Lama first re-settled in this village it was all but abandoned. Then the Tibetan refugees who successfully escaped from China revitalized the marketplace, the Indian merchants moved back to town, the fans and followers of the Dalai Lama flooded in, and the beggars flew in. Suddenly it was a bit of a boom town and the economics of the place got complicated.

It's neighbor Matt who is responsible for my new-found understanding of the beggar kingdom. He started his India trip with a small group tour of tourist-friendly places like the Taj Mahal and Jaipur. Along the way, his guides explained how the beggars are pretty much pimped out by their handlers, who will even fly them in to places for the duration of festivals, particularly religious festivals—which explains the great number of beggars in town last week during the celebrations at the Dalai Lama's temple. The lowest of castes is held hostage by their poverty, which in turn lines the pockets of their masters.

It's easy for me to relate to, which is why my bile rises with hatred for them all—the beggars, their handlers, the idiots who give them money and the idiots who don't. In my hatred I am still beholden to my handlers. And all the shit I've gone through really was simply for someone else to make money—access to which is still denied me. Part of it is because of my internalized revulsion at having any of my worth whatsoever equated with money. Part of it is successful brainwashing. Nothing renders us more insignificant and less powerful than poverty. Why would anybody believe the story of someone who has rarely lived above poverty level and who claims so little monetary worth for herself? Surely she is worthless.

To say that money is the source of all evil is to put it mildly. And my WTO research effectively reinforced my prejudice about the stuff. Just before the end of World War II, the global powers that be met up at Bretton Woods, New Hampshire, to discuss how to insure wealth for their Western countries. In a proverbial nutshell, it all had to do with lending poor countries money so they could afford to pay rich countries to build their roads, dams and other forms of infrastructure; and when that is all well and done, all the poor countries have to do is keep paying off the massive debts and ever-mounting interest. Welcome to the World Bank and the International Monetary Fund. This is a cavalier definition of a tragic situation that has rendered billions of people immobilized by poverty in countries in which the citizens have no access to their own natural wealth and resources. They also have no access to cultural dignity, food, shelter and healthcare for their families, or respect and recognition by the rest of the world. I learned about this and it was an epiphany. But instead of being exhilarated by my new-found knowledge, I went into a profound funk. Most of all, I realized that my ignorance made me culpable and that all my idealistic activism was way off the mark. All I could see were the waters in which I swam. I had no idea they were polluting the streams of the entire planet and that this river of capitalist consciousness in which I swam was nothing but a sleight-of-mind created with a few deep pockets in mind. Free trade it isn't. It's not fair, either.

It was Abraham Lincoln who warned: "As a result of the war, corporations have now been enthroned and an era of corruption in high places will follow...until all wealth is aggregated in a few hands, and the Republic is destroyed." Not only is the Republic destroyed (otherwise known as "Democracy") but so is the rest of the world. Corporate rights were not part of the democratic equation until 1886 when corporations were granted the rights of a "natural person." That's when the unnatural took over and growing money for money's sake became more acceptable than growing food, families and communities. It's been a downward spiral ever since because corporations are not human beings. They are bottomless pits of bottom lines. They live to consume, us along with everything else that comes before them—including earth, sea and sky. Only by rescinding the rights of corporations to be treated with the same respect as human beings will we ever be able to reclaim real human rights on the planet.

In researching and writing *Battle in Seattle* it was easy to connect the corporate dots "out there." The hard part was doing the connecting within my own life. It was a journey that brought me face-to-face with my own complicity in a system of destruction that I have rolled over for, and been rolled over by, for way too long. Not only had I woken up to my own personal slavery, now I was waking up to my complicity in everyone else's slavery.

That which had inspired the book to begin with—being part of the collective heart of humanity from all over the world that showed up for freedom on the streets of WTO Seattle—became a burden of guilt and shame. I remember expressing this to Sally Soriano, an activist whom I interviewed regarding the Northwest's struggle in the Fair Trade movement. She looked at me sternly and told me it wasn't my fault. What followed was a discourse on the meltdown of media integrity over the years; the corporate co-opting of "news" and the resulting distortion of values; the ways in which members of Congress come out of corporate life, become so-called "public servants", and then re-enter corporate life after leaving elected office, all the while making decisions that serve the private purse over the public good. It is a self-serving cycle of corporate culture that in ways subtle and not-so-subtle defines our lives as we have been trained and brainwashed to know them.

It was an illuminating moment for me and set me off on the interviews for the book that eventually restored my deep faith and hope in humankind. My research took me into the heart—and the many hearts—of civil society. It also took me into the heart of Christianity.

Two of the people I interviewed were Episcopal activists: Pete Strimer, who worked tirelessly for social justice issues—particularly for the forgiveness of Third World Debt, and Bishop Vincent Warner, who was so affected by the assassination of Dr. Martin Luther King Jr. that he left his career in business and advertising and entered the seminary. Both men had muscular, visceral theologies that embraced the deepest issues of social responsibility and justice.

On the streets of WTO Seattle, Bishop Warner marched with John Sweeney, president of the AFL-CIO, and California Congresswoman, Maxine Waters. The three of them marched together in the rain and stood in a circle around the exhibition hall in which the opening festivities were underway. They tied a yellow ribbon together to symbolize the chain of national debts around the world that are crippling so many innocent citizens; then they cut it with scissors in a symbolic act of cutting the chains of debt. Nobody paid any attention. The trio was not seen on the nightly news.

Pete Strimer was closely involved in Jubilee 2000—a global push of the Anglican and Episcopal churches to alleviate the debt crisis amongst developing countries. These three Episcopal ministers—Bishop Warner, Peter Strimer, West Davis—all inspired me to lose my angry, rigid criticism of Christianity. They opened my mind to the social justice at the heart of the teachings of Jesus. They taught me that the problem with Christianity is often Christians. They helped me to recognize that spiritually-based activism has been an essential part of every effective political movement ever undertaken. And that every effective activist, whether they admit it or not, is spiritual—committed to finding truth beyond the material and the measurable. And when the truth is known, people step up and do what's right. WTO Seattle was a watershed event for this global movement. But the media, owned and operated by a corporate bottom line, missed the whole story. Instead, they focused on the burning garbage can, a handful of "anarchists" who might just as easily have been working undercover, and a couple of broken windows. When these few images are replicated time after time on TV, they become the story itself.

Yet the real story remains, and it is this that compelled and propelled me through writing that book. I rode a wave of inspiration that I wanted to share with as many people as possible. The odd uneasiness of heart and spirit that I often attributed to my personal history, turned out also to be the unease that comes from living inside a social/cultural/economic lie. It really is the truth that will set us free. WTO Seattle unveiled the truth and set me free to face it. Perhaps even to be part of the message that so deserved to be delivered. Then, less than a year after *Battle in Seattle* came out, the world was delivered to September 11, 2001.

It was a call from a friend that woke me that morning. Instantly, I knew it was all over—that the gains made by the anti-globalization movement went down with the World Trade Towers. The demonizing began, all the borders went up, and all the work done to chip away the hold of corporate culture over human culture lost its slowly developing luster. September 11th, 2001, turned the world's attention away from the world—just when it seemed as though the world had a chance.

It would take years, civil wars, starvation, the tragedy of Iraq, and the massive threat of global warming, before attention would once again shift towards understanding the way the world works. My own work, too, took a nosedive. A follow-up book to *Battle in Seattle* got shelved in my mind; I quit writing and got a job driving a bus. Driving in circles around the island of paradise in which I lived seemed just about right. It rendered me poor and pretty much invisible which put me in league with most of the rest of the people on the planet.

But I'm not poor here in India so Thrinley and I spend our bucks on bracelets, necklaces and prayer beads made by two Tibetan women. It seems to me we should be paying five times the asking price. Afterwards we go to the Tibetan Handicraft Center where we buy handmade vests for ourselves as well as for gifts. The sewing machines and the sewers are quite evident and the women here are also proud of their wares—which are also far too inexpensive. But at least the money goes directly to the people making the products.

After our shopping spree, we drop the stuff off in our room and head down the long and winding path to the Library of Tibetan Works and Archives. Matt walks down to this library every morning for his classes in Buddhist Philosophy and he told us about a shortcut. But neither of us can remember the details so we stick to the road and its precipitous curves. When we finally reach the library the place has just closed for a two-hour lunch period. Precisely the amount of time we could spend here because both of us are teaching this afternoon. So we eat noodle soup and watch Indian women dressed in all their finery carry baskets of gravel on their heads and pass them off, woman by woman, until the gravel reaches a construction site. It's not clear what is being constructed but the number of women employed is impressive.

In India construction jobs are always prolific with workers. The roads need endless maintenance simply to keep them readily identified, propped up and passable. I've noticed the workers every time we've encountered the road between Upper and Lower Dharamsala. They work, sit around, work, sit around, work, contemplate something, work, look at their work, contemplate their work and one another, and work some more. It's work as life.

This breeds, of course, inevitable slowness. It also results in the embodiment of time. If we take time into our bodies it doesn't have to whiz by out there where we aren't yet. Always being on the way to do something or be somebody is exhausting. It's also a mind-fuck. Having avoided being in my body most of my life, I know this part of it well. Our minds are built to do whatever it is they need to do. And if the need is to avoid life and all its complexity they rise to the occasion like the brilliant stars they are. Most of my life my mind operated at warp speed to keep me from looking back and seeing anything out of the ordinary. I can quite honestly say that up until I was forty, it never rested. Then it went AWOL. "If you're going to make me work so hard without stopping, I quit," was its mantra. It needed exactly what those road workers need: to feel like it was in life, not in limbo. What good is a mind if it's not in life?

I know that's a dangerous question and I don't even try to rout out an answer. But I do know it has something to do with slowing down and seeing what's right in front of our faces. These construction women are so beautiful. Their filmy, flowing garments brighten the landscape like exotic life-size butterflies. Each woman moves with elegance, the big basket of gravel carefully balanced on the head and held with one hand. There is grace as the basket is passed on to the next woman, grace as she walks up the stone steps, grace as she dips slightly to facilitate the basket's removal. If we simply look at the job, it is repetitive, menial and undignified. These women transcend it all and transform it. They are embodying time with their beauty. In a land so apparent with poverty, they rise like Phoenix from the ashes. It is the way they live.

Eighteen

I t's Monday. Yesterday I didn't go to church. Last night I felt queasy. This morning Matt ministered to me at our breakfast table on the patio with some Vitamin C before he left for his Buddhist studies. Thrinley gave me some homeopathic *Nux Vomica* before she left with Tibetan friends to explore Lower Dharamsala. I was left to wallow about in my own moroseness. I don't know if I'm sick or not. Maybe I simply want a day of solitude, something that I am well used to on a daily basis and have had very little of since we started this journey.

This is a familiar push and pull of inclination. To be alone or not to be alone, this is the self-indulgent question. Nobody gets to be alone in India. The whole country is a study in human proximity. This is its greatest lesson in democracy because the unstated assumption underneath it all is that individual freedoms are public responsibility.

I encountered an example of this yesterday when I was fussing about the plight of an old and very disabled man who lives in a crude shelter on the edge of the street. It is no more than a plank with a tattered awning and a pile of blankets. He's asleep every time I walk by and there is no jar in which to deposit a few rupees. Now that the nights are cold I worry about his well-being; yesterday I talked about him to Nawang, our monk-in-leather manager. He looked at me quizzically, as though he didn't know who I was talking about, and I began to think he was being disingenuous. Then recognition crossed his face and he laughed in surprise. This time I thought he was being cruel and my confusion grew.

"No worry," he said. "The merchants help him."

It turns out the old man's been there for years under the care of the surrounding Indian and Tibetan business people who make sure he gets food and blankets and is well-covered at night. Help is offered by those in proximity. On the island where I live we pride ourselves in our sense of community. But it is an organized sense of community. A homeless old person sleeping outside, visible in a street-side shelter, would be considered an eyesore and bad for business. We take care of the needy by hiding them. By hiding them we don't have to face the rising tide of inequity and suffering that is increasing on our own shores. In India, nothing is hidden. Truth, in all its elaborate concoctions, is visible to the naked eye. We're all naked in its sight.

Yesterday I wanted to go to church and I also wanted to be a Buddhist. Today I want to be in bustling Lower Dharamsala with Thrinley and her Tibetan friends and I also want to be here, blissfully alone sipping tea. But I'm not a Buddhist or an Episcopalian, I'm somewhere in-between; and I am definitely not alone. The monkeys are nit-picking each other on the "May Peace Prevail On Earth" water tanks. The whole town is bustling about down below in the streets. From here I can see three small white fluffy dogs scampering about on three different rooftops. This might be solitude's finest hour: all alone in the midst of an exuberant community that knows no bounds of propriety when it comes to democracy, generosity or spirituality.

St. John's in the Wilderness, the Anglican Church I wanted to go to yesterday, is about a mile out of town on the road to lower Dharamsala. All day yesterday I wanted to go but the juxtaposition between Buddhism and Anglicanism was just too big for me to bridge. Or perhaps it was just too public. In my life away from India, on Sundays I can go to St. David's in the morning and to meditation at the Buddhist Temple in the afternoon and nobody knows. I don't keep it a secret, the worlds just don't overlap. Thrinley, my friend of fifteen years, knows about my inner pilgrimage to make friends with Christianity and why it's important to me. When I first started going to St. David's, Reverend West Davis knew about my Buddhist inclinations. As a scholar and a searcher himself, he was understanding and accepting. But that hasn't been true throughout my church community. I was once asked by a well-meaning Episcopalian, "How can you call yourself a Christian?"

This was a question I'd long asked myself, but not for the reasons of Buddhism, which is why I was questioned. The answers I had at-hand: Because I was trained to hate all Christian love as well as the Christian in myself and I had successfully fought back. And because my soul had been poisoned by shame and isolation and I had discovered that Jesus really did love me after all. But the person asking me this question knew nothing of my long and stubborn journey back to spiritual life so I had no answer to give.

In my own wrestling with it all, I'd read enough to know that religious scholars could see the heart of partnership between Jesus and Buddha, both in teachings and in personal history. Jesus was a Jew. Buddha was a Hindu. They both had religions created in their names, but neither of them was organizationally inclined to do such a thing themselves. Both renounced worldly wealth. Both believed in life after life. Both were itinerant storytellers. Both had transforming experiences at the age of thirty-something and went out in the world to teach us all to be nice to one another. Both had a clue that there was transcending beauty in the experience of life and only through the awareness of suffering could it be glimpsed.

In his book, *Buddha and Christ—Images of Wholeness*, Robert Elinor describes Buddha and Christ as "two masks of one transcendent mystery." Each, he says, represents "the beauty of holiness alive in love." His book is rich with imagery and an understanding of spiritual relationship between these two holy men. He writes, "Human beings move from self-centeredness towards the joy and peace of wholeness in both. Commitment to one need not exclude the other. Indeed, both may so inform minds and hearts as to make religious identity a process of interconnected Buddhist and Christian commitments."

Interconnected commitments. What is faith ultimately but a commitment to the unknown and the unknowing, no matter what the religion. Words are labels. Faith is faith. What I have faith in is meaning in life, which, by its very being, encompasses death. This is where spiritual healing has brought me. And it cannot be separated from the psychological, emotional, intellectual and physical healing that has carried me forward. My therapy was graced by Brian, who himself brings spirituality to his work and his life. It encompassed those to whom I trusted my body in touch. From the jolt of Shiatsu to the subtle, no-touch touch of Jin Shin, healing touch helped me to re-enter the physical realm of my own body as well as the body of the world. The synchronicity of grace brought people and places to me when they were most needed. Doors opened with perpetual offerings to my paralyzed self. My will, from its subterranean vantage point, made its way to the surface without my acknowledgement—it was the only way it could manifest. These are all interconnected commitments, some made by different parts of me, others made for me, and many made to me.

The merchants in McLeod Ganj who are caring for the man living in the street are making interconnected commitments on his behalf. And he is committing his helplessness to them. Who knows the layers of meaning this invokes in their lives? Meaning is relentless. It is a constant barrage of beauty in a world full of pain. This is what the Buddha discovered when he came out from behind the walls of his childhood palace. This is what Christ knew, when he said, "Love your enemy." There is something that transcends suffering and hatred. And it is available to us everywhere, all the time.

Yesterday, St. John's in the Wilderness was available to me and I couldn't rise to the occasion. The reasons are complicated: shame about the racist British colonialism that built the church; awkwardness about my Anglican leanings in this Hindu, Buddhist town; awkwardness about what to say to Thrinley. In short, my inner life resolutely resists exposure. It trusts no-one. The part of me that needs to exist and be recognized the most also needs to be held most secret. Perhaps this is why spiritual healing is so important. It is the end run of resistance. When it finally feels safe, all is safe. When the spiritual self has returned to the flock, the flock can frolic.

I think about my early Sundays at St. David's. Sitting at the back of the church, I was as dissociated as I'd ever been. It was a huge regression into fear, into the hypocrisy and arrogance of yet another religion that "knows best." I was there out of hatred. Yet I knew enough about myself to know that my hatred was much more of a problem than the Episcopal Church. West Davis, with his own resistance, skepticism and struggle, invited me to a church that was as full of questions as it was answers.

In November, 1995, I wrote a note of appreciation to West Davis about a sermon he gave about how we each have our own private intimate relationship with God. I thanked him for his unwillingness to judge and for how much I felt represented through his struggle and continually informed by his erudition.

He wrote back: *I thank God that you have found a supportive, "safe" community where you can just Be. A community where I hope questions are not only honored, but encouraged. It is my hope, prayer and intent that more and more St. David's will be a spiritual center where people can interact with each other in ways that are appropriate to their calling and the circumstances of their lives. I want to be part of a mixed community that embraces this rapidly-changing society and struggles together for answers to real questions that real people are asking. With you and others at St. David's, I want to be witness to the truth of Alan Jones statement: "The opposite of faith is not doubt but certainty."*

Alan Jones is the Bishop at Grace Cathedral in San Francisco where I took the labyrinth training with Lauren Artress. When Artress first talked to Alan Jones about bringing the labyrinth there, he told her she was ignorant. She shot back that he was unconscious. It was a story Alan Jones himself shared, rather abashedly, to those of us at the training. He had, as they say, "come around" in a big way.

Because uncertainty was allowed at Saint David's, I started showing up in the back row. Most of all it was an act of willfulness. A fist in the face of all that had isolated me from the human race. As the years went by, it become routine, symbolic. As more years went by I was asked to participate and my involvement in St. David's expanded. For two years I met weekly for training in Episcopal Fellowship Ministry with West Davis and a small group of people from the church. We explored the Bible, theology, philosophy and the ways in which our own struggles were interwoven with both faith and frustration. It was here that I first "came out" about my personal history to people I did not yet know well but to whom I felt a deep connection.

Then I was asked to take training in Lay Eucharistic Ministry which would qualify me to wear a white robe, read the Prayers of the People, and assist the priest with communion. This request was a shock. Before I knew what I was doing, I said "Yes." Not only was I growing into the sense of belonging in, and deserving to be, in church, I accepted a role of responsibility towards others who attended. This was the most powerful and most humbling of requests. I knew I couldn't treat it as part of my retaliation process. It couldn't be fraught with adolescent revenge. It was a duty I had to be grown up for; I had to take it seriously within my deep self. I had to feel its weight and the weight of what it meant to those who stepped forward for communion.

Suddenly I was no longer wrapped up in the never-ending details of my own private struggle. Suddenly I was offering the sacred chalice of wine, the symbol of the blood of Jesus, to those whose faith was precious, profound and immeasurable. And I'd better get it right. I was on my knees in a heartbeat and stayed there in my mind throughout every moment of my appearance as a Lay Episcopal Minister. It felt like a call of gravity. My whole body would grow dense with prayer: "Please, dear God, don't let me screw up." Eventually, it grew to be what I know as real prayer: a profound longing to be entered and filled with humility and gratitude in the face of this mystery and miracle we call life.

And just as Buddhism sent me into an exploration of Christianity, as I learned more about Christianity it gave me greater appreciation for Buddhism. Each led me to the other and continues to do so. Buddhism mapped out my mind, Christianity mapped out my faith. There are places where they overlap; there are places they diverge. But they are never out of relationship. I'm the one that gets out of relationship. And here in McLeod Ganj I don't have the wits or the wherewithal to counter my fear of the small god of judgment that is always on my shoulder. So I didn't go to St. John's in the Wilderness yesterday. And I feel lousy about it.

When Matt shows up after his meditation classes I give him a hard time about smoking too much. Even if he does, it's still none of my damn business. We lean out over the railing in the warm sun and notice things—like the enormous landslide across the valley.

"It was from last year's rains," Matt tells me. "But nobody was hurt and there were no houses lost."

He's only around long enough enough to drop off his books, have a smoke, get harassed, and head off to help fix someone's computer.

When Thrinley gets back in mid-afternoon, I'm still out on the patio being melancholy and trying to feel sick enough to warrant my day without moving. Thrinley introduces me to Norbu, her guide of the day who is a connection through Jetsun Kushok, the Lama-in-residence at the gonpa back on our island. Norbu's job in Dharamsala is as transcriber of a book his uncle is writing about his life as a Khenpo warrior in Tibet during the long ordeal of Chinese invasion and occupation. Norbu's English is excellent, but he hides his intense, observant intelligence behind a mask of reserve. He is evaluating us and I can feel it.

We are exchanging pleasantries when Dakpa bounds around the corner of the patio for his English lesson. He is animated, which for him means a fleeting smile of greeting and a quick sharing of his notebook. I introduce him to Norbu and Thrinley and then we retreat to our small room to share all the odd sounds of a new language. He reads his life-story to me over and over. He has translated my English into Tibetan and squeezed the words under my English words on the page. His animation deepens. He is fascinated by having the words to tell it. They make his experience real. They bring him to life. They light up the depth of his loneliness and isolation. They shape his loss. I am afraid that by giving words to his story he is entering its tragedy over and over again for the first time.

In the middle of our lesson, a young Tibetan girl comes bursting through the open door. She's the ten-year-old niece of one of the monks; she is brash, precocious and bi-lingual in Tibetan and English. She starts to get involved in the lesson and I worry that Dakpa will find it uncomfortable to be coached by a ten-year-old so I shoo her away.

"We're concentrating," I say. "Come back later. Go and visit Thrinley."

She shrugs in indifference and skips out onto the patio.

These sessions with Dakpa really have taken on the shape of timeless concentration. He focuses so intently it's as though he's literally wrapping his entire mind around the sound and the sense of language. When he leaves, Dakpa glances shyly over at Thrinley and Norbu. I sit down with them and we get into a talk about spirituality and reason.

"The proof is in the experience," Norbu says quietly.

Norbu, born in Tibet and orphaned at a young age, escaped from the Chinese invasion, trekked his way through the mountains, and lives here in Dharamsala with his spirituality keenly integrated with his intellect and his experience. All of this slips out between the lines of language and circumstance as the sky darkens around us and we decide, in casual Western fashion, to take Norbu out to the Namgyal Café for dinner.

So yesterday, I didn't go to church. But Thrinley and I did walk the few miles to the Bhagsunag waterfall and the ancient Hindu temple where frolicking, shivering children splashed it its freshwater pools. All day I reminded myself that spirit resides within, no matter where we are or what we are doing. But that small seed of longing to "go to church," remained fully intact, just waiting for its own small splash of attention.

I was in the middle of a labyrinth when I discovered I was mad at God and therefore there might be one. It was at St. Mark's Cathedral in Seattle. The great draw was at it again. I was in Seattle for the weekend to visit my friend, Martha. Somewhere I saw an announcement about a labyrinth workshop with Lauren Artress; something about it caught my attention, perhaps the words "spiritual path," perhaps because it was an event that intimated something mystical and psychological, and something else about emotional longing and walking in circles. I do remember that I was struck by the fact that Lauren Artress was both a psychotherapist and an Episcopal priest.

Martha had a workshop to attend that Friday evening and so off I went to St. Mark's Cathedral to see what this odd confluence was all about. There were things that Artress said that night—about the metaphor of the labyrinth, how we are sometimes in the middle, out on the edge, often lost, and sometimes found, on the path through our lives. Most of all, she said, just because we can never really see where we are going, it doesn't mean that we're not going there. She talked about meeting others on the path: sometimes we're glad they are there, sometimes we hate it; sometimes we're centered in community, sometimes we're isolated and looking out over the edge into the big friggin' void. Something about how the labyrinth held all of us in all our glory, vanity, innocence and guilt resonated deeply inside me and I decided to return for the workshop the following day.

I walked the labyrinth several times on that Saturday. I felt awkward, self-conscious, self-indulgent and far too self-aware for my own good. Towards the end of the day, I finally settled into a pace that was my own, slow and purposeful and from the inside out. Most of all, what I felt was weight, of my body and my life, of existence and persistence, of all the density of grief that was the lay of my inner landscape. When I got to the middle of the labyrinth, I sank under the weightiness of it all and sat down, right there, wherever it was. My head felt as thought it was too heavy for my body so I propped it up with my hands. I resigned myself to being there, splat in the middle of the labyrinth, forever.

It was through this fog of resignation that I heard the voice: "You are so angry with me, Janet." It was a big and soft voice; it, too, held resignation. I looked around with a start, and then with surprise; I could find no-one who had spoken to me. It was at that moment that I really heard the words: "You are so angry with me," and I knew immediately it was God. A God in whom I did not believe.

"Of course I'm not mad at you," I retorted in my mind. Then I started to cry. The God in whom I did not believe said ever so gently, "Think about it."

At first I thought this was the Wise One giving me the ironic once over. But inside, the endless brick wall between me and faith was being breached. It was then that I got the real message: If I am mad at God, I must believe in God. This was not a simple moment.

I cried a stream of silent tears, oblivious to the strangers walking by on the labyrinth path. No-one knew me. Like so many other experiences I had been drawn to, this one was true to the calling: it was a solitary pilgrimage through life that I was on. It had always been that way. Then something else shuddered through me in recognition. I hate God. I want to kill God. It was the futile helplessness of a five-year-old, a young child desperate for a reason, a small girl wielding the only power she had within her reach: a rage at God. And for all these years, ever since reason was lost to violation, she had been doing battle for us all. To be angry at God was the ultimate and only power she had left.

But God wasn't angry at me. This was all too clear. The presence in and around me reverberated with compassion. I was buoyed by it; I was breathing it; it was breathing me. My entire body and being knew I was being loved beyond meaning. What became instantly clear was that this ragingly indignant five-year-old had kept us alive; and she had also kept us from God. Her wrath had flared to life when we needed it the most. But throughout my life, when perhaps God, or the image of God, or the thought of God, or simply the very question of God could offer an affirmation of simple faith, God was not to be had.

Faith, however, was a different story because faith is nothing if not helplessness. And I was nothing, if not helpless. Along with God, my will, that incipient four-letter word that lays the foundation for a life in the Western world, was also not to be had. It was destroyed by the twisted minds of my abusers. Raging at God as a five-year-old was my last act of free will. The defining note of survival. It was then that faith took over.

I see all this through the lens of looking back through the telescope of time. And I see nothing but a stream of answers that responded to questions I had no chance of even asking. I see a helpless faith and the intervention of faith. I see an inarticulate longing for something that could never be known. An unfolding of something called "my life" over which I had no control and in which I had very little participation. Those who know me will laugh at this because I have a willful nature. She navigated us through lots of willful behavior; but she operated independently, like a hired gun. In 1984, when the Willful One ran out of existential steam and could not fight the forces rising up out of my unconscious, she scattered like dandelion seed in the wind. But she blows my way in times of need; she rouses us to act when there are dark forces to fight, like Jet-skis and other loud obnoxious forms of misguided power.

But it was in the middle of the labyrinth when I realized that "I" was mad at God and that this was a much deeper "I" with a much deeper meaning. The truth was that I'd never really thought deeply of God. "God" was just another word that could not be trusted. A weapon in the mouth of the undeserved. Yet I knew I had faith. But what, precisely, did I have faith in? This is the question that carries me to India, to the narrow bustling streets of Dharamsala.

My friend, Thrinley, was raised as a Catholic and it was this tradition she left for Buddhism. But Buddhism has a way of lending itself to the observer. Tibetan Buddhism is loaded with iconography, incense and ritual. It is very Catholic-looking. It's also rife with deities, which can be readily described as saints, as well as long flowing robes and long elaborate chants. Over the years, I've shared bits and pieces of my story with Thrinley and I know that this need of mine to know that Jesus loves me is one of those bits that are hard for her to understand. She doesn't ever say this but I can hear it in her mind. And as she's one of the most understanding people I know, my assumption is that this naïve, child-like need is not something I can readily share with the world at-large. Yet it's the most critical piece of it all.

Survivors of ritual abuse are most of all disenfranchised in childhood from the simple God-given facts of life that circumscribe instinctual motherly and fatherly love. In general, as human beings we are biologically wired to protect our offspring. When parents choose to prove their dedication to the greed and artifice of deviant cults over dedication to their child, it is a perverse and unnatural act and the results are perverse and unnatural. A lot of people don't survive. They commit suicide, or the small acts of suicide inherent in alcoholism, drug-addiction, homicidal tendencies, and other means of self-destructive hatred for self and other.

The years of therapy with Brian took on an unnerving approach to, and withdrawal from, seeing my life and being inside my life for the first time. Most of all it was an exploration through the voices, feelings, thoughts and contradictions of my inner selves. From the young ones who carried inarticulate grief to the old wise ones who carried detailed instructions for Brian, it was a rollicking ride through consciousness. And an unfolding of inarticulate faith.

Much of my therapeutic process took to writing. Hundreds of pages poured out encompassing everything from desolation and hopelessness to detailed spiritual instructions. There was a Wise One who reported how Janet was doing and gave Brian instructions: *Janet is right when she says it is important for her to be happy. Happy is not the right word, however. She should stop at the word "be." She confuses it with "happy." "Happy" as we all know is external and consistently fleeting. "Being" is a birthright and only those who have had it attacked would confuse this most natural state with "happiness." Watch out for this tendency, Brian. You cannot overestimate in others that which is simple and natural in yourself. If the feeling of "being" is not there it is not even missed and as it begins to manifest itself it needs the most tender and active reinforcement. If there is one place in which you have occasionally faltered in working with Janet it is in underestimating the power and vulnerability of this transition. You are facilitating the greatest of gifts. But the self has to practice feeling itself over and over. It is filled with disorientation as well as immense joy. Like the beginning of a muscle it must flex and flex until it reaches a sort of critical mass of existence. Then suddenly it exists. It knows.*

The Wise One spoke to me, too: *DON'T FALTER, JANET! I have been with you for life and Brian has been with you for another life. WE MEAN SOMETHING. Okay, Brian, I need neither awe nor thanks. Both are detrimental to this process. None of us are separate and gratitude makes us so. Janet, I do need your acceptance and you must believe in my existence. I know this is very hard for you. There is a fierce and fragmented independence that is most impressive—please give it my respects—but it does keep me from you and this I do not appreciate. Okay, go clean your house.* (I did) *Now, that wasn't much fun, was it? All the surfacing selves pushing you all over the place. Remember what Brian said about things not being any different than they've always been? The only difference is that now you are recognizing the shifts. This, of course, adds another element of confusion because now you are in there along with everyone else and nobody is getting realized except for short bursts of energy that are quickly replaced or dismissed. YOU MUST NOT DISMISS YOUR SELVES.*

The Wise One watched over us and came through only in the writing. I could not articulate him. He guided my ability to understand what was happening to me, and why. He presented Brian and me with permission to have a more fully realized relationship in a way that was critical to overcoming the biggest obstacle in my therapy: the feeling of being re-traumatized. Memories surfaced in ways wordless and experiential, which meant deeper and deeper levels of terror and shame. And Brian was witness to it all. This was when the therapeutic process turned toxic. I was once again being watched. As a child used in medical experimentation and child pornography, being watched was where the terror and shame escalated unbearably. That it was Brian made no difference: I hated him. I was deep in the throes of the re-experiencing the trauma and Brian became one of those "nice" people who, underneath the niceness, enjoyed watching me suffer.

I remember the look on Brian's face when my rage and accusations would turn on him. Within the experience of my past I could not distinguish the present. A memory really is good for something: It gives context to time, to learning, to the integrity of a self who can differentiate between the causes and effects of life and of death. It recognizes the difference between those who are on our side and those who aren't. When the feelings inside of shame and rage rose up from the ashes of forgetting, they didn't know the difference between the people who harmed and the people who healed.

While going through the journey with Brian, I learned that I knew more about how to die than how to live. This became explicitly clear to me one October day when I got lost in the mountains. I'd gone on a hike, got tired after five miles, and told my hiking companions I'd meet them back at the car. But going back on a little-used trail is a lesson in unfamiliarity. The trail got confusing so I sat to wait for my friends to return. They, in turn, looped back a different way. It started to get dark and after a moment of striking fear I found a soft place close by and settled down to die. Hours later, after my friends got back to the car and didn't find me there, they returned with flashlights and loud voices. I heared their shouts as in a dream. I had shut down into some suspended state of hibernation where, even in rescue, I could feel neither fear nor relief. I was simply prepared to die.

I was stunned when my mountain escapade opened my eyes to this affinity for dying. Very clearly I could see that I was more afraid to live than to die. That life itself had become a near-death experience and I was more comfortable with waiting for death to happen than with fighting for my life. Some memories are lies but lead to the truth. I always knew I'd had electric shocks "three times a week for a year" to help heal the nerve damage in my arm. I was five years old and got taken out of school regularly. It was in England and I'd been going to some "school" or another for a long time. When I first tried to put the pieces together, I'd equated my scar with some satanic blood ritual. Later, with more complete understanding, came the awareness of polio experimentation on children. Cult-raised kids could be trained to forget. It made us valuable, and it made our parents money. Many kids were experimented on, surgically and with electric shocks. Electric shocks eliminate memory, self and soul. Electric shocks create near-death experiences.

In therapy, my beginning memories blended together: blood, sex, adults watching me in a state of fascinated excitement. My body stretching in agony in ways I didn't understand. Nobody helping. Eternity filling up my psyche with endless terror. Convulsions in which my shoulders tried to reach up and rescue my head from its disembodied predicament. Paralysis. I was over forty and re-entering the body of my childhood. My mind was another story. Its hold on defining and creating my reality was ferocious. My self, slowly starting to wake up to *being*, had to face this gauntlet of opposition. It was coming to consciousness in a body of pain and a long-established mind of distrust, denial and the determination to prevail no matter who the emerging self was. This was beyond complicated. Only from years later can I look back and see the struggle and the ways in which my entire life was invested in not knowing about my life. I had learned how to give in to death. Giving in to life was the real test.

The self is a small and tender thing that requires very little to take its own unique shape in the world. It needs, in fact, nothing. But when it's violated and exiled from the body, it has nowhere to grow. It was the eradication of my self that was the goal. Mind-control insured that I would not be able to remember the medical experimentation, child prostitution and pornography that made me of economic use. I was a beautiful little girl. I had a beautiful little self. Giving in to life meant giving in to a small helpless self suspended in a state of innocence and perfection.

I remember being in my thirties sitting on various buses in Seattle, looking at the diverse array of people around me and marveling at how perfectly comfortable they were with themselves, how at-home they were in their bodies. How easy it seemed "to be." I knew then that I was a stranger to such a feeling. I was "being" in the world but I was not "being" in my self. I was to discover there was a very big difference.

In my readings by and about the Dalai Lama he often addressed the issue of self-esteem in America. The topic mystified him. How could someone not have self-esteem? The Dalai Lama is a very smart man. He converses with top scientists from around the world about topics of space, time and mind. Yet he couldn't understand the lack of self-esteem that seemed to afflict so many Americans. In Tibetan culture, love of the child is a community event. Children are held, jostled, played with and loved by everybody within reach. Self-ness is celebrated. Buddhism, with its sophisticated understanding of the mind and its machinations, is also firmly rooted in being.

What I know, what I have learned, what I am feeling here in India is that being-ness is a profoundly simple feeling that eluded me most of my life. For all the gains that I might have made in one way or another, nothing comes close to this feeling. I share it with everyone around me—the beggars, the monks, the German tourists and the Indian merchants. I am one of them. I am being here. In India, right now I am just one in a billion but somehow I am more than I have ever felt. I am part of the human community and this is what it is to know I have lived.

I have no idea how to communicate any of this to Thrinley. She knows a lot about my history but she doesn't know how much I carry with me. We are on an adventure in India, having fun as well as forays into meditation and spiritual reflection. This overwhelming experience of *being* falls outside the realm we are sharing and there is no language that fits. I simply slap a silly grin on my face and let my happiness at being here speak for itself—for my self. Right now, Thrinley's teaching English to Darjee and I'm out on the patio having thoughts and feelings I cannot describe. The sun is shining all over the magnificent incongruity of this small universe and I'm impatient to be part of it, to go out on the town, to celebrate my simple, insignificant place in the human race.

Nineteen

It's four-thirty in the morning and I am sitting out on the roof wrapped up in layers of clothes and the big blanket from the bed. The stars are brilliant in the night sky. I hear the sound of one dog barking, which seems almost as quiet as the sound of one hand clapping. The Geshe will be up here soon for his morning prayers and circumambulation.

The mountains are pure and black against the black sky and sparkling stars. I am filled with inarticulate gratitude and grace. The secret silence of being. It is as though the heartbeat of the universe is pulsing us all into life, into relationship with life, into the only thing possible—love—for it all, ourselves included. I'm snuggled back in bed by the time our resident monk climbs the stairs. When I wake up again I am in that state of delicious relaxation that tells me I actually trust the bed to hold me up. I am sinking into being here just in time to think about leaving. And it doesn't feel good.

Yesterday, Norbu told us that we must plan ahead if we want to be back in Rajpur, as scheduled, for Christmas. So today we are scheduled to buy bus tickets for a December 22nd departure. That's Kenneth Rexroth's birthday, I remember. It's also the birthday of the English professor boyfriend I had who tried to choke me on a regular basis. There is no end to the ways in which "once a victim always a victim," plays out its sad, sick song. Signs of recovery always lead to shocking, often unbearable, recognition of complicity in our own abuse. It's no surprise that for the last couple of decades, for years at a time, I've explored the far reaches of celibacy with dutiful attention to detail.

I estimate that out of the 7,000 or so nights since my first collapse into consciousness, I've spent more than 6,800 of them alone. I've gotten used to it. I have, in fact, grown fond of my own body in my own bed. The feeling of curling up to sleep safely until morning is something I never take for granted. Sleeping safely with someone else, however, is a different story. But this morning reverie through my rocky romantic life is distraction from what I'm really worried about—leaving Dharamsala on December 22nd. But it's almost a whole week away, I tell myself; I will be ready to leave. But I know it's not true.

I don't want to leave Dharamsala and I don't want to confess this to Thrinley. She is my friend and this trip would not have happened without her. I feel loyalty both to her and to our shared journey. I had no idea that I would also be accompanying my self and that I would see my selves in such overwhelming abundance and that I would begin to find whatever it is I didn't know I was looking for. But today we'll get our next week's bus tickets back down the mountain and I'll pretend cheerfulness and anticipation at Christmas in Rajpur.

In the afternoon, after we've purchased our tickets, Norbu accompanies us down to Lower Dharamsala where Thrinley and I hope to find Walkmans for our English students. We're briskly in and out of several shops until we find our small headset tape recorders; Norbu tests them for quality, and then tests the merchants for sale price. When he's satisfied, we're quickly on our way to the bus stop and back up the hairpin highway. Norbu had better things to do today, I'm thinking, as he bids us a quick and gracious goodbye in the town square. He strides off to the other side of town where he'll walk down another hill for a mile or so to where he lives and works with his uncle, the Khenpo warrior.

For the first time, Dakpa is late. My pervasive insecurity suggests that perhaps he doesn't want to come because I'm a lousy teacher. But I put out his Walkman on the small table and arrange alongside the picture book of everyday life we are using as opportunities for talking. It's half-an-hour later when he arrives and I am very close to taking my sad and sorry self down to get Thrinley so we can go somewhere and get chocolate. But it is Dakpa who is really sorry. It turns out his friend is very sick and he had to take him to the hospital. He also proudly and excitedly invites me to his place for dinner. I'm astonished and very touched as I know how little he has in the way of resources.

Our lesson goes well. We work inside our little room because the breeze is too cold to work outside. Dakpa holds eye contact with me and is less dependent on his array of books. And he loves the Walkman. As usual, he reads me his story first thing; then we get to the mundane exchange of daily conversation. We have also added some reading from the newspaper. Then right in the middle of things, the door flies open and the precocious young girl from the neighborhood says cheekily, "Are you kissing?" And then dashes away. It happens so quickly that I don't think Dakpa understands, but I do.

I feel a rush of shame at this young girl's words. A young Tibetan monk meeting in close proximity behind closed doors with a Western woman has all kinds of implications. My own habitual response is always to the dangers of sexualized circumstances, no matter how irrational, so I've been particularly careful in meetings with Dakpa. His emotional vulnerability is achingly painful and I don't want him to experience any teasing or derision from others about our meetings. But he seems oblivious to her words and we carry on unperturbed. As he leaves he tells me he can't come tomorrow because of visiting his friend in the hospital but will meet me the following day at five o'clock at the Green Hotel and take me to his place for dinner.

I search out Thrinley and drag her out for dinner to talk about this turn of events about me and Dakpa kissing. I tell her how worried I am that this little girl is spreading the word to her uncle and the other monks in our guest house that I'm somehow having my dirty old woman way with dear orphaned Dakpa to whom I feel most protective and motherly. Why did she think that we wonder?

I go over all the times of my meetings with him and then I remember the other day when I shooed her away and told her we were "concentrating." "Concentrating" could sound like "kissing," we think, and wonder if there is any way to set things right, semantically speaking.

No, we decide. It's far too complicated.

In her book, *Child Exodus from Tibet*, Birgit van de Wijer reports that since 1980 close to 20,000 children left behind their families in Tibet and escaped through the Himalayas to Nepal and eventually to refugee settlements in India. Thousands of other children died, were captured by the Chinese, imprisoned and often tortured, or adopted into slavery in Nepal, while attempting escape. But their parents know that if their children stay in Tibet they will be educated and brainwashed into being more Chinese than Tibetan. Escape out of Tibet is the only way Tibetan culture, history and religion will survive. Parents send their children to India to save them and to save Tibet. Some children escape of their own accord. They all trek through months in the mountains, arriving in Nepal with hypothermia, snow blindness, frostbite so severe it often requires amputation. How many die en route is not known. But still they flee. In her book, van de Wijer quotes from Claude B. Levenson's book, *la Messagere du Tibet*: "All strive for the same goal, a dream which some call escape, and others freedom, which some cannot define at all, and which all are prepared to pursue to the last of their powers, even at the risk of their lives."

What is this thing called freedom? And when do we know we have it? Surely it goes beyond the freedom to acquire and own things, so celebrated in the west. That's not why these children are sent off into the cold, lonely and treacherous unknown. Something speaks to the human heart when the spirit is confined and names it "freedom." And it must be pursued. No matter what.

My first encounter with the depth of this pursuit came in the early 80s when I was researching a play for the Seattle Repertory

Theatre's school touring program. Dan Sullivan, the artistic director there at the time, commissioned me to write a play based on the experiences of the Vietnamese and Cambodian "boat people" who were risking their lives to get to freedom. He was perturbed by reports of racism in the schools towards the young Asian refugees. In my interviewing process I discovered the same shattering fact over and over: the young people whom I was interviewing were in this country alone. They had been put on boats by their parents who desperately wanted freedom for their children. Freedom came even before family. After several students started to cry in interviews when I asked them about their parents, I quickly realized that I'd better get more skilful because my questions were triggering terrible grief and loss.

Although many parents of these children were eventually able to join them—thanks to enlightened and compassionate government policies and determined civil organizations—these kids carried all the weight of war and abandonment as well as the label of foreigners in a new country. All for freedom. Getting free of whatever it is that binds us is a long, lonely and ultimately mysterious journey. The freedom to be, whoever it is we are, comes with its own karmic territory. Healing means to find out what we're healing from. That in itself is a valiant accomplishment. Then comes the rest of life.

Just recently I read how, as a result of stringent and unforgiving post-911 laws, many Asian refugees, rescued by the government in the 70s and 80s, are now being deported because of misdemeanors that were once simply misdemeanors. Now they are cause for deportation. Who's to say rescue was a good thing when freedom turns upon those it has liberated and sends them back into captivity.

It is a familiar feeling to me. I recognize healing and I also recognize all the traps set along the way. Sometimes I end up in them and nothing looks or feels any different from the old entrapment. But, somehow, grace offers up a moment of liberation and connection and just a glimpse can break the bonds that bind. Yet for these Asian and Tibetan children, and all the other children in the world being banished from home and heart and propelled to "freedom" because of wars—economic and otherwise—it is often simply the freedom to suffer even more.

This afternoon I'm meeting Dakpa at the Green Hotel and from there he'll take me to his place and cook me dinner. Thrinley's student, Darjee, is fixing her dinner this evening, too. We wonder if it is an accident or if unbeknownst to us they planned it to be on the same day. Darjee was a monk, too, until his new life got too compelling. He's a handsome chap and immensely charming, and like Dakpa, he is a refugee from Tibet. Darjee, too, traveled through the desperate measures of the Himalayas to escape, leaving behind family, friends, and in many ways, a future. I know Darjee has suffered, and is suffering but I'm suspicious of him because he is so charming. And I feel protective of Thrinley because he is so solicitous of her.

Dakpa, who is so introverted and serious, is much easier for me to trust. What kind of stupid sense does that make? I know exactly what kind of sense it makes to me. In my childhood, the face of charm was a trick. It was a sign that I was about to be used and abused. Salaciousness has a charming and delighted face. I haven't given an inch in this regard. Whenever I meet an overtly "nice" person I am immediately on guard, wondering just how dark is their shadow. This is a pretty sick response, particularly in a country where niceness is the norm—prescribed and expected. The irony is that I think most people think I am pretty nice myself. I hide behind it, and mostly I feel it. But the truth of me is much more about loneliness and isolation, fear and grief. The other side of my truth, where faith and joy reside, is just as hidden. Why don't we wear our deepest stories on our faces or hint at them in the way we walk or talk? It seems that we would be so much more at peace in this world if we were to first share our heartbreak with one another, instead of the way we have overcome it, or forgotten about it, or dismissed it.

Over and over it is taught: We have to know suffering to know the end of suffering. This is one of those Buddhist conundrums that always seem to defy understanding. But I know exactly what it has come to mean to me. Suffering—entering it, being it, and knowing it—has led me out the other side where joy and devout gratitude for life reside. These extremes are no longer extreme to me. They are partners in something over which I have no control. And I am learning that only by allowing both can I fully experience either.

I'm fussing to Thrinley about not having a gift to take to Dakpa when I see a pair of burgundy sweat pants for sale at a roadside stall. They are a perfect match for his robes, which seem too threadbare for the cold evenings and wintry days to come. He never confesses to being cold but he looks way too thin to be warm. I buy them and Thrinley and I part ways to go off to our respective dinners.

"We'll have stories to share later," she laughs.

"I hope we won't be throwing up together," I quip back, knowing I will eat everything I am offered and not at all sure what the results might be.

I get to the Green Hotel fifteen minutes early and Dakpa is already there waiting for me—a clutch of onions and leafy vegetables in his hand. His smile is enormous and I read in it great pride and excitement. He leads me up the road a few yards and then we turn on to a wide dusty trail that cuts along the face of the ridge across from our Loseling Guest House. It's an immediate shift in landscape. The hillside is green and terraced with a scattering of small houses. We pass chickens and cows along the way and, unlike up in the town where travelers pave the way, all signs here are of a more permanent domesticity. Stone and cement homes, whitewashed and tidy, stack up on the hillside, geraniums blooming and laundry flying.

We walk for about ten minutes until we get to a small square cement building. It's divided up into two living quarters and Dakpa and his friend, another recently "graduated" monk, live in one of them. Their space might be eight feet-by-eight feet, certainly no more. Dakpa's friend, who is still in the hospital, has a quasi-real bed up off the floor about a foot. Dakpa has a thin sleeping pad right on the cement floor. The down jacket I gave him is on one end. His pillow has a Daffy Duck pillow case and there's a large map of Tibet on the wall above. On the other wall alongside his bed is a large poster of a bright yellow sports car. There's also a photograph of Dakpa in his robes in the snow. He gestures for me to have a seat on his bed. There's no chair, or room for a chair. The space that's left is taken up by two low tables, one with a hot plate and another with cups, plates and cutlery.

His friend's side of the room is meticulously tidy. A pink satin comforter is folded up with origami precision on one end of his bed. A large poster of London Bridge lit up at night is on the wall. Books and a few items of clothing are stacked neatly under the bed. Everything is at right angles to everything else. Dakpa is not the orderly one in this small room and somehow I'm glad of it.

There is no running water so Dapka goes outside to the neighborhood spigot and rinses off the vegetables. There is nothing I can do about my fear of intestinal mayhem but give it a spiritual talking-to. "So you get sick? So what? It'll be worth it." Somehow it's always worth it, whatever it is. And Dakpa's earnest desire to please me with a meal is already balancing out whatever distress is in store. My mind goes into contingency planning. Thank God we have a bathroom back in our room. Here's hoping I get there in time.

There is nowhere to prepare the food so Dakpa squats down and chops vegetables on a small stone chopping block. He's tall but folds himself up neatly over his task. He's skillful with the hefty cleaver and soon radishes, tomatoes, onions, ginger, garlic and greens are in neat piles in a big bowl. He brings a big pot of water to boil and pours in a variety of sauces out of a variety of bottles, none of which are identifiable to me. The man knows how to cook. He doesn't measure anything and there is an aura of confidence about all his movements as the vegetables are added and the soup starts to boil away in a most reassuring fashion.

I'm just about to ask him to show me on the map where he was born and where his escape route was when the next stage of cooking begins. Flour and water and salt are brought into play and Tibetan dumplings are underway. Suddenly I'm at a performance. It's not the mixing that counts; it's the kneading and stretching of the dough, over and over and over, that becomes ritual in this small space.

"I cook at monastery," says Dakpa. He smiles, obviously enjoying his expertise and its impact on me. Never have I seen dough so skillfully and lovingly tossed and rolled and stretched into obedience. The final stage involves flattening and stretching between thumbs and fingers until the dough is almost translucent. Then it's torn carefully into pieces and tossed into the roiling soup. Simmering is not part of this recipe.

While the soup roils on, Dakpa attends to the map and shows me Amdo, where he was born. Amdo is the most northeastern province of Tibet and he is from the most northeastern part of Amdo. It looks to be at least a thousand miles away from Lhasa where his final trek to freedom started. The Dalai Lama was born in Amdo and it has a long history of other auspicious Buddhist teachers and a vast network of temples.

Soon he has his few photographs out to show me. He has none of his family but proudly shows me his friend's family as though it were his own. He's taken me into his life because he has told me his story. I think about how often the writers in my memoir classes start out so estranged from their own stories; about how our lives happen in sound-bite disposable increments and how hard we have to work to re-claim the trajectory of our lives as meaningful.

Yet it is our stories that give us meaning. Indigenous peoples, with their centuries of experience in the oral traditions of story-telling, have been so much more successful at cultural self-respect than those of us who have abandoned our stories. Individually, our stories lead us to self-respect, as well as respect from others. I watch it happen in classes all the time: knowing one another's stories breaks down barriers, builds trust, and develops real relationship. Knowing one another's ideas and opinions has no such value. I can feel Dakpa's story taking hold and I know I will never see a young Tibetan person the same way ever again, or think of Tibet and its genocide without knowing its personal underpinnings. I will never be able to think about the Dalai Lama separate from Tibet and Tibetans. His picture is here on the wall. His image is illegal in Tibet. His people can be executed for having his photograph. My mind roils like the soup.

It's delicious, of course. Dakpa serves it to me in a large white bowl and I eat every bite. It's easy to express appreciation without using words found in a dictionary so I mmmm and ahhhhh myself through the meal. Then it's over and Dakpa efficiently washes our dishes and gets ready to walk me home. My feet and lower legs are asleep from sitting cross-legged for so long. While he's outside with the spigot, I carefully move everything awake so I can stand up without falling over.

On the way up the path we pass a cow nuzzling through a dumpster. Two handsome dogs sit regally close by. I am reminded of my animal rights activist friend, Ben White, who said his entire life was changed when he realized he was being regarded by dolphins. These calmly poised dogs seem to be quite carefully regarding us, along with the entire contents of the universe.

In India, I cannot seem to have an experience that does not feel weighted with some new version of consciousness. Finally, I might be losing my controlled mind.

Mind control works—and it keeps working. The more effective it is, the less likely we will recognize it and the more we will suffer. I have strange marks at my temples where electricity entered my head, a large scar on my arm from experimental surgery, small five-year-old fingers and a thumb that won't bend. To me these physical details are insignificant. Freeing my self from the internal, invisible struggle "to be," however, is momentous and life-defining. It is a struggle I lose every day, and in losing it, I am winning because I recognize it as a real struggle. I am doing battle for my mind, the one that is beyond control. The one that inhabits my body, communes with nature, communicates with higher consciousness, and knows I am already whole. This mind accompanies me but I want to be *of* it. I want to experience a through-line of time in which I stay connected to being who I am and to those whom I love. I want to remember my self in time and know I have been alive.

Here I am, walking up the path with Dakpa. His young life has encompassed suffering beyond measure. My own appears easy and indulgent next to his. Yet he is more whole than I will ever be. He knows he can learn and be useful in the world. He knows he has suffered, and precisely how. He remembers the cold snow, his mother's death, his father's sad, imprisoned life. He knows he can *be*. He *is*, without knowing it. For just a moment, I think he's lucky, and isn't that a mind-fuck?

When I get back up to the room, Matt is on the doorstep. He wants to go out for dinner so we go to Jimmy's next door and I eat another meal. Matt is anxious to talk about writing. He wants to write a book, he says. So, just write, I tell him, and then keep writing. I am ruining my time with Dakpa by eating yet another dinner. But it feels a bit like Matt is losing his mind, too. So, what's an old girl to do?

TWENTY

The profound simplicity with which the Tibetan elders so lov- ingly engage in the world is also mirrored in the lives of some of the most profoundly complex Tibetan teachers. Today we are going to visit Tushita, a meditation and retreat center founded by one of the most beloved of Tibetan teachers, Lama Yeshe. He was born in Tibet in 1935, entered the Sera Monastic University in Lhasa when he was six and studied there until he was 24 when he was forced to flee to India during the Chinese invasion of his country. In 1967, he went to Nepal where he established Kopan Monastery, near Kath- mandu, in order to teach Buddhism to Westerners.

It was a pivotal moment in the history of Tibetan Buddhism's influence outside Tibet. In the 1960s and 70s in America, going to Nepal was part of the countercultural scramble away from the social restraints of the fearlessly mundane 1950s, and the grotesque ex- cesses of violence of the Vietnam War in the 60s. Hippies ran away and traveled. They met Tibetan monks who loved them, laughed with them, and taught them how to see "either, or and holy both." The word began to spread of these astonishing teachers of the mind and their robust humor and loving acceptance. And as the word spread, so did the Tibetan monks and their teachings. There are few countries in the world that do not now have active Tibetan Buddhist centers of spiritual activity. The Chinese invasion sent them out of isolation; the hippie invasion welcomed them with open arms, hearts and minds.

Matt started his round-the-world trip with two weeks of silent meditation at Tushita. It was also his first entry into Buddhism. His appreciation for his experience there is buoyant and he wants to show us the place. It is a few miles up the road, around the hill, through pine forests and steadily diminishing signs of human activity. It's a wonderful day to walk. Clear skies, warm sun, and very little haze. Matt says there's a short-cut trail up and over the hill but we stay to the dirt road as it winds its way above the small village of Dharamkot. We encounter the occasional cow and small band of monkeys but very few people and no careening buses or roadside capitalism.

Tushita is closed as a retreat center for the months of December and January but Matt knows the caretaker so with a little luck we'll be able to go inside the dining area, library and temple. It doesn't matter though because the buildings and grounds are lovely and welcoming. Through the trees is a long view past layers of hills down to the high plains of India. The shining white stupa seems to float above the ground, as does the elevated walkway around it. Flags fly in various weather-worn shades of color in the trees and across thresholds. It's like coming across a jeweled cottage in an enchanted forest.

Our luck is good and the doors are open. Inside, Matt goes off to visit with his friend and Thrinley and I are left to browse around. I go right to the small library. At home my shelves are stacked with Buddhist tomes, all of them different but with one thing in common: they all explore the inconceivable scope of the mind. The mind is a most curious and mellifluous event. For years, I experienced my own as fragmented and anguished as it sought a way through to survival. Yet in my Buddhist readings, long before my own mind disintegrated in despair, I read about a mind that was a most precious jewel in the heart of a most precious flower. It radiated a reality of pure love and infinite joy. My books on Buddhism sat on my shelves like sentinels when I could no longer open them but they were never closed to me. And when my mind returned to life, they were still there.

But the Tibetan books were not only about the mind and its un-ending metaphors. Teachers like Lama Yeshe were able to quickly relate to circumstances in the West. In the 60s and 70s there was war inside and outside the country. Between Vietnam and the Civil Rights movement, between the assassinations of John F. Kennedy, Martin Luther King Jr. and Robert F. Kennedy, between ducking nuclear missiles from the Cuban missile crisis and bullets at Kent State University, the world was inflamed.

We all craved something that made sense beyond the world we could see and hear because so much of it seemed insanely self-destructive of person, population and planet. These Buddhist teachers, escaping to the West from Chinese brutality and genocide, brought us ways to see and understand the brutality in our own world and in our own minds. It was a convergence zone of peace and possibility, all held in-waiting within the healing power of our minds. This is what Matt is drawn to in today's world and I am reminded that the important questions are ageless and it is only when we stop asking them that the world diminishes in beauty and in meaning.

The Buddhist books on the shelf in the Tushita library bring back a rush of recollection and along with it a rush of realization about how much I've learned and forgotten over and over again. No matter how hard I've tried to re-train my mind away from its deeply entrenched pattern of operating in the ruts of fear and isolation, I know it is a habit I will be breaking over and over for the rest of my life. Yet here, and now, pleasure and joy are palpable. That this place called Tushita is here, day in and day out, lending itself always to the realization of perfection in the present moment, available to us all, like the monk on the mountain, is another jewel in the mind of remembering.

When Matt finishes his visiting we go out to circumambulate the stupa. The resident dog appears and ambles out to join us. It's business as usual in the dog kingdom; they are always herding us humans in spiritual circles. I remember my dog, Buck, and his insistence on exploring beautiful places and his everlasting assumption that he was loved by everyone he met. This dog has the same demeanor. He calmly looks us over and then sits down at the entrance to the path around the stupa to watch as we walk in small, clockwise circles. Our circumambulations begin in silence and spontaneity;

I'm wondering when we will stop and which one of us will take the determining step away from the path. I feel too buoyant to be prayerful, too aware of the deep blue sky, the forest greens, this gem of a place, and my own being-ness, to bow down to eyes-lowered reverence. I want to skip and be silly.

It's Matt who stops first. "I feel faint," he says, stopping in his tracks. His face looks a little paler than usual and he is hunched over in what appears to be anguish. The dog comes right over to his side and looks at him. Matt sits down on the stone steps and it is as though the spiritual wind has been knocked out of him. He seems bereft and I wonder if this reminder of his two weeks in meditation is too much to reflect upon now that he's back being a young man on the move around the world. The dog is poised above him on the stone wall fixing Matt with a most direct gaze. We're all silent. Then we decide to head back, slowly. The dog walks with us along the trail to the edge of the property and watches as we take the short cut down many steps to the road. He's there still as we turn the corner.

We're all very quiet on the slow walk back to town but Matt decides he needs a Coke and some rice to help his stomach. Spiritual comfort food, I'm thinking, but don't say anything. I don't envy Matt's predicament in the world. Only in his mid-twenties, he's already burned out by the computer game programming job that consumed his days and nights for years. More than anything, this trip of his is a dive out of virtual reality into substance – spiritual and otherwise. We go to the rooftop restaurant where he indulges accordingly and Thrinley and I eat the best egg rolls ever rolled.

When we get back to our digs we discover we've been moved out of our rooms. Thrinley has way more equilibrium than I do about this turn of events. My heart drops like a lead balloon and it's my turn to become bereft. The monks have moved all our belongings to a cold dark room on the floor below. It has a view of a cement wall. They are nonplussed.

"The workers come," we are told.

This is an annual occurrence it turns out. A crew of Indian workers shows up to paint the place and if they aren't given free reign when they arrive it doesn't get done until next year.

"How long will it take to do our room?" I ask, trying very hard to keep the dismay out of my voice.

"Two days, maybe four," is the answer.

Reading between the words, I know it will definitely be longer.

I am pissed and also heartbroken. I love our little balcony room with its windows on three walls and blue and pink covers. There is no way I can muster any Buddhist equanimity about impermanence and attachment. I'm in mourning, and but for Thrinley's matter-of-fact acceptance I would have gone right out to look for a new penthouse suite. But we love these monks. Loyalty, too, has its place and I give in to this new scenario as though I, too, don't do attachment.

The truth is: attachment is precisely what I need to learn. I remember reading in some Buddhist tome that you can't overcome your ego unless it's a healthy ego. The same goes for attachment. You can't give it up unless you know what it is. I was in the midst of learning attachment to our lovely little room and my lesson got rudely interrupted. And Dakpa is due to arrive any minute.

I'm still a bit disconcerted by the accusation of "kissing" but have decided not to give it any attention. The immediate problem is that I can't work with Dakpa up on the roof because of the workers and we for sure can't work in this closed, dark little room we have just inherited. I go downstairs to wait for him and enlist the translating skills of Nawang to help me explain the situation to Dakpa. We can't really work in the lobby because it, too, is dark and there are people coming and going, including the boisterous and curious young girl.

It's Dakpa who suggests the rooftop café across the alley. But instead of going all the way up to the roof, we settle down with our books at a quiet, corner table inside on the second floor. We are stared at and both of us opt for even greater concentration than usual. Dakpa says "no" to food and so we drink chai and go through all the steps of our English lessons as though we are the only two people on the planet.

This town is famous for its auspicious resident His Holiness the Dalai Lama, and infamous for its many layers of exploitation by, and of, Westerners. We flock here out of some sort of spiritual desperation and become fodder for monks desperate for a way out of exile. Learning English is part of it, so is finding a financial sponsor. At least I'm not a sexy young thing, I'm thinking, as the opinions and judgments leak through the ethers towards us. I've seen young monks escorting young women around in a kind of prideful arrogance. I've seen mature Westerners in postures of pathetic subservience to men in robes. My inability to trust the motives of anybody has lots of fodder of its own. But I know I can trust this exchange with Dakpa because we are both orphans, abandoned by those who could have loved us into greater ease with ourselves and the world.

"He's so intense," Thrinley commented after a meeting one day.

And he is. Our meetings leave me awash in grief, not only about his heartbreak but also about the heartbreak and loss suffered over and over by the millions of people on the planet displaced by power and greed and racism and just plain thought-less-ness. We are so oblivious to one another. Waking up to what's really going on in the world is learning to live in a nightmare while all around us is paradise. Or perhaps it's learning to live in a paradise sustained by someone else's nightmare. It's confusing, to say the least. And Dakpa represents it all. I feel the weight of knowing his story, and most of all, of him knowing I know it. He's spoken it, written it down, and read it over and over. And in doing so it has become real. I am witnessing his life becoming real to him and it is familiar and unfaceable terrain. It is where we are bonded.

After he leaves, Thrinley and I can't face an early evening in our new room so we grab Matt and go to the movies, which turn out to be in a darkened room behind a café. The screen is wobbly and the image far from crisp. The film, which is really a TV special, is *Red Flag Over Tibet*, the history of how Tibet was "discovered" by the British and eventually invaded and destroyed by the Chinese. I can hardly breathe at the end. Whatever size of tragedy you like can be found right here in Dharamsala—on screen and off. Afterwards, Matt goes off to play and Thrinley and I go to Jimmy's for dessert. She has Chocolate Squishy Cake and I have Banana Toffee Pie.

When we get back to our room there is a note from Dakpa stuck to the door. Between us, we decipher the writing. His sick friend got sicker and Dakpa has to go and be with him so he can't go to the Norbulinka temple with us in the morning. We're supposed to meet up with Norbu at noon. I want Dakpa to be there. He has been starting to relax a bit. His life, so sheltered by suffering and hardship, seems to be taking on new horizons as he encounters two mothers on the loose, Matt's jovial adventurousness, and Norbu's Tibetan kinship. He was really looking forward to this outing. Yet another layer of upset gets plastered on my psyche.

And something else is happening, too. Buddhist that I am, I am longing to be here in Dharamsala for Christmas. The "wanting-it-means-you-can't-have-it-conundrum" is having its way with me; but the calling to stay on is growing louder and louder. I am not happy about leaving with Thrinley on December 22nd and I don't know how to tell her. I'm all restless about this as I climb into bed in our cold and miserable new room. Our upstairs room was cold but it was also open to the night sky and all the sounds of life I can't hear from here. I lie in bed without my earplugs and realize that I am in physical and psychic discomfort, surrounded on all sides by tragedy. But I do not miss my life at home. What the hell is that all about? I live in a place of extraordinary beauty. I have friends whom I love and a life rich in time for reflection, recreation and whatever else that appeals. Why does it feel that only here is there meaning? Has my history simply made me a junkie for suffering? Is the suffering world the only place I can call home?

I fall asleep into these questions, thinking of Dakpa and Norbu and their stories, and all the stories in the world that remind us who we are, and who we aren't.

Twenty-One

We have no way of reaching Norbu to tell him that Dakpa can't make it on our planned jaunt to Norbulinka today so Thrinley and I go out for apple-ginger pancakes at our favorite rooftop breakfast joint. I woke up way too early this morning after way too little sleep. I was up on the roof before sunrise but didn't last long because of the cold so I retreated to the dining room where it wasn't too early for the monks. I drank tea and wrote in my journal while they swept and polished and the Geshe did his brisk and prayerful circumambulations. Now I'm eating my favorite apple-ginger pancakes cooked to thin and crisp perfection. We read the *Hindustan Times* and soak up the sun and the light and the morning surroundings. Down below and across the way a man comes out of his house in what appear to be his pajamas and brushes his teeth for a long time.

In Dharamsala, the sun arrives with instant warmth. There is a dramatic difference between being in the shade and in the sun; it is unlike any experience I've had of early morning. I am reminded of all the stories I've read of mountain climbers in the Himalayas and realize I am sharing an extremely modest version of what it is that they, as well as the intrepid Tibetan refugees, experience. Light and dark as signs of life and death—here it is the most literal of metaphors.

We wile away the morning and at noon go back to the Loseling to meet up with Matt, Norbu, and Tsering for our planned outing. Norbu is quick to pass judgment about Dakpa's absence. We can't go without him, he pronounces. We'll go to the Norbulinka another day. I am so happy to hear this that I hardly feel my disappointment about not going on an outing. But this, too, is short-lived.

"Well, what should we do?" asks Matt. "After all, we're all here."

It is decided we'll do a field-trip for lunch in Lower Dharamsala. Our destination is Andy's Midtown Restaurant which is as Indian as it gets, despite Andy, whoever he might be. The place is up a flight of stairs and packed with Indian families. Our tablecloth is plaid and our meal is extraordinary. Each of us gets a plate with five or six entrees on it, all of them ensconced in distinct and delectable sauces of their own. Then come side dishes and several platters of different types of bread for us to share. We laugh a lot and I notice Norbu relaxing and enjoying himself in lively discussion with Matt. Still, I don't think Norbu knows quite what to make of Thrinley and me. He understands Matt, the young traveler, but precisely what we're doing here is, I think, a bit of a mystery to him. He has yet to be spontaneously engaged with me in conversation.

After lunch we go to the Museum Kangra to see miniature paintings, pottery, tapestry and folk-artifacts dating back to the fifth century. The art is nearly all within reach and we are the only visitors in this place. It's priceless stuff we are looking at in this very modest and meandering museum with its one guard at the front door. The small exquisite details in the work reflect the ways in which nature, love and spiritual life were celebrated as intricate and precious.

When we get back outside I look up to see the Dalai Lama's temple in miniature out on the end of the high ridge of McLeod Ganj, itself dwarfed by the looming and snow-clad Dhauladhar Mountains. I can't leave this place and I still haven't told Thrinley.

What is this thing called yearning? It's not a thought, or desire, or wanting. It happens inside my body, as though instinct in the cells. It feels almost magnetic in its nature, drawing me towards something for reasons that are as elusive as the feeling itself. I am yearning to stay here and I can't articulate why, to myself or anyone else. I also want to be a good friend, and responsible to this journey Thrinley and I are on together.

One feeling is very familiar: My yearning to be here is not something I *want*. I *want* to be a good friend and responsible. I can want these things because they are a response to someone else's want. But actually *wanting* to stay longer is too wrapped up in the deeply absorbed belief that wanting means not getting. It is an equation that has ruled my life—from men I've loved to education I've wanted— the wanting itself is sabotaged as it happens, so is whatever it is I want to want. The big exception to this rule is in the realm of spirit and faith. When what is wanted is of spiritual significance, yearning takes over and makes it happen. I have experienced this over and over. It is as though the protectors who have been with me throughout my life enter me and turn want into yearning. They make possible what is impossible. They keep me on the healing path.

After the first year and a half of working with Brian and running away from home until I could run no longer, a great yearning for silence took over. As the language of my life fractured into its million pieces I knew I had to be quiet. I also had to support myself. Suddenly there was the job in the paper calling for someone to cook at a year-long silent Buddhist retreat. Within weeks I had sublet my half of the house, packed up Ethyl, the old Volvo, and moved to Cloud Mountain where Gen Lamrimpa and Tibetan Buddhism took me under their spiritual wing.

People, places and predicaments showed up in my life in ways that were entirely unexpected. They led me to safety, to solace and always to the next stage in my healing. But they were never conscious choices. A conscious choice meant "to want" and to want meant not to have. This is a conundrum truly understood by only those who have had their selfness shattered and fragmented and sent into hiding. It took years of therapy with Brian before all the truths of my paralysis became apparent. The ways in which I was experimented with through electric shocks, sensory deprivation and isolation, mind control, sexual abuse, the separation from the natural bonds of parental nurturing, all took a toll in different ways.

There is another book to write about the organized and systematic ways in which the human mind and body have been experimented with by everyone from government-sponsored scientists to sex slave traders. There are a lot of us survivors out there, coping with life and our lives the best we can. Having neither the vocabulary nor the stamina to tell our stories, we keep ourselves secret out of fear, helplessness and shame. Always on the chaotic and creative path, struggling to circumvent the destruction of our wills, our souls, our very selves. Looking back and recognizing the ways in which this convoluted and unconscious way of living took over my life is a lesson in gratitude and grief, mind-over-matter, and miracles.

To write about my life I must write about miracles. They have been there at every turn, leading me through a life blessed with a faith I could rarely feel. Faith. I give her a name. She found meaning in everything and tried to lead us there. Sometimes she succeeded and I was suffused with a reverence beyond language, suspended moments in which order and grace glowed through the world like a breeze through the body. Faith. She led me to poetry and prayer, to necessary strangers and essential friends, to teachers and students, to trees and the sea, to soccer and the stage, and to Brian. And she also led me to Cyrus, my young friend who died far too soon.

In 1988, after my time cooking and retreating at Cloud Mountain, I moved back to Seattle where my first job was writing a rape-prevention play for Alternatives To Fear, a local non-profit that taught young women how to say "no" as well as how to put up a good fight if they got assaulted. One day, at the end of this project, and at the end of my income, I was in the Alternatives To Fear office when a friend there handed me a tiny two-line classified advertisement. A writer/editor was needed for a seafood catalog. I sent an irreverent two-sentence letter of interest stating that I knew very little about seafood but I loved to eat it. I included a few articles I'd written—including pieces on soccer that I'd had published in *Sports Illustrated* and the *Seattle Weekly*—and got myself an interview. John, the publisher of the seafood magazine, turned out to be a man who loved the written word even more than he loved fishing in Alaska. He hired me. It was a life-changing moment. To this day, he, Martha, and their daughter, Zoe, are part of my extended family of friends. And when I met them, I met Cyrus. He came into the office one day with his sister, Zoe. He was frail looking, fair with freckles, and shy. He had an almost translucent appearance that, unbeknownst to me, was the face of his illness.

We did a few things together, Zoe and Cyrus and me. My job entailed some research so one day we went to the Seattle Science Center. Cyrus, who was perhaps eleven at that time, was courtly towards me and protective towards his sister. He had an ageless quality emanating from a direct and compassionate gaze that is less rare among children than it is among adults. We didn't know each other well but there was spiritual camaraderie, an affinity that I knew instantly.

It was several months later when I found out that Cyrus was recovering from brain surgery, that he had a tumor removed and that his prognosis was still indefinite.

In December, Cyrus went to the hospital for tests. His surgery and all his treatment had not stopped the malignancy. It was growing again and there was little they could do but experimental things that meant hospitalizations, which he hated. It was the beginning of the last six months of his life.

By that time, I was two years into therapy with Brian and just over a year into uncovering the dark history of my life. I was bone-frightened and the world as I had known it no longer existed. Everything I did felt as though I was doing it for the first time. A new part of me was "out" and she knew nothing about the things we already knew or could do. She was out in another truth, hand in hand with fear and shame. How could she possibly have the right to befriend Cyrus? The surfacing memories were destroying all the integrity of my existence as a "good" person. As all the bad was surfacing; all the good was suspect. And all my spiritual yearnings became lies.

I agonized over this in therapy with Brian. Every visit to Cyrus was wrenched with fear. It was a blueprint of my pathology: I did not deserve to be a good person; any manifestation of my spiritual faith was a lie; I was a lie. And here I was, being called to connect spiritually with this young man as he faced his death.

Over New Year's I went to a meditation retreat at Cloud Mountain. Alan Wallace had come up from Stanford to lead it. It was my first visit back to Cloud Mountain since my year-long cooking experience, and as a guest this time, I was free to sink into the luxury of silence and structure. Three days of quiet in the country to meditate, reflect, and to eat somebody else's cooking. Cyrus was everywhere. In the sky and forests he would no longer know, in the meals he would no longer eat, in the language he would no longer speak. Everything he would lose as he lost his life was precious around me.

I talked to Alan about him. "What should I do?" I asked. "I know he will die yet I must not interfere with hope. His family is rooted in it; it's all they have."

Alan looked at me for a long moment. "This is between you and Cyrus," he said. "Do what you have to."

Cyrus and I had a spiritual connection to honor, and hope, that essential life-force of the living, was not on the agenda. We were to help each other somehow, and only we knew how.

An entry in a journal from 1978 reads simply: *Dream. How survivors should teach. "I'm dying," is the underlying knowledge from which everything must be taught.*

I remember how startled I was upon waking. Dreams of death and dying had filled my nights and my journals for years, but this one was different. There was no fear or horror, none of the personal attack of a nightmare; it was simply a mandate, a voice of authority in my sleep. There was resounding autonomy to it, as though it was lecturing to me urgently and purposefully. I woke to a voiceless authority inside that said, "Do something. Help Cyrus." And then the rising demons, "You don't have the right to help Cyrus. Help Cyrus and you will die."

Being with Cyrus was an invitation to spiritual recovery. And it was reached only through terror. Inside me, the battle that I was in to lay claim to the good in me raged unrelenting, escalating with every decision to be of service, to help. I could only believe the lies: The good has been taken out. I am filled with bad. It is good to be bad. God has gone. I am special. I am perfectly bad. That intrinsic sense of self, the palpable reassurance that what is good in me truly does exist is missing in the survivor of systematic abuse. It is gone, and if it is looked for, you will die.

Cyrus became an epiphany. He was the reason I got the job, the reason I was facing my deepest fears, the reason I was being challenged into recovery. My newly defined internal management system, painstakingly constructed with Brian's help, could see how the opposites were at war, how twisted my thinking was and how much there was to learn. So I began to actively do the opposite of what I felt. When the nihilistic voices inside said, "Don't call and ask about Cyrus," I did. When they tried to sabotage me from sending a present up to his hospital room, on the third try, I did. When they tried to trick me into keeping a respectful distance, I barged in uninvited and determined. And there was never a moment when I was not afraid.

Cyrus's family was private with their ordeal. The immensity of their tragedy was inconceivable; what could an outsider do? Yet I was compelled to be spiritually present, to witness the spirit of love within Cyrus and to allow my own spirit of love—fearful, unacknowledged and banned—to begin to breathe.

I was in Long Beach, California, the day he died. Not knowing what to do, I drove out to Joshua Tree National Park, about 150 miles east of Los Angeles. It was a hot, smoggy day and I remember how the light brightened as I drove through the curtain of smog between two mountains and into clear desert air. Because it was summer, Joshua Tree was pretty much empty of visitors. I parked my car and went climbing into the immense red boulders. Somewhere I sat looking out over a wide desert distance. Two ravens circled above my head and landed on a nearby boulder. Then I went to another area and climbed again; the two ravens went with me. I didn't know how to pray then; I just talked silently and out loud to my friend Cyrus. I couldn't get to grief that day but the presence of the divine was everywhere—in the brilliance of the air, the silence, the sound of ravens' wings as my two companions kept close. I took a photo of them and when I got it developed there was a streaming rainbow of light coming down out of the sky and across the red boulders upon which they perched. It's a photograph that accompanies me as I write.

Cyrus, Cloud Mountain, Gen Lamrimpa, Saint David's, Dharamsala, His Holiness the Dalai Lama, they are all miraculous accidents in a life never lived on purpose but in some profoundly mysterious way firmly rooted in faith. This trip is unfolding my faith and there's not a damn thing I can do about it.

Going back up the mountain from our shopping jaunt to Lower Dharamsala, Norbu lets us take a van—along with eight other people. Thirteen of us are squeezed into an eight-passenger vehicle. The driver looks to be thirteen years old; his driving is actually sedate. There's even time to read a roadside sign: "Life is short. Accidents make it shorter."

When we get out in the little town square of McLeod, Thrinley goes off to teach Darje English; Matt goes to find his friends; Norbu and I have chai and talk. I tell him about my time at Cloud Mountain, about Gen Lamrimpa and the year-long Tibetan Buddhist retreat. "Gen Lamrimpa was in retreat for seventeen years in a hut somewhere near here," I say to him. "I would like to see him." And it is as if magic has spilled out of my unsuspecting mouth. Norbu regards me with a sudden and intense interest. "Yes," he says. "You must. I think I know of him." He writes down a name in English, Jamphel, and repeats the writing in Tibetan. "Very well known," he says. "Very special person." And his eyes light up with respect and reverence.

Gen Lamrimpa is an honorary title and I never took the time to remember his "real" name, so this could certainly be it. My odd reluctance to search out this man who had such a profound impact on me so long ago dissipates in the face of Norbu's authoritative enthusiasm. I ask him if he'll take me there and he says "yes" as though it is his divine duty. It's that old wanting conundrum: I wanted to see Gen Lamrimpa but to want led to the quicksand of not having; so when Norbu quickly started wanting for me I was free to want because he wanted first. I see this cascading series of wanting moments as absurd and idiotic. It's becoming a tiresome view of inexplicable and unpardonable paralysis. How can I still be so vulnerable to such wrong-thinking after so many years of work to get over it all?

By the time Norbu heads home we have made a date to go up the mountain to find Gen Lamrimpa. Very soon I must tell Thrinley that I have decided to stay on a bit longer simply because I want to. And it doesn't get any more complicated that that.

TWENTY-TWO

Today I am going to church. I told Thrinley and I also told her I've decided to stay in Dharamsala until after Christmas. I didn't ask her if it was okay until after I told her. I didn't even say I *wanted* to stay on; I said I was going to. I know there are sensitive ways to say things about changing plans and perhaps it being a disappointment to her and leaving room for discussion and all kinds of other skilful means but they all got lost in the fear I felt. If she'd hesitated in agreeing, I would have capitulated in a heartbeat. And I didn't want to. So I didn't leave room for any discussion until after I said I was staying. I suspect this is a useless exercise in mental masturbation for any normal person but for me it was a whopping gigantic milestone of immense significance.

Thrinley, of course, was nonplussed. She might have been a bit surprised but she didn't show it. We talked about the logistics and how she can't stay on with me because she really does need to get to Rajpur to participate in the birthday preparations for Sakya Trizin. And Norbu will be going with her so all will be safe and smooth.

All this resulted in a kind of giddiness and I am feeling it this morning, even when the cold reaches my bones as the first feeling of a hovering winter becomes evident. What if I get snowed in here? What if I can't get to Delhi in time for the flight home? What if I am never heard from ever again? There is no shortage of "what ifs" to contemplate but they don't dampen my state of euphoria about staying on. All I can hope for is that we get to move back to our room upstairs before Thrinley leaves and I am on my own. Otherwise I might have to sleep with Matt.

It's quiet in town when I set out for Saint John's in the Wilderness, which is about a mile down the treacherous road to Lower Dharamsala. But because I'm walking this time, I finally get to pay attention to the scenery. It's a serene, gently treed hillside. There are no buildings along the way and very little traffic at this hour. I've given myself plenty of time to get there before the service starts so I don't have to walk quickly or even think quickly. There are no beggars to face or merchants to disappoint. Inside and out, it's as quiet and alone as I've been since arriving in India. But suddenly I'm joined by a dog.

He arrives out of nowhere and takes up the walk with me as though he is mine. Right alongside, he trots. Like a guide dog, I'm thinking, as we exchange pleasantries—he with his tail wag, me with my surprised greeting and gladness. He's quite handsome, with a healthy light brown coat and a jaunty, focused step. My own step gets a bit jauntier and I express my appreciation to him as we go. I was very aware of being all alone on this walk, and suddenly I'm not. We walk the mile together as though he'd taken me to obedience classes and I think about my old Lab, Buck, and his unconditional love, loyalty, and ability to eat an entire pie without taking a breath. I wonder if this is him, reincarnated within walking distance of the Dalai Lama's pantry.

Saint John's in the Wilderness appears through the forest and it really does feel like it's in wilderness, even though we are but a mile from town. The delicate fir trees have been left to grow freely and the burial mounds bring a gentle rolling green to life. The old stone presence of this Anglican Church is both formal and friendly. It looks as though it belongs here and I am reminded of Saint David's Cathedral in Wales and its humble location in a small valley surrounded by small hills. The cathedral doesn't loom over the landscape in some sort of omnipotent statement of Christian power and might. It settles into place and is discovered like a hidden treasure. Saint John's feels the same way. It blends into its environment—an array of subtle greens and grays, stones and trees. Christianity was once like this—nature and human nature in partnership. "Not even stewardship," a Celtic Christian theologian once said at a workshop I attended. "It was partnership."

He went on to speak of the ways in which early Christianity honored nature and original blessing, not original sin. How women were part of its very fabric and celebration of life at its core. It all changed in Nicea, when it was decided that Christianity would be based in Rome, where power and might and maleness were already culturally, historically and architecturally in place. We say the Nicean Creed every Sunday at Saint David's on the island where I live. But I am always thankful to that workshop in which I recognized myself as a Celtic rather than a Roman Christian. Dominion over nature always seemed like such a misguided principle. "Nature bats last," is a bumper sticker statement I saw somewhere.

The British constructed Saint John's in the Wilderness in 1852 and it was one of the few structures in the area that survived the 1905 earthquake. The only thing damaged was the bell, which fell ringing to the ground. Otherwise the church was left intact. Lord Elgin, Viceroy and Governor-General of India in 1862, is buried here.

As soon as we turn down the path to the church my four-legged companion bolts off to explore. It's as though he knew we were coming here all along and now he's free to roam while I do whatever it is I do inside the place. As so much of what is happening to me on this trip comes with built-in significance, his behavior hardly seems unusual. I enter a church dense with silence, and a Morning Prayer service underway. I take a seat in a pew at the back and notice the colorful dahlias decorating the front of the church. There are wooden beams heavy overhead supporting a high curved ceiling; and stained glass windows illuminating the youthful and muscular innocence of Jesus as he is baptized by John; and a beautiful Mary, her arm flung across her forehead in a gesture of apprehension and supplication, her eyes alert and knowing.

I think of the enormous task it must have been to get these windows here and I am impressed, until the weight of colonialism and its exploits raises its reliable head. This conflict has not been lost on me throughout this journey but I have been unable to find criticism at every turn about the colonial influence, maybe because it lends itself so much to my personal history. I was born into an odd confluence of Welsh-ness and English-ness and even though historically the Welsh have hated the English with great passion—some perhaps still do—the "Englishness" of Great Britain leaked across the borders into Scotland, Ireland and Wales, just as it did here in India. I am of that particular culture in which a kind of elegance was perpetrated on places and people that weren't interested in acquiring it. Yet it remains elegant just the same. I remember the curved colonial balcony in the hotel in Majnu-ka-Tilla and how it thrilled me in such an odd way.

There is only one other white person in the church, a young man sitting in the pews across the aisle from me. He appears comfortable and familiar with the congregation and I wonder if he's a regular here. Everyone else is Indian, including the minister who is lighting the candles on the altar. He's a small man wearing white robes and a long red drape across his shoulders. When he turns to us his face radiates peace and tremendous kindness. As he surveys our gathering of perhaps forty people, his eye rests momentarily on me. He says the word, "Welcome." Then he speaks in Hindi, with warmth and gentleness in his voice and a kind of humble merriment in his being. A regal Indian woman strides up to do readings from the Bible. Her voice is as commanding as her presence and her authority an expression of real righteousness. There is no doubt in this woman, and no doubting her, either. Her husband and two daughters beam at her proudly.

When the minister regains the pulpit, he regards me once again. Then he begins in halting and fractured English, "I am the caretaker here. I am not the priest. I am here to love God with you all and to welcome you to here." I feel my presence as an intrusion and a burden. I had hoped to be invisible, to blend in with the crowd, but my foreignness is being graciously accommodated—even as it excludes others—and there is not a thing I can do about it.

He doesn't give a formal sermon, but instead talks to us about Christmas carols and their history. And in-between is singing, sometimes in Hindi, sometimes in English. I find out that *Silent Night* was written as a poem one Christmas Eve by a young Austrian priest who then asked his friend to write a guitar accompaniment for the next day's service. He tells us about the *Fantasia on Christmas*

Carols written by Ralph Vaughan Williams, an English man who was Charles Darwin's nephew. I know about Vaughan Williams because of his transcendent *Fantasia on a Theme of Thomas Tallis* and his voluntary enlistment into the medical corps in World War I. His second wife, poet Ursula Wood, described him as an atheist who eventually "drifted into cheerful agnosticism." I had no idea he was related to Charles Darwin, who was himself a religious scholar and a man who had faith in both evolution and spirit. Then we sing *Amazing Grace*, written by John Newton who was the captain of a British slave ship before he became an abolitionist and a man of the cloth. It was Newton who inspired the intrepid William Wilberforce in his twenty-year struggle to get the British Parliament to ban slavery, which they did in 1807. I'd always wondered about the words in *Amazing Grace*: "That saved a wretch like me." I had no idea the song originated in Britain and that its author was a man spiritually devastated by his role in the slave trade. Finally, our caretaker-minister shares with us a story about a hymn written by a Korean man who, out of great hardship, wrote a beloved carol, the name of which I do not understand. It is after this story that his tears well up. The whirl of spiritual contradiction, multi-racial devotion, human despair and God's grace all presented to us from the heart of this humble man. By the time we sing *Morning Has Broken*, I, too, am in tears.

At the end of the service, our minister who is not a minister comes up to me with a big welcoming smile and a grasp of my hands. I can feel his warmth, physically and otherwise.

"You come back tomorrow," he says. "We practice for Christmas."

But tomorrow I am going up the mountain with Norbu to search for Gen Lamrimpa and I have no idea when we'll be back. I also have no idea what it means to practice for Christmas; but I do know I'd like to be there.

"I'll try," I say, and thank him for the lovely service.

"I'm just the caretaker," he says. "For years I care for the church."

His love of this place is as palpable as the warmth of his grasp.

When I get outside, my four-legged companion is sitting on the top of a stone wall. He comes over as soon as I notice him and then trots alongside as I explore the graves, many of them marked with Celtic crosses with their sacred circles incorporated into the stark right angles. The monument to Lord Elgin says he was sixty-two years and four months when he died. It was installed by his wife, Mary Louisa, and recounts her husband's history as Governor of Jamaica, Governor General of Canada, and High Commissioner and Ambassador to China amongst other "high offices."

I have just experienced the gift of Christian love offered by an Indian man in an Anglican church on the outskirts of a town that is home to His Holiness the Dalai Lama and the Tibetan government-in-exile. And the biggest monument here is to a British upper-class colonialist who loved Dharamsala and wanted to be buried here. I am in a Thin Place and it is making me dizzy with its mysticism, its incorrigibly incorrect and correct politics, and its absurdity. The only thing that makes any sense is the dog.

It doesn't take long before all the parishioners have left and I'm left alone with this swirling craziness and perhaps for a moment I get it. In a Thin Place the veil between worlds loses its density. The church needed the Brits; the caretaker needed the church; the Dalai Lama needed Dharamsala; the wife needed Lord Elgin—although I'm not sure India did and I know Jamaica didn't. The moment of Christianity needs Buddhism to appreciate the irony. The moment of Buddhism needs Christianity to appreciate the mysticism. It's all Buddhist Emptiness. And emptiness is just another word for inextricable Celtic interconnectedness. None of it has inherent meaning without the "other." Except maybe the dog and we all know "dog" is God spelled backwards. It doesn't get any thinner than this. I feel as though I'm in this graveyard with Jesus and Buddha and they are both laughing out loud. Maybe God is, too.

Why are we here, after all: to dissect meaning or to celebrate it? If I try to dissect what it all means—from the holocaust of my childhood to the definitions of Buddhism and Christianity—all I am left with is the chill and disconnection of intellectual analysis. But if I celebrate it—from the personal grief and loss to the complexity of religious contradictions—I am enlivened with meaning. It tells me I exist. It reaches into me with its mystery and mirth. It sets me on the path without a map and sends me on the way. The Celts had small boats with sails and no rudders. They trusted in spirit to fill the sails with meaning and direction. And in some way, as powerless as I've felt throughout my life, it is spirit that has filled my sails and sent me here and there and wherever it was that would help me heal. And spirit sent me to Buddhism. And the Dalai Lama sent me to Christianity. If becoming whole means becoming stuffed with contradiction, who am I to argue? Maybe India needed Lord Elgin after all. He certainly needed India. After all, he wanted to be buried here.

It has been a momentous morning at St. John's in the Wilderness and I have no idea how I will speak of it. Saint John the Baptist is himself described by scholars as the boundary between the Old Testament and the New. He was of the Thin Place. He also announced himself as a "voice in the wilderness" and preached as well to the wilderness in the lives of the people. He went into the wilderness to fast and to pray. He ate locusts and dressed in rough camel hair robes. He was mistaken for the Savior yet never wavered from his role as humble servant. He baptized Jesus while feeling as if he had no right to do so. And Jesus loved him and respected him. Then John was betrayed and beheaded. There is no end to wilderness, nor is there an end to the voice in the wilderness.

It's after noon when Dog and I set off back to town. When we reach the spot from which he first appeared he disappears back into his secular life. And I do the same. I go off to find Thrinley, hoping she hasn't already gone off to lunch. I want to tell her that I want to eat Tibetan momos and drink Indian tea; and I want to be a Christian even if I am a Buddhist.

TWENTY-THREE

It is three-thirty in the morning when Thrinley's voice, harsh and urgent, wakes me from a deep sleep. As I surface I realize that I was having an intensely sexual dream and the last thing I want to do is wake-up. But Thrinley is uttering the magic word, "Fire." I shake myself away from my erotically aroused body and its secret dream and try to pay attention to whatever it is that's burning. Just remember, I'm thinking as I scramble into my shoes and start contemplating my exit strategy. Just remember the sex. But first I have to remember my earplugs; they are still in my ears. This explains why Thrinley's fire narrative sounds as though it is coming through a pillow.

It all blurs together in seconds of awareness. I don't have to get dressed because I am dressed. Sleeping in our clothes, or at least in a version of our clothes, has become routine. I yank out the earplugs.

"Somebody knocked on the door and yelled at us to get out because there's a fire across the street," says Thrinley.

She's already got her canvas pack stuffed with whatever she wants to save. I'm still evaluating. I whip the small flat pouch with my plane tickets, passport and pink green card from under the pillow and put it around my neck and under my clothes. The camera, some warm socks, my current mystery, the book Matt lent me, my note-book, all get tossed into the pack along with whatever fleece stuff I can find. I also rescue a small bag of gifts for friends back home. Dashing into the bathroom, I grab my contacts and toothbrush. All in about 45 seconds and all through the haze of sex.

The dream, which was so gripping, has not let me go. Fire and sex all roiling together in a life and death panic of departure. And all I want to do is climb back into bed. I find myself actually aggravated at Thrinley for waking me up. Hell, she might even be saving my life. But the only sex life I have these days happens in my sleep and this dream was worth a little smoke inhalation. I don't tell her about it though. It packs too much power and I know I want to think about it for awhile before it gets claimed by language.

As we scramble out of our room, the Danish woman down the hall calls to us in a panic. She is terrified and doesn't have a flash-light. When we reach her, she grabs my arm fiercely. She's seen the fire out of the window of her room and says it's enormous, lighting up the sky and getting brighter every second. We pick up our pace and make a slow dash down the stairs. When we get out to the al-ley we come up against a wave of people coming towards us, all of them carrying things—boxes, big plastic bags, arms full of clothes and furniture. Just as we are evacuating, the rest of the community is arriving for safety and safekeeping. I barely register the irony of this situation; my fear is riding high and my rational mind is miss-ing in action.

"They're crazy," I think. And am immediately awash in my lack of faith and fortitude. Sex is easier to think about. As we navigate our small alley and arrive out on to the street, I see the bucket bri-gade in action. The fire, it turns out, is yet one more block over but the buckets of water are navigating up our street and through yet another alley before they reach the inferno. We follow the crowd to the spectacle. It's a nightmare. The flames are vicious in the night sky; the sound roars around us. I have an image of some large stor-age tanks containing something inflammable less than twenty yards away and my survival instinct shifts into high gear.

"We're out of here," I mutter to Thrinley and our newly acquired Danish friend. We turn and head towards the home of the Dalai Lama. After our first hundred-yard dash towards safety it becomes a stroll. I pretend there is nothing, anywhere, for anybody to worry about. We engage in civil conversation. Our new Danish friend says she is writing a book and has been doing so for about ten years. It is about spirituality.

Slowly, the night sky takes over. Away from the fire it's dark and nothing competes with the stars and their brilliance. It's peaceful, too, as though nothing unusual is happening, as if there is no fire raging just a half-mile away. I'm aware that we are walking away from being useful—although I know there is little we can do to help and our Danish friend needs our reassuring presence.

At the Dalai Lama's temple we find a balcony corner that looks out towards the fire in one direction, and down into the valley in another. There's not much to do but watch the fire's glow in the distance and wait. I am still embroiled in the dream of sex with the man whom I was absolutely sure I would forget in India.

It was five years ago when he landed on my doorstep one winter's day looking for his daughter. Attraction breached the short distance between us, a moment of recognition that went far beyond control. I wanted to ask him to come in and make love. Instead I was cold and inhospitable. "Your daughter went to the beach. She'll be back later." I didn't invite him in.

And so began five years of thwarted love, misguided intimacy, flagrant hostility and an entire human cell-realm of fear. The only place anything worked was in my dreams. He was much younger than I, handsome as sin and steeped in the physical. He also had a fine mind, wrote haiku and had a love of language that was greater and more informed than mine. Divorced for many years, he had moved back to the area to make amends with his kids. This is when our paths first crossed; at least, that's what I thought. But my dreams knew otherwise.

I began to have dreams of youthful adolescence in which he and I ran and played in fields in England and Wales. We fell down with fumbling kisses and delicious heart-pounding yearning that neither of us knew what to do with. All of teenage romance unfolded in those dreams and me along with them. They were literal dreams about the two of us in some earlier innocent time.

In waking time, things were different. For four years, intimacy grew between us and we grew barriers to intimacy. Only the dreams prevailed. In my dreams, we grew up, until the romance between us became sex, sex so driven and complete that I would wake utterly aroused, and sometimes rippling with orgasm.

These were impossible dreams to share with him, mostly because I was afraid to appear seductive. And even if I wanted to be, I didn't know how. What I did know was that I wasn't making the dreams up. They were taking me through my sexual life as if for the first time. They started in an innocence I could never know and took me through the landscape of my very own sexuality—sexuality I had never been able to own in my waking life.

Eventually, our real-life relationship was lost to other places and people. But I never stopped dreaming about him. Going to India was supposed to help. Now I'm wandering around Dharamsala in the middle of the night escaping from a fire and steaming from the dream. Like all the other dreams, it was more real than real. The thought, long established and reflected upon, was that perhaps he and I had known one another in other lifetimes. Or perhaps I was dreaming about a lifetime yet to come.

I can't talk about it, not even to Thrinley, not even here in Dharamsala, where lifetimes blur together in karmic array and disarray. I came to India to forget, and I had. The dreams, however, were not about to forget me.

"Ahhh, fuck," I'm thinking as we negotiate the dark steps of the Dalai Lama's temple. "Is nothing sacred?"

It's very quiet here on the temple grounds. Dawn is a hint on the horizon. Early morning practitioners arrive for their morning circumambulations and we decide to go back and check on the fire. There have been no explosions; nor has the fire's glow risen in intensity. Our new Danish friend is nervous but comes with us anyway.

As we get close to the site, onlookers are packed in every direction and a few young members of the Indian army are standing around looking almost bored. We squeeze past antique-looking fire engines as we wind our way towards the fire, which is, we discover, devastating in its destruction but now under control. Our friend goes back to the hotel. Thrinley and I go in search of refreshment.

The little café near the temple has just opened and we order scrambled eggs, muffins and for the first time in India, coffee—in the form of powder and hot water. On the wall is a poster:

As We Think So We Become: The thought manifests as the word; the word manifests as the deed. The deed develops into habit; and the habit hardens into character. So watch the thought and its ways with care; and let it spring from love, born out of concern for all beings. The shadow follows the body and never leaves it. In the same way, as we think, so we become.

The shadow of this fire is growing larger even as the fire goes out. Thrinley and I sit in grim awareness of how many lives have been irrevocably damaged by this tragedy. It looked like an entire hotel and a dozen or so businesses were destroyed—all of them Tibetan-owned. The fragile balancing act of economic interdependence has just taken a severe blow.

"We have to do something," says Thrinley.

And all we can come up with is money.

After finishing our breakfast we go to the bank and I raid my Bank of America credit-card for five hundred dollars and get a huge pile of rupees. We find out where the family that owned the hotel is staying and deliver the money to a very humble abode tucked away down some stairs and behind a stone wall. A cow is the only sign of life in the courtyard.

The wonder is that no-one was hurt in the fire. At least, that's what we are hearing. And the flames were somehow prevented from spreading, more thanks to the rapid bucket brigade than the fire engines from somewhere in lower Dharamsala that only slowly found their way up the mountain. Someone says that one fire engine had no pressure to push the water through its hoses. Five hours after the first flame and the apocryphal stories are spreading like wildfire. All we know for sure is that now there is even more suffering in the streets and it won't be put out with the fire.

I remember that other dream: the signature dream beginning my therapy with Brian about a fire that could not be put out. As soon as it was tamed in one place it would surface from underground somewhere else. I was continually running for help as it increased in demonic power and became more and more ruthless in its sudden appearances and raging voraciousness. Finally, in the dream I was assuring a small girl that help really was on the way and that she could trust it. Now, here I am in Dharamsala, twenty years later, discovering how true it was. I got help and the help was trustworthy. I wish Brian was on my shoulder here in India where my journey through the fire of recovery and healing is holding me in such good stead.

The innate sense of self is such an omnipotent thing, the only thing more omnipotent is that which can destroy it. This is the ultimate power trip—the ability to destroy the self of the other. There are countless ways in which this has been attempted throughout history. And they have all been eventually defeated by the power of the human spirit to love and seek freedom.

When I was interviewing Ben White, the man who created costumes for the sea turtles who benignly roamed the streets of WTO Seattle on behalf of their own continuity, he said: "There are two basic rules of consciousness. Rule number one is that life will out, no matter what. And rule number two is the main rule governing human society: Everyone wants freedom. And they will eventually get it. No matter what." He believed that all political struggles are spiritual; we are all fighting for that elusive version of freedom in which we can all be our fully human beings in our human bodies.

When I was on the streets of WTO Seattle I was in the midst of people from all over the world laying claim to be who they were in the lives they had created. They wanted to be free to farm, to provide for their families, to live on sacred land, to have the right to be human in the ways that were culturally and historically meaningful. Brian was on the streets of WTO, too. I didn't know this until months after the event when it came out in a therapy session. So when writing *Battle in Seattle* I interviewed him by email. I'd moved to the island by then and my therapy was intermittent. Brian wrote about how much we need wholeness in our communities in order to survive: "A wholeness in which we would no more exploit someone, be it for labor or profit, than we would attack one part of our body to make another part more comfortable."

For those of us struggling with the effects of mind and self splitting abuse, healing comes about only when we stop attacking one part of our mind to make another more comfortable. It took me many years to understand this and many more to accept it. My normal day-to-day self would not relinquish its hold because it was powerfully invested in keeping me going. Any other version of selfness was a threat to its very existence. It built up a huge resistance to variations on time and circumstance and gamely kept us going through all the emotional upheavals and meltdowns that defined my daily life.

I have gained tremendous love and respect for my "system" and it is something I fought bitterly. "No way am I a fucking system," was my mantra. But the truth is: I am. And it's a beautiful system. Elegant and resourceful. When, finally, after many years of therapy, my "normal" self was able to look up and see the inner guides, the gatekeepers of information, the anguished and suspended children, the holders of the truth, and its own shining role in all of our survival, it was able to relax and allow some wholeness to begin. The isolation, grief, shock, loss, fear and fragmentation leaked out through years of overwhelming and inarticulate feelings. For me, they were as necessary as rain. They nourished my soul and made way for knowing. But understanding how my mind was working to survive was a bigger challenge. Being normal is the key to appearing normal. In the normal world as I knew it, abnormal was aberrant, certifiable, shameful and unacceptable. But there is nothing normal in India and that's the norm. Here in Dharamsala, this morning's fire will perhaps hold a blessing somewhere in the future for those who are suffering today. In the meantime, we hope a little money will help.

After breakfast, Thrinley and I head back to the guest house. The fire site is reduced to smoldering rubble and the streets are filled with anxious people. As we go down the alley to the Loseling we pass the same stream of Tibetans, this time carrying out all the goods they had brought from their burning shops to store in the lobby. The monks are still preparing tea and food for those who had taken refuge in the night. There's no way we can go back to bed so Thrinley settles down to do her prayer practice and after a shower I go out to circumambulate the temple. Today's the day I'm supposed to meet Norbu and Dakpa at noon to go up the mountain to find Gen Lamrimpa. I am preparing myself for postponement and disappointment.

The fire and its aftermath might define the day but Norbu still shows up at noon ready to help me find Gen Lamrimpa. But first we must find tsampa. "It's traditional," he tells me. And off we go in search of a bag of barley flour. Tsampa has sustained Tibetan life for centuries and in doing so has become a spiritual icon. It is sustenance as well as the sign of sustenance. One cannot search for one's teacher without first searching for tsampa.

We go to the obvious places, the small quasi-grocery stalls that sell mostly potato chips and sweets, but there's no tsampa in sight. We go down some stone stairs to a wobbly open courtyard where a cow munches on the only thing growing and find our way to somebody's door. Nope. No tsampa today. Norbu looks uncharacteristically stymied. Then he nods his head to himself and off we trot yet again. We wind our way through the labyrinth of the Dalai Lama's temple grounds to a kitchen door where a Tibetan woman greets us with reckless, abandoned joy. She is surrounded by tsampa and happily sells us five pounds.

After meeting up with Dakpa, who is coming along for either enlightenment or entertainment, I don't know which, Norbu negotiates us a ride part way up the mountain to the Tibetan Children's Village, a large compound of school buildings and playing fields high above McLeod Ganj. It's a landscape of natural beauty perfect for children in exile from their families, their country and their culture. It feels happy here, a Shangri-la for children.

This was Norbu's first home after his escape from Tibet. He knows the surrounding hills and speaks about the freedom, the discipline and the care he received. The place pulses with happy memories for him and for the first time I see Norbu carefree and lighthearted. He is home. He lost everything. Then he gained everything. His steadfast calm and seriousness give way to the remembrance of play. It is like seeing his secret self.

Dakpa, quiet as usual, is looking up the mountain. His robes don't quite look appropriate for the climb but his body seems to be more than ready. Mine, however, feels leaden at the prospect. It is straight up. The trail is meager if it is, in fact, a trail. And I have no idea how far, how long, how hard it will be. I remember what Norbu had said to me during our tsampa search, "It's not supposed to be easy to find your teacher." He was mischievous. Now I see he wasn't kidding.

As we start up the trail, we encounter a man coming down. He turns out to be an old friend of Norbu's, a caretaker at the children's village. They engage in a brief conversation and Norbu reports that many of the monks are in southern India where His Holiness has been teaching. Ah, yes, His Holiness the Dalai Lama. When will he be back? And is there any possibility of seeing him? They are not questions I've uttered in Dharamsala, partly because of my ingrained inability to want what I want. Partly because it seemed spiritually incorrect. I came on this trip to accompany my friend Thrinley and to experience India. Tracking down the Dalai Lama on purpose was not on my agenda. Nor was the cascading flow of connection to my colonial past, my spiritual history, my churchly confusions, my fragmented inner selves, and to this newly emerging self that seems to be experiencing life for the first time. I have come home to nearly 50 years of connection to a man whose life had been a beacon to my lost self, yet the idea of actually seeing the Dalai Lama, right here where he lives has not even begun to take hold. This sounds disingenuous, I know, but it's true.

I'd lobbied to include Dharamsala on our itinerary because it was home to Tibetans-in-exile; because it was high in the foothills of the Himalayas; and because it was a familiar word in the vocabulary of my friends who had traveled to India. But the deeper draw was happening where everything of importance takes place in my life, outside my conscious daily mind. There was success in the control of my mind because whatever "I" wanted was doomed before it could be conceived. But my guides, operating inside and out, made sure we got what we really needed—first of all to survive, and most of all to triumph. I am recognizing this on this trip. It ripples through my body like a big fist of "fuck you!" A huge roar of rage and reconciliation. Rage at the perpetrators whose arrogance led them to think they really could get to me; reconciliation with the parts of me—inside and out—that conspired to keep us whole, to keep us going, to keep us creative and to keep us alive. Now all I have to do is get up this friggin' mountain.

The caretaker friend of Norbu's tells him he knows of Gen Lamrimpa but sometimes he goes abroad. There is, however, a meditating monk who will know everything; all we have to do is find him. This appears to be a simple feat for Norbu who sets out with confidence up the mountain. We climb non-stop for about an hour. Each step impossible but still I keep up. There is stubbornness in being a sixty-year-old white woman hiking up a steep slope with two young, fit Tibetans, one of them carrying my five pounds of tsampa. At some point it's all I can do not to break out into hysterical laughter. It's raining and there's thunder close by. I'm full-body muddy scrambling up the face of this mountain, grabbing on to anything more tenacious than I.

It's Dakpa who strikes out ahead of us and conjures up the trail out of thin air. And the air is thin and getting thinner. Soon it will be as thin as his robes. But he looks happy, too. And moves like the wind, which is also on the rise. My whole life feels compressed on this hillside. It is all I can do not to die on the spot.

When a cluster of mud, stick and stone huts appear so does my utmost relief—until Norbu says we have to go still further and higher. The huts show no signs of life. These monks must be basking in the warmth of southern India with the Dalai Lama. The monk who is still here and who knows my Gen Lamrimpa is, of course, living up above this community of itinerant snowbirds. He doesn't leave the mountain. We keep climbing. It keeps raining. The three of us are drenched to the bones. At any moment I expect to see steam rising out of the ashes of my exhausted burned-out body as it becomes one with the mud, the mountainside and the mystery of whatever it is that has brought me here.

It's Dakpa who first finds the hut with a bit of smoke rising from its roof. He respectfully waits for Norbu to find the actual door, which is somewhere behind a mud, stone and tin wall. I hear an animated conversation. Then Norbu comes out to tell me that Gen Lamrimpa is indeed abroad, in America. Probably Seattle, I'm thinking. Where I'm not. But we are invited in for tea. And when I go around the stone wall to meet the meditating monk, he takes one look at my dripping wet and muddy reality and bursts out laughing. "You should have come on a better day," Norbu translates. Right. As if I had a choice. I burst out laughing, too.

I look around. There's a small stone room off to one side of the hut and in it is a small wood fire burning in the corner. Two cats sprawl close by. Smoke has blackened the walls, the floor, the ceiling. There is no reason for the outside room that I can see, unless perhaps it was the first home to this meditating monk and is now home to the cats. The larger room, into which he welcomes us, is made of stones brushed together with mud. There are stone shelves, a pad upon which to sit, and an altar where the color and imagery of Tibetan Buddhism brighten the room like a small sun. On the wall there is a worn poster of the ego's struggle with the ox and the path of transformation. Our monk gestures us to sit and bustles about making tea.

The room is no larger than ten-by-ten feet. A small wood stove warms us and heats the water. He arranges cups in a row. His burgundy robes wrap around him in a flourish with one arm and shoulder bared in tradition. He is muscular and vital in his movements. His energy is too big for this small space, perhaps too big for the universe. It emanates from him like a force of nature, more sexual than spiritual. Not a directed sexuality but a pervasive presence of sexuality. The sexuality of creation. The abundance of life continually reproducing itself in every atom of existence. Is this what happens to monks on top of a mountain? They get sexy? I think of those long-ago words of poet Kenneth Rexroth: "The entire universe depends upon a monk meditating in silence and solitude on the top of a mountain." So the universe depends upon this man who sits up here all by himself being sexy. What a waste. My mischievous little mind gets the better of me, until the shadow of sex, its abuses, its exploitation, its antithesis of love, bring me to spiritual attention.

Sex. Sex is supposed to happen at night, under the covers as well as under the cover of darkness. For me, as a child, sex just happened. It had nothing to do with me yet it wrecked every possibility I might have of sex as an adult. It was tainted; I was tainted; every potential lover was tainted. When this finally fully dawned on me, I was in my forties, alone, and looking back. I'd had more than ten years of therapy with Brian and I could finally see what he meant when he leaned back in amazement one day at something I'd said and told me in a very gentle voice: "You are so sexualized, Janet."

I had, of course, tried to sexualize us in ways large and small. But he is a therapist of tremendous skill, insight and integrity and was always in full professional control and empathy as he protected me from myself. I don't remember precisely the moment's cause; what I remember is his complete awe. He hadn't fully realized the depth of my estrangement. After all, for years we had worked to destroy the psychological and spiritual chains of abuse, mind control and defilement. Yet I was still bound by sex as love, sex as real, sex as measure of worth and existence. It was branded into my small child body more deeply than I was.

Throughout my years of therapy, there were moments when I could finally see that I needed to act. Getting up the courage to walk three miles around Green Lake in Seattle, just like everybody else, was one of those moments. I was re-entering my body. Going to the Cloud Mountain Buddhist retreat for nine months to cook was striking out for silence and the acknowledgement of the spiritual. Writing the letter to my parents saying that I would be disengaging for awhile because I needed a little time to think about things was a huge and defining moment. They were moments that were all mine.

The sex moment came one Sunday after church in 1995. I went home to the small log cabin where I was living and had an "aha" moment. I was fed up. It was time to reclaim my sexuality. I would have sex on Sundays. All I needed was a partner.

I was manager of the County Parks at the time and was living through the winter in the cabin at the park I loved. It was on a tiny cove on the west side of the island, a place where our First Peoples came for shelter and sustenance when the land belonged to everyone. Some precious person had gifted this place to the county years ago and it was revered by generations of campers from far and wide. In the winter it got very quiet. The land restored itself after being loved to death in the summer; animals came back and the silver winter skies brushed the place with spiritual luster. I loved that park. What better place to heal the bruised psyche of my sexuality.

We don't always know what we know the most. Some people know their parents love them before they know the word "love." I had always known that I was loved by nature. The solace I felt in open places had deep roots in my childhood when the smell of low tide and the sound of seagulls meant I was outside. I was safe. In recent years I had begun to articulate to myself that this relationship with the natural world meant something. It was real. It didn't translate into the names of things, like specific trees, birds and seaweeds; it was a feeling of being at home, of being happy, of being in love. So why not have sex where I feel most loved?

So, after a careful search, I found my partner—a lovely old madrona tree that reached out over the sea from a high bank. It was on a back trail, hidden from the road through the park and the parking areas. It was private there. It fit just right. I could straddle one of its trunks, lean forward and wrap my arms around it and hold on. A small ridge rose just where it counted and if I took the weight off my feet my communion with the tree was complete. It held me.

It felt pretty weird at first. I knew how to masturbate so that wasn't difficult. My clitoris had been introduced to me by foreign fingers long before I knew I had one. Pleasure is pleasure, even when it's abuse. But the sexual fantasies that always accompanied my forays into masturbation were violent, impersonal, degrading and very, very satisfying. I never used sex toys or invaded myself with anything; I simply attended to my clitoris and let my mind roam its secret recesses of sexual depravity and humiliation. I recreated the sexuality of my childhood. To heal, I knew I had to retrain myself, to imprint sex as a possibility of love and love as a possibility of life. My tree had a mighty big task ahead of itself. So did I.

I'd searched it out for its privacy, but most of all for its spirit. My madrona had a well-established survival instinct. The bank upon which it prevailed had been eroded by wind and sea yet it accommodated the pressures and kept growing. Its limbs reached out in welcome and in freedom, even as its trunks had rooted themselves in ungainly stubbornness in the ground. And it was smooth. I could lean into my most delicate places and stretch out my arms and wrap around its thickness without fear of splinters or scratches.

A madrona is a magnificent tree; and it's always defining its relationship to life. It sheds its thin papery red bark, exposing a deeper greener smoothness. It sheds its leaves in the fall; it has bursts of white flowers in the spring and sprays of red berries in the winter. It is a tree for all seasons and on the island where I live, it thrives in the salt spray that sends other trees inland. It's a survivor and it thrives.

At first, having sex on Sundays was a reflection of my past. I could get only so far with the physical stimulation, then my mind would take over and all the old abusive connections clicked into place. The orgasms were intense and physically satisfying. The psychic hangover was dark and draining. It was just like all my relationships with other lovers. I was the problem. The behavioral loops would not let me go. How could I change patterns of behavior over which I had no control? But I didn't give up. Throughout the winter, rain or shine, every Sunday afternoon and sometimes in the dark, I communed with my tree and my sexuality.

The change began when I started to realize that the tree was alive. That its smooth strength was offering itself to me, that it was vulnerable and tender. It was real. I started to feel like an exploiter, subjecting this lovely living thing to my aberrant imagination. One Sunday I felt sad and apologized and started to cry and was filled with grief and remorse. It was then that I stopped sexually acting out on the tree and started to feel relationship.

Slowly its grace entered me. I rested my cheek on its smooth trunk and caressed its smooth sides. I learned how it felt to wrap my arms around it. And the places where I touched, touched back. Instead of being overwhelmed by violent erotic imaginings, the simple sensations of the tree and me began to be enough. Some sort of innocence rose up between us and I started to understand that sexual yearning really does start in innocence, that it can be innocent. That this body of mine, getting older all the time, could find its way back to the moment where it, too, could be innocent. So, to the very best of my and the tree's ability, I began to heal my sexuality. Finally, the pure experience of pleasure had become a match for my defiled imagination.

One Sunday afternoon in April, when the park was coming back to life with occasional visitors, I was in the midst of deep intimacy with the tree. By now I'd advanced to a wider invitation to nature. I was inviting in the sea, imagining the waves filling me as they rolled in, great waves of sensation inside partnering with the outer sensation of the tree as I let the feeling of orgasm grow from the inside out. The strength and power of what sex can be entered me with such force that I gasped out loud. Then I heard someone laughing. I wanted to disengage from the tree and the sea but I couldn't. It was too late; the surge of orgasm was bigger than even my embarrassment. Over the ecstatic edge I went and on went the laughing. It must be somebody I knew, I was thinking, even in the midst of the best sex I'd ever had. Otherwise surely they would have turned away and left.

As soon as I could, I scrambled off the tree, straightened my clothes, and turned around. Nobody. Then I heard laughing again.

And looking out over the cliff, into the sea below, I saw a big old seal laughing right at me. It was as though I'd finally graduated and the mighty professor was chuckling out his approval. I started to laugh, too. Realizing in a moment that all I was missing was humor. Getting back my sexuality was serious business, but only if I could get to the humor of it all.

I learned a lot that winter. Even though I had no opportunity to practice what I'd learned with a mere mortal man, I knew I'd reclaimed my sexuality. That it was finally mine and would be from then on. I also got the courage to feel the child in me, the small one whose violation defined the tragedy of exploited sexuality. Her loss of innocence was complete but finally I could mourn the loss and move on. Now I'm high on the mountain exploring the hinterlands of spirituality and once again it's sexuality that I encounter and that encounters me. From all the way up here I can hear that seal laughing.

Our monk is laughing, too, as he fusses over us with tea and attention. I present him with the bag of tsampa which Norbu had quickly handed to me as we arrived at the hut. I give him the envelope with rupees that I had prepared for Gen Lamrimpa. I take out the note though, and ask our monk to pass it on to Gen Lamrimpa. He doesn't open the envelope but puts in on his altar, quickly and casually. He pours cups of tea, stirs in powdered milk, and serves us with a big mischievous grin across his beaming face.

With the tea comes conversation in Tibetan between Norbu and our monk. Then I am invited into the discussion. I ask questions: How long have you been here? How long will you stay? "I hope until I die," he says via Norbu as translator. Then he adds with a big laugh, "I hope I don't get sick." I look quizzically at Norbu. "If he gets sick he will have to leave here," he explains. Our mountain monk has been in meditation in this stone and mud hut for five years. He asks me why I'm here and I tell him the short version about meeting Gen Lamrimpa at Cloud Mountain retreat center. What I don't tell him is that I was living in shame of existence back then and what haunts me to this day is the way in which I was unable to reach out and touch Gen Lamrimpa's hands goodbye at the airport when he returned to India. I was early in my descent. His presence in my life had been profound but I didn't feel as though I had the right to know him, or to be acknowledged. My fear all these years has been that at that moment of departure so long ago when Gen Lamrimpa reached out in affection and kindness to us all, and I couldn't reach back, I was perceived as rude and disrespectful. It's a selfish worry, I know. But I want the chance to reach back, even if it is 20 years late.

It took being in Dharamsala for all this to rise up out of my memory and for the dots of my healing journey to be connected. I had to travel to the other side of the world to find the threads that weave together my inner life. I had to climb this mountain to understand the power of the path through the valley of descent. How I got here—that I got here—is nothing short of yet another miracle. As I sit in this stone hut, confronted once again by spiritual joy in the face of tragedy and deprivation, I wonder what it's going to take for me to finally really get it. The inner guides started doing battle for my mind long ago when it was first besieged by experiments that distorted my experience of life, undermined its meaning, and disintegrated the "selfness" that is a birthright to us all. The parallel reality—that I am here, have meaning and innate ontological existence—was carried by guides who lived in an inner sanctum of secrecy. And they won. They have always won.

In Tibetan Buddhism, the fundamental perception of reality is that it is good. No contest. It's what the Dalai Lama has stood ground for throughout the long ordeal of Tibet and Tibetans. "Have compassion for the abusers for they know not what they do." It is a refrain of Jesus, too, this assumption that good will prevail. The creative force *is* the power of the universe. It came first. Otherwise there would be nothing to destroy. Why would humankind be fundamentally otherwise? When we know the truth—whether it's about child prostitution or global warming—we want to be part of the solution. It is only natural. It's this that was brought home to me on the streets of WTO Seattle. It's this that I've come face-to-face and soul-to-soul with in India. It's this that confronts me here in this small dark room full of light. It's this that cannot be translated by Norbu. Because we cannot be taught to breathe, life breathes us.

In this small dense space the universe spins. For two hours we talk about religion and activism, about how they once could be separate but not any longer, about the transformation of the world, about Tibet and China and WTO Seattle, about the reach of peace and justice into a world spinning in despair. But there is no despair in here. Norbu translates and participates; his own views, informed by his own suffering, are compassionate and insightful. I am hearing them for the first time.

Then the monk turns intently towards me. His questions to me deepen with curiosity. His gaze becomes more and more penetrating. He is wearing a woolen hat emblazoned with Nike across the front. Enlightenment is nothing if not incongruous. I think about how often I've wished that Tiger Woods would drop the Nike swoosh in favor of workers' rights and global justice and here I am facing the damn thing on a meditating Tibetan monk in a mud hut on a mountain in India. And he wants to know what I know. I gaze back and cannot say a word. A current of something deep and heavy passes between us; then he nods as though he's heard every thought. I am aware of Norbu waiting for me to say something, of Dakpa huddled in the corner, and of the impossibility of language in the face of our deepest realities. This monk has gone inward in search of riches and found them. I am loaded with nothing but the excesses of grief and disillusionment. I know nothing.

A dense silence surrounds us. Dakpa huddles in a corner by the door, looking frightened. He really is fresh out of the monastery. His studies were of Tibetan art, language and culture. He has not yet entered the Buddhist mind. And here we are enveloped by it, besieged by it, conquered by it. Presence of mind.

I think of that old Taoist saying: "Those that know don't say; those that say don't know." This mountain monk knows. His solidity in this small space speaks volumes about the world outside. About the price of progress, the descent into consumption, greed and materialistic mayhem that has become life-at-large in the known world. Yet it is in here, in this unknown world, where the evolution of the spirit and the mind's brilliant ability to create happiness spill forth with overwhelming intention and inevitability.

Then he beams at me mischievously and I get the profundity of this moment, of all the moments that have drawn me to spirit, to strange searches and struggles, to a path that cannot be seen. His humor, his delight, his dedication to a world that defies every materialistic value we have grown to love spills over in excess. It comes over me in a wave of recognition as all despair is shattered by careless uninhibited joy. Life is joy, his mind ripples. There is no other way. All the grief of Tibet, of the Dalai Lama and his lost people, of my own lost self, get swallowed up in this moment. Life is joy. Even when life sucks. This swirling conundrum is reconciled in this moment and I'd damn well better know it.

Silence re-enters the room.

I think it's time to go, I say to Norbu.

Yes, he says to me. We share in a jovial leave-taking. As I make a final turn towards the opening of the hut, the monk stops me. He hands me a very small plastic bag full of reddish-orange-colored barley. Norbu translates. He says he will pray for you. I put my hands together in a gesture of gratitude and respect. The monk's eyes twinkle with humor and he waves us away with some laughing words. "Next time come back in better weather," Norbu translates.

Outside, the storm is still in charge of the mountainside. We slip and slide downhill and I know I have been changed. I also know that everything is still the same. My struggle is my struggle. It's what I came into this life with and I'll be taking it with me on my way out. But, for perhaps the thousandth time, I have been informed of the perfection beyond struggle, of the perfection that, if I'm damn lucky and pay attention, I can hitch a ride on out of my life and all will not be lost. Yesterday it was the humble Christian servant in the church; today it is the Buddhist monk on the mountain. They are both gifts of faith, of joy, of compassion, of love in action. One serves others directly in ways that can be named; the other serves the ineffable consciousness within which we all interact—with ourselves, with one another, with everything that is alive—seen and unseen.

On our stumbling way down we stop and pay our respects at the stupa shining magnificently bright and white in the midst of this mud-hut community. When we reach the Tibetan Children's Village, the rain is thicker and Dakpa's robes flap wetly against his bare arms and legs. But there is a lift to his step, whether because we are re-entering his known world or leaving the unknown one I don't know.

Norbu is now back to business, focusing on being a responsible guide and getting this weird white woman back to McLeod. Yet I know he knows, too. Ever since I'd asked him to help get me up this mountain, his spiritual muscle was activated and in charge. He trusts most that which is beyond the tangible, that which compels us to do things beyond our understanding. I feel the strength of his wisdom even as he once again becomes efficient in the world. I am filled with inarticulate love for both these young men. They have born great sorrow and it has quieted them and matured them. I feel safe in every way. Even as the electric wires crackle and spark their way across the fields from the violence of the storm.

TWENTY-FOUR

Thrinley leaves tomorrow for her night-long bus ride to Rajpur and the preparation for Sakya Trizin's sixtieth birthday. It seems ages since we were in Rajpur and ages since his birthday was the reason for this trip. Sixty years old is ancient. I am sixty years old. This is a fact that gets lost on me daily. All the steps of my healing have led me backwards—to reclamation of childhood selves and lost identities, to surfacing emotions appropriate only to youth, to a small and silent self delighting in a world it is only just discovering. In every respect but physical I have been growing younger. Reconciling this with my aging body is no picnic. Life is beginning just as it is beginning to end and this wreaks havoc with my sense of reality.

On the way to pancakes we walk by the site of the fire. It is nothing short of devastating. The amazing thing is that no-one was hurt and the town didn't burn down in its entirety. Ten Tibetan businesses were destroyed; a hotel, and five residences were reduced to unrecognizable rubble. Everyone is rallying around to help. Indian merchants pooled money to help the Tibetan merchants who lost their businesses. They also offered rooms in their hotels at no charge for those Tibetans in need of housing. This is a big deal for lots of reasons, mostly to do with economic competition.

There have long been mutterings about what will happen to the Tibetans in India when His Holiness the Dalai Lama is no longer alive. His presence here brings tremendous stature to the country as well as to the Tibetan refugees who now call India home. Without him as a leader in the world, as well as in the community, any number of dire possibilities arise. On a global scale the Dalai Lama's presence is a beacon for peace and the possibility of peace in the world. But after he is gone, who will pave the way for a peaceful and cooperative life for the Tibetan people in a country not their own? As exploitation increasingly threatens the survival of Tibetans and their culture in Tibet, going home is not yet an option for them. But it could be. And if it happens, the whole world will once again have its Shangri-La. The place where happiness rises out of relationship to all that's beautiful in the world and all that remains a mystery.

In his book, *The Art of Happiness*, written with psychiatrist and neurologist Howard Cutler MD, the Dalai Lama says, "The antidote to greed is contentment." Undoing the infrastructures of global greed will take nothing short of spiritual revolution. Our path to survival has been paved with hatred and fear. Having been raised inside such structures, I know all too well how they succeed, even when they ultimately don't. Fear is the end of beauty, the end of happiness, and the means to the end of faith.

My own fear has become a sign of something wrong. Training my selves to unearth the causes is a spiritual task and there is no end to the process. I have to work hard every day, whether I want to or not. I have to live inside my past just enough to understand how it is informing my present. Only then am I able to plan and look forward to my future. Every day I have to recognize the traps in my own mind and find my way to beauty.

It is the same for the outer demons we all face in this world. We have to work hard every day to keep them at bay, to keep the prevailing infrastructure of greed from defining our own lives. How we do this has everything to do with finding contentment, unearthing it, sometimes literally, in our daily lives. Rooting it out from under the mess we have made, bringing it out into the light. Knowing that we are more than how we are defined by others, that we have more when we have less, that contentment is a deep secret we can all share and when we do we serve life as well as one another.

I had to wake up to the depth of my personal self-hatred in order to heal. And then, when I discovered the depth of my complicity in the way the world does and doesn't work, I had another layer of self-hatred to work through. But self-hatred is a bust. And according to the Dalai Lama, "very, very dangerous." Because self-hatred means we hate what is good in ourselves as well as what is bad. We deny the spark of Buddha, the glimpse of God, the nature in our nature that insists on life in all its manifest forms—whether or not we believe in life after death or reincarnation. Life will out. And if we're not part of it—consciously and otherwise—we are part of all that is death-dealing. And what's the payoff in that?

I am in a cavalcade of realization on this trip and there are no excuses left. Watching the way the fire tore through the lives of the people in this town, how they responded so quickly to their own and one another's needs, how out of the ashes rose compassion and generosity, how tragedy was both experienced and averted, I am reminded yet again that every moment is a transcendent moment. Being sunk in the mire of my own mind is a dead-end for me and for whatever good I might have to offer. "Get over it," is the voice booming in my ear. "And get on with it."

We are lost. Thrinley's been to the house once before but she was with Norbu so she wasn't actually looking for the place. Now we are. It's one of those "around the next bend" experiences and it's driving me around the bend. Thrinley doesn't even remember what side of the street the place is on. Given the twists and turns of the road it's not all that surprising, but still I am irritated. We are off to meet an auspicious man—Tsering's father and Norbu's uncle—a Tibetan freedom fighter, the Khenpo who left his life as a young monk to take up weapons against the Chinese invaders. And we are late.

Thrinley finally gets through to Tsering on her cell-phone and to our utter relief, she answers. She comes to meet us, smiling and happy, and leads us the rest of the way. The house is stone and tucked behind a wall and a yard wild with bushes and small trees. We enter through the kitchen, and the high ceilings give a formal feeling to this home which might easily have been built by the British. The windows are few so it's quite dark inside, but the feeling is one of warmth and activity. Tsering goes to tell her father we are here and then takes us into his study which is also a library and his bedroom. The high walls are all stacked with bookshelves. Tibetan artifacts and Buddhist icons fill the top shelf; books fill every other square inch of wall space. A lot of the floor space, too. There's a desk piled high with folders stuffed with papers and more folders stacked on shelves. The room is regal with the written word. It's also ornate with colorful Tibetan thankas.

Thupten Namgyal rises carefully from a big chair to greet us. He's a man in his late-seventies, a big man whose strength is waning physically but whose presence has expanded exponentially. His gaze is compelling, his handshake firm, and his power implicit. This is going to be interesting, I'm thinking, as we are introduced. The warrior is still in this man, not as aggression but as perception. I feel him looking right into me, assessing what he sees, and evaluating all the strengths and weaknesses I have ever possessed and will ever possess. His uninhibited intensity surpasses that of the monk of the mountain, who honored some form of social decorum by keeping his power to himself. Not this man. I know enough about the history of the struggle in Tibet to know that he has given up everything: his sacred relationship to non-violence; his youth; his heart and soul for the cause of Tibet.

As Tsering goes to get her older sister who will be translating for us, our host settles back comfortably and with a slight and bemused smile regards us both. I consider regarding him back and then quickly think better of it. He is bringing his vast history to bear upon this moment. I have a vast history, too. I know we meet somewhere in the realm of tragedy but he has quite likely killed for his country. This means he lives inside the intolerable, reconciles the impossible, and has no patience for mere mortals. He twinkles at us. We twinkle back.

The silence grows more eloquent and then something mischievous erupts. It's always like this with Tibetan people, no matter how somber and serious the moment, the threat of levity is always hovering. Life itself is cause for joy, no matter what the prevailing pomp and circumstance. To take one's own individual self terribly seriously is quite laughable, which, unfortunately, is a lesson I might not manage to learn in this lifetime. I manage to be serious even when I'm sick of taking myself seriously.

Tsering returns, introduces us to her sister, Kunchok, and then asks us what kind of tea we would like, Tibetan or regular. For years I've read references to Tibetan tea and its butter and salt ingredients but have never had the opportunity to taste any. Even the Tibetan restaurants here serve Indian-style tea. So Tibetan it is.

Kunchok is gracious, composed and beautiful. She's a member of the Tibetan-parliament-in exile which means she's following in the footsteps of her father, who, after fighting the Chinese well into the 1960s, finally faced the futility of the struggle and escaped to Dharamsala where he became politically active in the exiled Tibetan government. Thupten Namgyal was part of the first group of Tibetans to go back to China for an official visit in representation of His Holiness the Dalai Lama. And he is a scholar. He spent years helping to create the Tibetan constitution, now waiting for its opportunity to serve the Tibetan people. His research took him deep into understanding the various constitutions of many governments—contemporary and historic. One he respects immensely and used as a model is the Constitution of the United States of America. And it is this that he wants to discuss with Thrinley and me.

Here we are, on the run from the warmongering George W. Bush and associates, and our distinguished Tibetan host wants to talk about the wonders of the United States of America and its president. "A wonderful country," he informs us. "Wonderful."

Thrinley and I glance at one another surreptitiously. I think of the effort we went to in order to neutralize our appearance of American-ness. And here we are: confronted by a Tibetan Khenpo warrior exhibiting an unwavering respect for the country. Does he know how the brilliance of the U.S. Constitution is being undermined by fear-mongering and war-based economics? Does he know that habeas corpus is under attack, freedom of speech curtailed, that there's domestic spying at-large and an insidious diminishing of individual rights at home and human rights abroad. I remember my time as an election monitor in Ohio, where voting machines weren't working in the early morning when hundreds of African Americans showed up to vote before going to work—and couldn't.

It was overwhelming grief I felt back then and it is overwhelming grief I feel right now. The promise of the United States of America, the courageous vision of its Founders, the genius of the constitution and its fundamental respect for the rights of the individual to pursue life, liberty and the pursuit of happiness—all sabotaged by an economic mandate that puts the bottom-line ahead of the human being. Capitalism and democracy have become synonymous and we've all become blind to the consequences. Everything I learned while writing *The Battle in Seattle* comes flooding through my mind but I can't stop even one coherent thought long enough to groom it for expression. Our Khenpo warrior friend is in love with the U.S. Constitution and he assumes that George W. Bush is in love with it, too.

Thrinley and I attempt, rather weakly, to make the distinction between Thupten Namgyal's idealized vision of the country and our own experience of its wayward path. But the truth is we need this man's optimism, the reminder of the impetus that founded the United States of America as a beacon of freedom, hope and possibility. Where will this optimism come from if not from a remembering, a re-visioning, a reconciliation with the ideals upon which the country was founded. This warrior of a man is holding out the hope and promise of the United States as a model for the hope and promise of his own lost country.

Our Khenpo warrior leans back on the couch and surveys us from the magnitude of his knowledge. Thrinley and I, in mysterious unison, capitulate to his wider mind, his more informed intellect and his dream of American freedom. This man has studied all the constitutions of the world and the U.S. Constitution is his favorite. He incorporated much of it into the constitution he helped create for Tibet, a country so tragically betrayed by so many. Now he is here in this house at the behest of the Dalai Lama who has asked him to write his life history. It is this task that Norbu attends to each day as he translates and transcribes Thupten Namgyal's Tibetan into the computer. And it is this task that Norbu neglects when he takes us here and there, including tomorrow when he will go on the bus with Thrinley to Rajpur.

Tea is served. It really is salty and buttery and it provokes in me an almost automatic nausea. I don't want to be rude so I sip often, ingesting only a fraction each time.

Back in our cold and dark room Thrinley and I crawl into our respective beds wearing our fleece vests over layers of other things. I wear a hat. Our monks gave us double the amount of bedding but there's dampness in this new room and it chills in a way that our upstairs room, with all its windows, doesn't. Up there, cold as it might get, there's aliveness in the visible night.

My history, of being closed in and in the dark, is never far behind my experience and I hate it. It's become one of those litmus questions in my life and perhaps the real reason behind all my searching. How will I die? With the fear and isolation and hatred that defines the life underneath my life? Or with the light, the love, and the faith that is the mystery underneath everything? It seems I am still too vulnerable to my surroundings. It seems that I can be triggered in spite of all I have learned, all I know, and all I have been given.

"I could die right now and be happy," is the thought that comes, often when I'm flying above the beauty of the earth, or writing something that I know is true, or watching my son be happy, or basking somewhere suspended in sunlight in the forest at the water's edge within the smell of fir and the sound of the sea. Its opposite, "I would hate to die right now," is always related to fear and constriction, something in my body that is powerful enough to control both my mind and my spirit.

I have a long way to go before gaining equanimity about death; and this experience with these two simple rooms illustrates it firmly. And tomorrow night I'll be in the dark room alone. Sometimes I think the most difficult loss to my childhood was my imagination— that elusive gift of consciousness that invites us to imagine the light room at the top where beauty streams in and reminds us who we are. It's that room I want to be in when I die and creating it in my imagination might be the only way in.

It's Buddhism that has helped my imagination come back to life—imagining the realms of light, the peaceful stream of universal consciousness flowing through the back of the cave, imagining the valley of flowers, the mountains, and the warmth shimmering below the cave's entrance. Imagining dying.

The words and deeds of Christ: loving our enemies as well as one another, treating our neighbors as ourselves, being wary of money and power, being charitable—they all guide me in living. An arbitrary heaven or hell does not invite my imagination. Even though the hell realms of Tibetan Buddhism are furious and frightening, we are invited to see them as aspects of the mind, not ultimate destinations.

So these two religions and philosophies of life, the way of Christ and the way of the Buddha, weave their way through my past and create my future; they are individual and indispensable. Snuggled under this mound of blankets, I think about Thupten Namgyal and his heroic battle for Tibet and the ways in which his heart and mind had to expand in order for him to fight for his country. That's a warrior, I'm thinking, as my own small-mindedness struggles away in its very small rooms.

TWENTY-FIVE

Thrinley leaves this evening and I am aware of it all day. We have created a comfortable traveling world around ourselves and it is about to change. My emotions are mixed. So much has happened to me on this trip and most of it has happened internally, out of sight and sound. I am so glad for a few days of solitude in which to absorb it all and reflect upon the many levels of meaning and their impact upon who I am and who I think I am. I'll also miss the safety and security of Thrinley's presence.

I go off to circumambulate the Lingkhor and leave Thrinley to do her morning practice. Today it's earlier than usual. It's colder than usual, too. On our local mountain peaks there is snow on the lower slopes and the sky above is a deep and startling blue.

The morning walk through the streets of this town has taught me everything about the intimate details of sustainability in a town with little infrastructure. I'm happy to see the streets edged with mounds of food peelings and other organic disposables because it means the cows, monkeys, dogs and rats are getting their morning meal. I know that on my return trip it will all be gone and the Indian and Tibetan merchants will be out sweeping the street clean in front of their stalls. It's daily bread that binds people together in this town.

I know there is nothing romantic about poverty. I also know there is nothing romantic about wealth; even if it is seductive. And for one moment in my life, I felt precisely how seductive wealth can be. I had gone on assignment to Maui with Fabio for a few days to an exclusive private and "spiritual" spa operated by a woman who claimed to have the voice of God.

It was four days of non-stop individual attention which included astonishing food, massages, hot tubs, psychic counseling, and Fabio, in all his physical, and it turns out, intelligent, splendor. Our hostess structured each day with meticulous attention. Devoid of being responsible for my hourly life, I slipped into a fugue of passivity. At first I had enough composure to question it all. But there came a moment when I actually thought, yes, I deserve this. I must be better than the rest.

It happened during a long, multi-course meal we were eating outside under a warm Maui night sky to the tune of two exotic Hawaiian dancers and singers. The wine was lovely. It all went to my head in great luxurious detail. Ahhhh. Yes. I really could get used to this, I thought. But it was the next thought and feeling that really got my attention. A great sense of entitlement took over. It was a feeling resonating with "special-ness" in which luxury felt like my own personal birthright. Some scrambling bit of awareness at the outer edges of my mind tried to put up a red flag of resistance. But I was gone. I could feel the lap of luxury enveloping the inner and outer reaches of my being. It was exactly what I deserved. This meant, of course, that for someone else, living in poverty was exactly what they deserved.

It was the Great Breach between the experience of my privileged and sheltered self and the experience of the rest of the world. Once this separation is in place, the life of the "other" is hidden, consciously and otherwise, or it upsets the apple cart of privilege and the delicious feeling of natural entitlement. Although my *SPA* job took me to places of great luxury around the world, it was the moment in Hawaii with Fabio that took me to the place the Buddha left when he walked out of the palace and into the streets of suffering and never turned back. This is a landscape which the Buddha and Christ shared. They were both engaged actively with poverty and the idea of poverty. They both knew that there was truth and teaching in poverty that did not exist in wealth. The Bible is full of such references. And the first step to what we know as the life of the Buddha was taken when he left the palace and his life of luxury.

This is a curious crossroads for me because as a child I was trained to be powerless, which meant first of all a separation from money. All my life I have been ashamed at my shame about money. I have been viscerally unable to equate myself with any form of monetary worth. It has severely restricted my ability to belong in a society in which earnings equal identity. My livelihood has been undertaken through a wide variety of jobs that have dropped out of the sky or been manifested by my survival self. Only one has come out of the inner me: teaching writing. When I'm with my memoir classes, I'm with my self and my story and it is story that I treasure and yearn for from others. Writing has saved my life and saved my life for some sort of posterity in my memory and it is this that I know is lacking in this world. When story is written, and writing is given its free reign, something sacred happens. In an ever-disposable sound-bite society, stopping to enter our stories, and the layers of our stories, is stopping the rising tide of destruction of human life and spirit. We need our stories and our stories need us. It is the only way through to a future.

Here in India, stories are everywhere. They are visible and complex. They jump out from alleys and doorways. They sleep in alcoves, dance in the temple, prostrate in worship, beg for sustenance, beg in deception, dress in the outrageous color and finery of outrageous poverty, spiritual accomplishment and market savvy; and they spill out in unending detail. It is how I feel inside, a continuous never-ending mess of detail in which survivable truth can only be found in the connections. Taking anyone of them as "the truth" of me means murdering most of me. Perhaps that is what we do when we insulate our lives from the lives of others. We murder them in our minds.

At home I live in such a state of separation from all the mess in my life—from bodily waste to electronic excess. Yet it all goes somewhere and affects something. Here in Dharamsala there's no separation between immediate life and its leftover consequences. After all, if the dogs didn't get fed they would be ransacking in desperation and menacing the streets instead of lying back peacefully in communion with all available rays of sun. Today I count five of them sprawled out together in front of a rolling metal door already warm from the sunrise. The dogs are happy here; they belong to the community. They reflect a satisfied life to everyone who strolls by. They have enough to eat, a place to sleep and just enough unencumbered attention to relax into the fullness of the dogs they are. We should all be so lucky.

I marvel at it all as I start my circumambulation around His Holiness the Dalai Lama's home and temple compound. The early morning light is bright on the red, green, yellow and blue Tibetan letters that make up Om Mani Padme Hum written on stones on the hillside as I round the first corner. Tibetan flags in the same colors fly between trees, their backdrop the Himalayan Mountains. The Jewel at the Heart of the Lotus is everywhere; impermanence is everywhere. They are at once opposite and the same. A dizzying happiness accompanies me. I feel as though I could fly.

When I get to the array of prayer wheels and small temples I am stopped in my tracks by a large gathering of chanting Tibetans sitting on the ground. They are facing the path I am on and responding to the leading chant of a robed monk seated at a small prayer stool. It comes to me in a rush: All this time I have been arriving just a bit later than this and missing these morning prayers. I stand by the big prayer wheel unsure of my next move. It feels rude to continue across this spiritual stage as though nothing else is happening here. I would have to stroll in front of a long line of praying Tibetans looking right at me. So I simply stop. I feel awkward and conspicuous with no graceful recourse in sight.

About five minutes later the entire group rises to their feet, almost as one body, and moves into one long line. An elderly man comes over to me and gestures me into the line. His eyes are dancing with glee and a huge smile beams across his face. Then he reaches out to my hand and opens his own. He has a fist full of tsampa and he pours a portion into my hand and turns me into position. "Watch me," he gestures, and he joins in with the chanting group for less than a minute before they all raise their arms, chant a final phrase, and toss the tsampa high into the air. I understand just in time to participate with my own toss. There is a big communal laugh of appreciation and I am surrounded by laughing and congratulatory

Tibetans before they continue on, spinning the prayer wheels on their way around the rest of the path.

If spirituality doesn't result in joy and generosity it is a sham. That's the message I get in a heartbeat. All the layers of erudition that accompany the religious quest don't stand a chance in the face of this moment. It is as simple as a smile, and as complicated.

So much trust has been lost in our world; and along with it has gone all that is sacred between us. I can name this and it terrifies me. What possible reason is there for the reductive, competitive, consumptive society that has taken us by storm and rendered us profane? How does it serve the evolution of the human heart and spirit?

There's a steep hill before the final curve of the path out of the Lingkhor and there's a seat there for those who tire from the exertion. This time around I sit on it, joining two women elders who are catching their breath. And they really are elders, bent and wizened, with bright black eyes in their weathered faces. These women escaped from China through the mountains; every elderly Tibetan I see has a story to tell of loss and suffering. Yet it is joy and happiness that they share. This has humbled me in the past; here in Dharamsala I am downright shamed. So much of my life lost to my lost self, so much introverted anguish and isolation, so much self-involvement. I know it has been necessary, that I would not be alive if I hadn't been granted this healing journey over these past 20 years. But I am shamed just the same. And I know that shame, too, serves no-one.

The streets are all tidy when I walk back through town. When I get back to our room, Thrinley's already packed and organized for her departure. We gather up the monks from the guest house for a photo shoot on the roof. Even the Geshe comes along, followed up the stairs by his little dog. Altogether they are a rather imposing bunch. Nawang looms tall in his leather jacket; the others—the monk who wears a knitted hat, another whom I've never seen smile, one who is always smiling, and several too shy to make eye contact—all cluster around the Geshe seated in his flowing robes and Thrinley in her flowing wool poncho.

We have found a home here and a modicum of acceptance and even affection from these monks who see so many types of travelers and tourists come and go. They have anchored our stay here in meaning. From the meticulous sweeping and cleaning to the morning circumambulation and pots of steaming strong tea, they have served us with unpretentious grace and good humor. I know each of them is learned and deeply committed to spiritual practice. Yet to them, everyday common sense and practical purpose is also an embodiment of spiritual grace. Chop wood, carry water, sweep the stairs, flip the pancakes—they all add up to the Great Present. Be Here Now: they are the easiest three syllables of Buddhist principles and the hardest to do. Because being here now means being here to everything everywhere for everyone. Not just ourselves.

Dakpa shows up for his English lesson and without prompting, immediately reads his story aloud. It's become a ritual and each time he reads it he owns it more. He's bridging the Great Language Divide with a few fickle vowel sounds and a handful of reliable consonants. Globalization is nothing if not breaking into one another's languages and breaking up our own. What we really need today is an international language of indigenous insight and wisdom. Perhaps one of those languages that have a thousand words for "sky" and no word for "I." But then, where would I be?

All this life trying to get to "I" when it really isn't all that useful, that's the really big irony. I remember that long ago article about psychology and Buddhism and how important it is to have a healthy ego before you can effectively leave your ego behind. The state of no "I" equals the Big Emptiness. But the other emptiness, the one that the "I" never inhabited, is hollow and meaningless. It has no reverberations of self or boundaries of body.

I recall this meaningless emptiness from over many years. After family gatherings I would be hollowed out by a suspended and desolate depression. To link the two events—family and depression—was not a connection I was capable of making. Just as I was never capable of asking questions within this family. Not only did I not know how to ask, I did not know that I did not know how.

This is a difficult state to describe. I had a questioning mind and had used it to write plays and poetry and articles but never had I turned it in the direction of my family. Nor had I ever written a word about my family, nor any family of my imagination. A gap I never even began to question. Even now, years into uncovering and recovering, my family exists in a world without me. A world in which I never existed. I long to sit down with my brothers and ask them questions: What was I like? Where did I sit at the dinner table? Did I have friends? Did I play? Did they tease me? What did I wear? What did I like? Did I have birthday parties?

One question still haunts me like the wind. Where did I sleep? It was in Vancouver, British Columbia where I remember my first bed. I was fourteen. In one house in Montreal I remember lying on the floor in an alcove at the top of the stairs listening to a discussion my parents were having about me with another man and woman. She's very lovely, said someone. Yes, said my mother. I was perhaps ten. I was being bargained for. I have no idea where my bed was. I do know there was a dark room with no windows, a low ceiling and a mattress upon which women would have sex with me. At more public gatherings, the sex was with men. In between were all the measures taken to make me one of them—or nothing at all.

In Montreal, my father went to New York and brought me back a bracelet. In Montreal, my mother greeted me at a train station and on the way home asked, Aren't you glad to see me? These two odd occasions I remember because I was so startled by them both. The bracelet was beautiful—all rhinestones that stretched around my wrist like precious jewels. I was only a little girl and I got this wonderful present. I could not believe it. And I never did. I knew there were no wonderful presents in my childhood.

I could not believe the other either. I had returned from staying with people in the city. I got off that train and walked on sticks toward my mother. My arms were sticks, my head was a stick; I was dead. In Montreal my mind was toyed with and I was used for child prostitution and pornography.

"Aren't you glad to see me?" my mother asked. "Give me a kiss."

I remember the shock I felt. Suddenly she wanted a kiss—as though she was really my mother and I was really her little girl. Inside I could feel the lie of it all, the pretense. I reached up and kissed her cheek. I was already making myself up from minute to minute. Finally, at the age of 60, I am no longer doing it. I can let myself go.

The biggest tragedy about the abuse we suffer is that it renders us unable to let ourselves go—for our own sake and for the sake of others. We get caught in a web of self-survival so dense that any strands of connection to the outside world, to any reality beyond the confines of our own mind, including those we should inherently love, are inaccessible.

But the disintegration in my family is profound. The poisoning of normal has alienated us all from one another. My brothers are unwilling, unable, and unready to talk about the depth of the darkness and disintegration in the family. I do not blame them. It has taken me all these years and a whole lot of therapy to accept the truth of our family and to heal into being. And I was their big sister; I was supposed to be there for them. And I left. It is not my brothers' fault that they do not know how to love me. My responsibility to them is my healing. The brothers I love now are the innocent boys I knew when we were all small within a family system over which none of us had any control.

Over the years, the language about systemic abuse has changed. "Satanists" has become "deviant social groups" and the understanding of the mind-control experimentation has become sophisticated enough to really help survivors undo the damage. My interpretation of my experience has changed, too. At first I tried to see my parents as crazy cultists. But the gaudiness of blood-letting rituals and a frenzy of satanic chanting did not fit the profile of my parents as I knew them. But medical experimentation did, and so did using me as a money-making enterprise. And I had always known I had received electric shocks. It was the reason I was taken away from school as a small child. And my father said Nazi things that I can remember. And his disdain, and my mother's, too, for joy, for affection, for anything lighthearted and spontaneous between anyone and anything, was stark and memorable. As were their lies. For years, I was told I fell through a window and cut my arm. Later my father told me "my brother did it." My parents' entire relationship to me and about me was fabricated. Once, when I showed my mother a photograph of my son, she said it wasn't him. It was as though I had to be discredited about my own experience in every way.

Yet my parents never denied my abuse, nor did they ever contact me after I made the decision to take what I thought would be a temporary break from them. I was, however, contacted by a psychiatrist who said my mother was worried about me and thought I should make an appointment to see him. I didn't. Shortly after, my mother moved to Florida.

I then heard that some members of my family thought I should be committed. My father, however, wasn't one of them. He died in 1993, after taking himself off the medicines that were keeping him alive. When he stopped eating and drinking, one of my brothers called me from the hospital and told me my father was dying. I was by his side for the last 20 hours of his life. I cried at his bedside, touched his head, and held his feet as they grew colder and colder. The nurses nodded at me approvingly. "He's been too alone," they said. I helped him die peacefully, bringing to bear all my Buddhist practice. Hearing is the last to go and the left ear is the last to hear, say the old Buddhist monks. I whispered prayers and told him I loved him, even though it was the father I never had whom I loved. This father had sacrificed his daughter to experiments, exploitation and extradition from the human race.

All the grief at never having a father poured out at his bedside. I told him it was okay and that he would find peace. He never opened his eyes—until the moment of death when they flew open in a startled moment of recognition. Words of love and light and beauty were in the room as my father exhaled his last breath. I won. And when, in his very final moment, his eyes flew open in surprise, I imagined that the light, too, had won.

I was surprised to feel daughterly pride at the way he disciplined his departure. It was as controlled as the way he lived. Two of my brothers arrived right at the end. One of them said to me, "Good work." Then we went our separate ways yet again. My father did not exclude me from his will. He knew what I was up against, and why.

I can feel the power of the darkness of it all, the Nazi arrogance, the denigration and ridicule of all that is human with feeling. It goes beyond hatred to something more chilling—a final and ultimate dismissal. It's this that has been hardest to face, that I am, in ways, one of them. This is the ultimate irony—that getting back my light means getting back my dark. But I had to be "made" to be dark. The real light of my beginning self only seemed to disappear. And I have found my deepest self to be in a state of being-ness that I can only describe as prayer. Precisely what was trained, drugged and brainwashed out of me—a sense of inherent goodness, an expansive individual self that knows connection to the beauty of the universe—is what finally remains. I am not a bad person. I have peeled away the evil; and what is left is the "I" inside the jewel of the heart of the lotus that can finally give up and let go of itself.

But now I have to let go of Thrinley. She is my friend, my spiritual sister, at times like a daughter, and perhaps, like a mother. But that is only something I can guess at.

My mother. I knew her as a word, *mother*. I knew her as a bitter divorced woman who finally needed me. I knew her as the mother who could not get out of bed for weeks at a time during her last and unwanted pregnancy. I knew her as the mother who had a kidney stone operation and, upon coming home from the hospital, berated me for the dust on the window ledge in her bedroom. I was fourteen years old. For three weeks I had taken care of my brothers, the house, my father, the meals and the cleaning. I went to school every day, too; and took exams. I was so proud that I'd been able to do it all. Surely this time, I thought. But no, there was dust on the windowsill, couldn't I get anything right? For weeks afterward, I would continue to take care of my mother, and everyone and everything else at home. But after that dust-on-the-sill moment, somewhere inside I knew I would never, ever, get anything right.

It was a diatribe of diminishment. I was too fat. My hair was a mess. I always looked tired, terrible or miserable. Why was I so awkward? Why didn't I do it better, whatever it was? My father's routine commentary was about my "behind." It looked big. The truth was I was slight, weighing in at around a hundred pounds at five foot three when I was fourteen. I was pretty. And I was neat. My mother saw to it. She cut my hair her way, with bangs too short, and she made my clothes. I looked exactly the way she wanted me to look and it was always wrong.

Even after my parents' divorce, when I was my mother's entire and only emotional support system, her invariable greeting was,

"You look tired, Janet." After which would begin her litany of hatred about my father as off we would go to yet another doctor's appointment about something. I never knew what. She simply dissembled into a state of physical, emotional and psychological despair—and I could be counted on.

I could always be counted on. It was what I knew most of all how to do. My four brothers counted on me before they could say my name. And after they could, I was always there for something they needed, whether it was praise, appreciation, money or a roof over their heads. Not long ago, one of my brothers told me that the family disintegrated after I wrote the letter of separation from my parents. But nobody, not one single member of my family even called me to ask what was wrong. Was I okay? Why was I doing such a terrible thing? And I was left with a question of my own: How could I have caused disintegration in the family when nobody gave a damn about me?

If love is anything, it is a glance. A glance that simply says, "I am glad to see you." I see it in the eyes of my friends, in the eyes of children I don't even know, in the eyes of lovers, colleagues, acquaintances, dogs and sometimes in the mirror. It is a glance that comes before words. It is a glance I never knew from my parents. But that is a lie. It is a glance towards me that grew in my father's eyes after his near-death experience. A glance I could not abide. The "good" me, who, for forty years, had created love in the world in which I did not exist, could not face my father's glance of simple acknowledgement because it would unveil the artifice of me. The artifice that kept me in the family.

Long unable to face that I meant nothing to anyone, I instead made them mean something to me. It's what survivors do; we create what we cannot face having lost. I was treated with deep and abiding indifference. So I created a self that would give to my family what I was not getting, acknowledgement first of all, and love. I had to get it from somewhere. Otherwise, perhaps, I would have hated them. I write this but I don't know it. Somewhere I got goodness. The good love of my grandmother took hold deeply and early. Some of it came from my guides, tenderly protecting the goodness of my core self and working like mad to keep the rest of me connected. Some of it came from the "good girl" I created to counteract the ground of badness upon which I knew as my own. It was only after I'd faced the abuse done to me that I could face the creation of the nice, thoughtful "me" that everybody in my life took as true. It's complicated. Whenever I try to describe and explain the map of my mind and the inchoate geography of my body, I am stymied by the reality of it all. It is as unbelievable as nature. And as true.

When I wrote that letter to my parents from the coast of California, somewhere in-between the wild ocean and the endless sky, I was part of the grace of nature. I was separating from my family into that grace. And although I had no idea I was separating for good, it was an act of complete and total and catastrophic proportions. It named me on my way. And it was spontaneous, like the irrevocable splitting away of ice from an iceberg. There was no going back. And going forward was defined by tides I couldn't feel, winds I couldn't see, and obstacles I couldn't name. And I told no-one. Not even Brian knew that I would write that letter, that I was writing that letter.

It was during my exile in Oakland, a weekend away to the Montara Lighthouse Hostel. On Sunday I drove south to the curious corner on the coast near San Gregorio where bikers stop for beer and BBQ and there is an art gallery. I was reeling and unreeling from what was being revealed in my life. The only place I could go to begin any shape of acceptance was to the sea. I wrote the letter in my old Volvo Ethyl in a parking lot by the tavern. I was afraid of solitude and I was afraid of people. Writing that letter was the most courageous act of my life. And I don't even know who wrote it.

I was slipping in and out of my selves so fast and so unconsciously that it was a kaleidoscopic existence. Every moment was a shift in time, place and circumstances of self. The one who wrote it was calm and polite. The one who made not writing it impossible was fierce with reality. There was no option. She gave my hand nowhere else to go but to the words that would make the rest of my life possible. And this time, she was a "she," a grizzly bear of protection, a roaring ferocious one who would not let anyone stop that letter from being written. And it seems that I mailed it from there, that day, along that blistering and beautiful coast.

I am in awe of that grizzly she-bear. How she rose up and filled all of me with that inevitable, irrevocable act. It wasn't an aggressive letter. It simply said I was having a hard time and wouldn't be seeing my parents for awhile. Most of all, I expected a response. The shock of their silence started me believing that which I could not believe. It articulated the truth in a way that no words could come close.

I think of that: How would I feel if my son sent me a similar letter? I would be in a wailing mess of harangue and communication. I would be sorry for everything—whether I'd done it or not. Nothing in my life would mean anything as long as that terrifying silence prevailed. It would take all meaning out of my very existence.

After many years, I came to understand how that first and lasting silence from my family said it all. What I did get was proxy attention via a sister-in-law. She would call me to have lunch and ask questions. She was as "nice" as I was. But I knew enough to keep my counsel, to listen, and to wonder why she was there. Later I found out she was involved in the family move to have me committed. They feared I would write about them and destroy their lives. Institutionalizing me as "crazy" was easier than making a phone call to ask me what was wrong.

My four bothers are absent in this book because they have been absent. Each of them suffers in his own way from the legacy of life in our family. Each has his own story to tell. Their stories aren't mine. The image I have of our shared childhoods together is that we were a small band of survivors fighting for existence against the looming shadow of our parents. It turned out I was on my own. Over the years, however, some reconnection happened, always around death.

Within a year after I sent that letter to my parents, my mother moved away from the Northwest to Florida where she would live for the last 23 years of her life. We would see each other once before she died. It was a reunion made possible by the same brother who had called me out of compassion to our dying father's bedside. As I write this I feel the awkwardness of naming and not naming my brothers. So I will use "younger" and "youngest." They are the two brothers with whom there has been heart and human connection. The other two brothers remain unnamed.

"Mother is dying," my younger brother said, when he called me from Florida where he'd flown earlier that day. She'd had a heart attack and a brother older than he, who had legal control over our mother's affairs and her physical well-being, had pulled the plug on her life-support system. Then my younger brother did a magnificent thing: He bought tickets for me and my youngest brother to fly out to Florida to see our dying mother.

My youngest brother had suffered tremendously over the years. A dad to three lovely children, he encountered his own personal grief and trauma about his own childhood as his children were born. He experienced a despair bordering on suicide that drove him to be in touch with me when he was 35 and I was 50. I was still fragile then, but I knew enough to be helpful, and I wasn't too fragile to love his children. Our contact had been sporadic over the years, but reliable.

Now, he and I would go to Florida to see the dying mother who, a few years earlier, had screamed racial epithets at his wife and children after he'd spent thousands of dollars to take the family to Florida to see her. He had wanted his children to get to know their grandmother. It was an event that haunted him. But both of us wanted to see our mother before she died, wanted, perhaps, to know we had the courage to see her.

My youngest brother got there ahead of me. It was 9:30 on a Monday night and I was on my way to the airport when I retrieved his cell-phone message. "You need to know it's really bad here," he said. "Really bad. Call me before you get on that plane."

I pulled over, just before the freeway entrance and returned his call. It was after midnight in Florida. He'd flown through last night to get there; that he was still up was not a good sign.

This time he was in tears. "It's really awful," he says. "I don't know if you should come."

But my baby brother is crying and there is my mother. "Don't you want me to come?" I asked.

"Yes," he said, "I need a friend." And now he is sobbing.

"I'll be there," I said. "But I've got to hang up right now and get to the airport."

Some kind of psychic invincibility propelled me down the freeway. I knew I was going to have to be strong to make this trip. I also knew there was no choice for me. I decided to hell with some distant twelve dollar a day parking lot and drove straight to the roof of the expensive parking lot at the airport where I knew I'd find a space. I got there and immediately shit in my car. It happened so suddenly that I had no chance of making it from the roof of the parking lot, into an elevator, and down to a bathroom. It was an explosion and it was a mess.

I remembered the long-ago call from my ten-year-old son after I'd gone off to yet another writer's event and left him with someone who I thought was trustworthy. "You missed the explosion of my stomach at the airport," he told me across 2,000 miles. "You missed it." I was young and still stupid to my own life as well as his and said I hoped he was feeling better. Now, 30 years later, I'm sitting in an explosion of shit at the airport and I know I can't take any of it back, ever. I left a mess behind me and now I'm really stuck in it and the metaphor not only blindsides me, it stinks. I started to laugh. And I realized that this trip to say goodbye to the dying mother I haven't spoken to in more than 20 years is going to be a doozie.

Thank God it was dark. Thank God, He, She or It has a sense of humor. Thank God. It's something I'd learned over many years to do with reverence. Now I was doing it with a vengeance. I will figure this out; I will make that plane; I will rescue my brother; I will see my mother; I will.

It was a long way between that car seat and the airplane seat. Getting cleaned involved various contortions of body, mind and newspaper—the *New York Times*, to be exact—and a pair of old jeans blessedly discovered in the trunk of my car. It took me half an hour to clean up body and car, all the time wondering where the security surveillance cameras were pointed. Then, when I finally dashed to check-in, the computer wouldn't give me a boarding pass. Turned out I was a security risk. I didn't have the time or the courage to ask why. Maybe my every move had been caught on some security camera; maybe because I wrote *Battle in Seattle*, maybe just because. A woman punched things into the computer for several minutes, appraised me carefully, and finally said I had "permission to board." I got on that plane and expected it to explode on take-off.

When I got to Florida, my youngest brother met me at the airport, his composure intact. My mother was alive. She had, in fact, revived right after being taken off life-support and had been moved back to a convalescent center. We drove straight there.

When we walked into her room, it was full of brothers and brothers' wives. "Hi," I said, not looking anywhere but directly into my mother's eyes. I took her hand. My mother had grown tiny and was as frail as a bird. But after getting out of the hospital and back to the convalescent center, she'd immediately resumed smoking. So the first thing we did was wheel her outside for a cigarette. It turned out that her deathbed would be months away.

During my visit, all four of my brothers were there and some ugly things happened. The brother who'd pulled the plug, the one who wanted her to die as quickly as possible, saw my Janet-come-lately arrival as interference. So did another brother. They both look at me with hatred. But my mother could no longer look at me with hatred. She simply wanted to have her lipstick on, her hair combed and the clothes she liked to wear. All the things a daughter could do. But not this daughter. My mother had cast her lot with the brother who'd pulled the plug and there was nothing I could do about it. He had total control over all her affairs and was her legal proxy. He kept a proprietary vigil over my mother, reminding her constantly of her frailty, keeping me at bay.

"Are you my Janet?" my mother asked during our first few moments of private time together. She was glad to see me. Glad I was there. "Can you get me out of here?" she whispered. Hearing the broad reaches of the question, I instead responded to something I could do, or thought I could do. "Would you like to go to the beach for dinner?" I asked.

Her eyes lit up. "That would be wonderful," she said.

I got permission from the staff at the convalescent center for us all to take her out to the seashore for dinner. It was only a few miles away. In my Pollyanna mind I imagined a kind of reunion, a rehabilitated time with my brothers, a place that left the past 20 years behind and found the greater past, where we were all in this together. But the brother with all the legal control was outraged at my interference and wouldn't allow my mother to go to the shore, the place she loved most. He swooped in, bullied me physically chest-to-chest with his rage, and used his legal status as my mother's medical proxy to bully the staff as well. He caused such uproar that we were immediately categorized as a "problem family" and ushered from the premises.

I'd battled for my mother's getaway but I had no legal standing.

"If you don't leave, we'll call the police," they told us.

So my mother was left behind, alone with the brother who had pulled the plug, wondering about her dinner outing and where did we all go?

It was then I decided to call the Florida Elder Abuse Hotline. I had only a day left and I could see what was happening: this place of isolation; the dark room in which my mother was assigned; the overworked staff intimidated by a brother who poisoned them against the rest of her children; her lack of control over her own financial resources—resources that could add comfort to her life. Up until recently, she'd lived alone and happy in her condo, playing bridge with her friends, swimming in the pool, smoking, drinking and socializing. These were things my mother always put first. In some fierce way, she always fought for her self. But now, what was left of my mother's life was about to become a greater hell.

"Can you get me out of here?" She asked again and again, to me and to my younger brother.

"Do you want to come back to Seattle?" we asked.

"Yes," she said.

We conferred and agreed that between us we could care for her. As we spoke to my mother there were moments in her face when composure became confusion and a flash of something shocked filled her eyes. But she still knew control. She still had the old feisti-ness that at one time erupted into rage and violence; now it seemed full of dreadful pathos and loneliness. I wanted to hold her and com-fort her. All that long time ago, when I was born, she lost me, too, as I had lost her. And I saw something else very clearly. When, so very early on, she gave up her bond with me, she gave up the mother's bond with all my brothers. I could see no glimpse of maternal con-nection to any of them. We were all awash in the aftermath of life-long abandonment. In many ways, I was the lucky one. I'd broken the bonds of fear and rejection. It took all these years of healing, but I could now look at my mother with a compassion I really felt.

"Would you please get me out of here?" Her question hung in the air. But we had no recourse, no legal standing to say "yes." Nei-ther did she. I hoped the Elder Abuse intervention would create a different playing field for her.

A wonderful man came from Florida Elder Abuse office to me-diate a round-table discussion with us all—my mother, her five children, and staff from the convalescent center. The brother in legal control tried to prevent my mother from attending. But she had already expressed her wishes to the Elder Abuse officer and he insisted she be brought to the table. My brother's custodial presence, however, was evident. He sat by her side, smiled at us mockingly and whispered in her ear. Our mediator gained from us all that he could. My younger brother and I voiced concern that her financial resources were not being used to full effect for her well-being. We talked visiting rights, the right of family to receive medical information and the right of my mother as an elder in the State of Florida. The mediator had interviewed my mother privately and assured her she had the right, and the capability, to do whatever she wanted. At that table, weighted with lifetimes of suffering, my younger brother asked our mother if she'd like to come back to the Northwest. She bristled defensively in her old way, "Why should I?" she asked, even though, in private, she had beseeched us to take her "home."

In light of it all, her question was legitimate. How could she possibly know that she had three estranged children, now adults, who could actually care for her, kindly and compassionately? How could she know there was love in the world?

My few days in Florida were full of moments that would have been pathetic if they weren't so profound. When my younger and youngest brother and I put photographs of our selves and our children in my mother's room, they were immediately removed by the other two brothers. I went out and bought my mother a super soft blanket for her to touch and an electric candle that warmed essential oil of lavender to help alleviate the terrible smell of illness and dying that permeated the place. She loved them both, and they, too, disappeared within hours. Those of us in the family who had struck out for something healthy in ourselves had no standing in the face of the cynicism that prevailed. I had been gone from the family for more than 20 years and I had no recourse in my mother's life. The most we could do was get assurances that the convalescent center would keep my younger brother informed about my mother's condition, and he would in turn pass on the information to me and to my youngest brother.

On the last day we were there, my youngest brother and I were allowed some private time with my mother—at the bingo table. She asked us questions, about our lives and our children. I saw a tear in her eye, quickly wiped away and credited to an allergy. I could feel the wail of grief rising under my skin and wondered if there was a moment anywhere in the universe that could hold it all.

Later that day we flew home across the country, leaving behind the younger brother to battle on for my mother. He and his wife knew the psychic battle would be great. But they, too, had no heart or stomach for what was happening to my mother. They hoped to have an impact. Maybe they could bring her home.

I had gone to Florida filled with the fear that had defined my childhood; and I left as my mother's protector. I had done the right thing. I was whole. I was heartbroken. I called Brian from the airport and we spoke about it all. I had used everything I had learned in order to be there fully, with all the parts of me rising and falling to the occasion. I had held nothing back but my grief. I could feel the vast journey I had taken to freedom. I felt triumphant. What I had held out for as a small child was real love. What I created to survive was the artifice of love. And in my healing, I had come full circle.

Some terrible things unfolded in the following months. Because of the decisions made by two brothers, my mother died isolated and all alone. Three of us could have helped her final months be comfortable, and perhaps even redeeming, but two brothers played out their hatred and we were deprived of helping her. And she was deprived of our help. In Florida, not even children have a right to information when a parent dies. And, as it turned out, the convalescent center did not honor their commitment to keep us informed. I, my younger brother and my youngest brother did not even know she was in decline and getting close to death. By keeping her isolated in Florida, my brother insured himself total and ultimate control. It is here where I see the terrible legacy of the family playing itself out in dark and treacherous ways. It is here where love ends and rage begins. I still have a lot of work to do.

There are volumes to write about my therapeutic process with Brian. I had not heard of "cult abuse" when my own disintegration process started. I had no context for the experience I was having. Putting the pieces together—of things I remembered, re-experienced and reconnected—has happened on so many levels of body, mind, heart and spirit that it is nearly impossible to distinguish them one from the other. Brian's patience in those early years, his acceptance of the overwhelming and helpless grief that was my life, saved my physical life. His skills and insights into treating my traumatized self brought emotional relief. When I ask Brian about this process, he refers to Pierre Janet, the French psychologist who, in the late 1800s, was one of the pioneers in linking events in childhood with trauma in adulthood. He was the first to give names to "disassociation" and "subconscious." Some professionals see Pierre Janet as the real founder of psychotherapy, not Sigmund Freud.

Brian's expertise about the ways mind-control programming works was crucial in getting me through the final stages of reclaiming my self in my life. He gave me very precise tools to defuse the fear and immobilization that accompanied my ever-growing ability to be my core self. A core self that was never supposed to be known, or felt. They are tools I use every day to ground myself in my body, and to ground my body in time and space. My inner world is a negotiation between my inner guides, who want me to win this battle, and the outer forces of fear, hatred and cynicism that try to co-opt my experience. There is a formula to mind control. Thanks to those who are courageous enough to share it, there is now a formula to combat mind-control.

To help someone heal from the abuse of mind, body and spirit requires a whole lot from a therapist: professional expertise in posttraumatic stress and disassociative identity disorders; an arsenal of techniques to combat the fear and mistrust that marks the survivor of cult and mind-control abuse; an understanding of the wounding of the soul; endless patience; all kinds of resilience; spiritual self-awareness; faith in goodness; and uncommon courage.

Trust in instincts is also a great gift. It was an instinctive comment from Brian—at just the right moment—that woke me up to a turning point in my healing that made all the difference. It was at the end of a session on the telephone during a time when I was struggling to make a leap of faith in the seemingly miraculous effects of the techniques he was using to help me experience, more and more, the great feeling of "being." (To say that I have had trouble accepting help would be the understatement of the ages.) "Janet," said Brian, "Sometimes I think you hold on to the pain because it proves how bad the perpetrators were. And that if you get better, it will somehow make what they did less reprehensible." He said it to me almost casually; but even before the words were fully delivered, his observation riveted through me with truth. *YES!* That's exactly what I was doing, had been doing, and would still be doing if Brian had not trusted to say it. I was filled with a shattering and liberating euphoria. The prison gates were imposed from within as well as without and only I could unlock them. With his help in that brilliant moment, I did.

Later, I asked Brian what made him say that. "Instinct," he answered. But it was an instinct I could trust, born out of years of therapeutic relationship, and timed to perfection. It was an instinct that delivered me to the rest of my life. I knew I was in it for the long-haul in terms of cognitive reconstruction and fear-wrestling. I also knew that real healing meant joining in the fearless flow of life that was my birthright. Holding on to the pain meant holding on to the annihilating forces that had held me hostage in their parallel and pointless universe.

I let go.

TWENTY-SIX

Thrinley left last night and it was sadness all around. Her student, Darjee, was there to say goodbye and he couldn't muster even a hint of a smile. Tsering, Matt and I waved her and Norbu away in the bus and in spite of myself I was worried about their trip through the night, down the mountain, around the treacherous curves, and always in the face of the insanity known as driving in India.

Now I am on my own. So, I go to the library.

As I walk through the trees and down the hill, I see two young girls and a young boy coming my way. As they get closer, one of the girls appears to be holding her hand out to me. I immediately brace myself for the begging experience. But right in the middle of my consternation I realize that I am being offered bright pink cotton candy. This young Tibetan girl, maybe seven or eight, is so thrilled to be eating it that it must be shared. Something about this moment stops me in my all-too-worn-out tracks. How many lightning strikes of expectation gone astray will it take before I stop giving in to old, ignorant, rigid patterns of responding? From cotton candy to love, I was trained to turn everything good that came my way into a threat. And it worked. I do.

Whether or not I will ever fully get over this I don't know. But I do know that I will die trying. The thin air is crisp with cold as I find my way along the shaded trail to the library. I'm on the path Matt walks every day when he goes to his Buddhist Studies class. He is devoted to his classes and no matter how hung-over he is in the morning, he gets there in time every day. He is probably there already. The small square in front of the library is quite empty and once again I am struck by the bright beauty of Tibetan architecture. I wonder where the Tibetans got all the pigments for their paint. The wild barrens of the high plateau of Tibet are stark; but somewhere color was hiding underground and somehow they found it.

There's a dog sprawled in sleep on the steps to the library. His body drapes in supplication to the winter sun. He doesn't blink as I ease myself by. I pay a few entrance rupees and wander the halls of this auspicious and ordinary library. Auspicious in that it is a repository for more than 80,000 rare and treasured Tibetan manuscripts, books and documents; 6,000 archival photographs and hundreds of Buddhist statues, thanka paintings, and other artifacts. Ordinary in that it invites all of us in, whether we are distinguished scholars, curious tourists, young people on pilgrimage, or lost souls in search of life.

This Library of Tibetan Works and Archives was built in 1971 by the Dalai Lama and is part of the complex of buildings that are home to the Tibetan Government-in-Exile. It's a cultural resource centre as well as a renowned research library. Most of all it is preserving and protecting what is left of a civilization that knew no boundaries between spirit, politics, culture and justice. All that was Tibet is represented in this building, and all that it will be as Tibetans spread out across the globe in search of home. It is a massive and incomprehensible tragedy that Tibet is no longer home to the Tibetan people, that Tibetan monks and nuns are imprisoned because of their faith, and that it is illegal for Tibetans, abandoned and at-risk in Tibet, to own a photograph of the Dalai Lama. The genocide perpetrated by the Chinese government and directly and indirectly supported by governments around the world, is a crime against the human race and the future of the human race.

Until we wake up to the abuse that is done in our name and say "no more," collectively and absolutely, we leave it to the survivors in this world to strike out for freedom and justice in our name. And it's not fair. Survivors—whether of crimes of collective genocide or individual brutality—are at a serious disadvantage when it comes to issues of political impact and social justice. For one thing, we cry too easily. And for another, the fact that we've actually survived means that we are working too damned hard every day just to keep it together, let alone save the world. If those in the seats and cultures of "power" in operative society would just wake up to the real power of grief and the nature of suffering, we might have half a chance of preserving the human community for future and better times. But it won't happen without an upheaval of biblical proportion—on the streets, in the environment, and in the minds of us all.

I go down a hall, open a door marked "museum," and carefully peer in just in time to see a most elderly monk lower his eyes away from examining me and my entrance. He goes immediately back to his engrossing work, which looks like translation. There is no one else here.

Every religion has its icons from when time had time to carve and sculpt and paint and honor all that is timeless. In this small modest room, the life of an entire race of people is held in sacred trust. Ancient books, scrolls, paintings and sculptures are on these shelves and walls; the mind, in all its various guise and brilliance, is on display. I am in the holy presence of all that it means, and has ever meant, to be human.

I feel a secret kinship with the old and silent monk who is in his own world and letting me be in mine. We inhabit our solitude together. I think about Rilke's writing about the sacred responsibility that lovers have to protect one another's solitude. But why not extend it to all who live? When we do, the other can never be overlooked, abandoned, exploited, violated or abused because solitude is sacred and we can only greet it with our own.

In the center of the room, behind glass walls, is a big sand mandala on a table. It's the Kalachakra, the Wheel of Time, an astonishingly elaborate colored sand illustration depicting the sacred dimensions of earth, mind, body, cosmos and the universe of consciousness. It's a complex image painstakingly created over many days by a team of monks trained in the discipline. They build it grain-by-grain of colored sand into a visual masterpiece of design and meaning. Historically, it's an activity that has always been held secret, but the Dalai Lama, wanting to lift the veil of misunderstanding about this sacred

Tibetan Buddhist ritual, has sent the Wheel of Time into the world. We even had one at our county fair.

For five years throughout the mid-nineties I was the manager of our county fair. It was a juggling act of major proportion, involving getting along with everyone in our island community—from farmers, artists and musicians to politicos running for office and eccentric driftwood collectors. So, why not have a Tibetan Buddhist sand mandala? We invited the Namgyal monks to come to our fair.

For four days, people stood and sat silently in the corner of the fair building and watched as this beautiful rainbow of colored sand was carefully sifted, grain-by-grain, into a sacred geometry of design. The monks were so focused on their task that it felt like we were all voyeurs to solitude and to the spirit at work and at play. On the last day they performed a ceremony and swept the sands together. Then we all walked a mile down to the beach where the sand was carried out and cast into the water to the sound of all of us chanting our hearts out for world peace.

Ritual.

It has the power to destroy and the power to heal. Getting back to rituals that honor life and beauty and connectedness and the power of creation to far outlast the power of destruction is a true homecoming. This power is manifest in all the nooks and crannies of Dharamsala. All of life here is a creation ritual—from the monks chanting prayers in the temple to the dogs sprawling in the sun. It's all a big meditation on our behalf. This is where my religious skills of discernment fail me. I find it impossible to believe that the world's religions don't, at some very critical place, join up in celebration of unity. Nothing else makes sense.

When I leave the library I do so with the utmost quiet. I don't want to disturb the old monk so deep in concentration. He has protected my solitude and it's the least I can do in return.

As I'm walking back up the hill to town, a fellow in a small car stops and offers me a ride. It's one of the Indian men who own the cyber café where I go to write home. I'm grateful for the ride and take it as a sign to email all my friends and relations. Out of the spiritual fire and into the frying pan of mundane and daily life.

That's what I miss back home: the blatant interrelatedness between the sacred and the profane, the celebration of the crazy conundrum of consciousness that is life. This whirling diversity, from the depraved to the divine, is recognizable to me because it is a reflection of my inner world. But the ways in which opposite realities hang out side-by-side without trying to change one another is an epiphany. For twenty years, in and out of therapy, I have been trying to negotiate my inner selves, trying to integrate my personality into something continuous and recognizable, trying to become "normal." Here, nothing is normal. I fit right in.

When I get back to the guest house, I am greeted in the lobby by Nawang who wishes me a cheerful "Merry Christmas" and gives me a present and a card from Dakpa. Then he issues instructions that it is time to move back into the old room upstairs. "Merry Christmas" has never sounded so good. I race up to the patio penthouse and throw my arms wide open to the sky and the mountains and the madness of it all.

TWENTY-SEVEN

They have great cakes in Dharamsala and Matt and I are searching them out for our Christmas Eve daytime dinner at his friend's place in Dharamkot. Matt has invited me to join him for this event and I think I'm grateful, although I'm not sure. I was ready to spend the day on the beloved patio, drinking tea, writing in my journal and daydreaming about life as a dog in Dharamsala. Matt, however, caught me at my reverie and spirited me away. We get boxes for the big creamy confections and set out on our walk to only-Matt-knows-where.

We start on the road to Tushita and after about twenty minutes head off on a trail across the hillside. Another twenty minutes gets us to a house of cement, color and wrought iron. There's a patio area out front where food fills a big low table and young people are sprawling around eating and chatting.

I'm wondering why Matt invited me along. I thought there would be two or three people at this afternoon dinner but this is obviously a party and nobody is over thirty. Then I find out from one of the young people that the Dalai Lama is coming back to Dharamsala today. Maybe right this minute. I am so pissed I could spit. Here I am at a gathering of young people all infatuated with themselves and one another when I could be back in town welcoming the Dalai

Lama home. The yearning to see the Dalai Lama has been kept at bay by the circumstances of his absence. With that no longer in play I am suddenly obsessed with the possibility. It turns me into someone who doesn't like these lovely people who have so kindly included me in their Christmas dinner. But I'm not confident enough to find my way back so I sit and suffer.

It is 3:30 by the time Matt and I head back to town. As we walk, I chirp on in friendly fashion about nothing of significance, feigning obliviousness to my pissed-off impatience about the afternoon. Then, as we walk through town, Matt suggests we buy a Christmas present for the monks.

Okay. Fine. Be nice. See if I care.

I am, of course, struck by the perfection of his suggestion.

"Let's get them a thanka for the lobby," says Matt.

"Yes, let's," says I.

We go in to the thanka shop where beautiful Tibetan Buddhist hangings of all sizes and deities fill the space with brilliant color. They are all made by monks who also run the shop so it's fair trade in all directions.

"How about Chenrezig?" says Matt.

"How about Chenrezig," says I.

After my forty years of Buddhism and his four weeks, it's Matt who can say "Chenrezig" and know that it's the precisely right deity for the occasion.

Chenrezig is the embodiment of compassion, the One Who Gazes Upon the World and Sees the Suffering, the One Who Refuses to Become Enlightened Until Everyone Else Does. Including me. And that's the sobering thought-of-the-day.

Chenrezig has anywhere from four to one thousand arms because two arms is not enough to hold the suffering world. Neither is one head. It is said that Chenrezig's head broke into eleven pieces when he became overwhelmed with the needs of so many sentient beings. His Holiness the Dalai Lama is believed to be the earthly manifestation of Chenrezig.

Chenrezig has other names, too; Avalokiteśvara is the Sanskrit version and it's a word I learned to say years ago when I was cooking at the retreat center. A-val-o-ki-tes-vara cried so many tears of compassion for the plight of us all that the millionth tear gave birth to the lake upon which floated the lotus that gave birth to White Tara, the Mother of Liberation. It was no accident that I memorized the difficult name of the deity that cried a million tears and could not stop.

The Chenrezig we select for the Loseling monks has four arms and is bordered by two layers of beautiful brocade. It comes ready to hang with a protective silk covering the color of saffron. It is beautiful and expensive. We'll give it to the monks tomorrow, Christmas Day. They are already thrilled because Christmas coincides with a commemoration day for some special historical teachers and they will be eating chicken, beef and "pig." It's an immensely rare culinary occasion to which Matt and I have been invited.

We are pleased with ourselves when we get back to our rooms. I give an English lesson to Dakpa and then head off for the Christmas Eve service at Saint John's in the Wilderness.

I don't do Christmas well. No matter how well I prepare, it is never enough to save others close to me from my meltdown of mind and emotions. I am an undercurrent of cynicism and repulsion, a mire of self-hatred and hatred, a child's urge to excitement and pleasure accompanied by a child's heartbreak and disappointment. I love the season because it is full of heart and generosity. I hate it because it is a trick. I spend money wildly. I get lost in irreparable grief. I try to be good, to hold to some sort of equanimity as the good tidings go by. I fail at every attempt to do so. At no other time of the year does desolation so effectively do its dirty work on me and on my relationships. I get totally fucked up and there is not a thing I can do about it.

If one is analytical, this holiday meltdown makes perfect sense. The litany of my upbringing—that I am beyond bad and there is nothing I can do about it—triumphs at Christmas. It tells me that I am a lost cause, that healing is a lost cause, and that the world is nothing but lost causes trying to fool themselves into some gruesome representation of good. I understand the idiocy of all this when my own personal undercurrents get the better of me. But it doesn't make the feelings go away.

This struggle to feel at home in the generative world, to feel as though I belong in the human family, is invisible. I am perceived as grown up, responsible, creative, accomplished, active in my community, intelligent and sensitive. These are easy things to see. What is invisible is the feeling of defilement that shadows every gesture towards being "good," towards what I "love," towards "life." I write these words in quotes because sometimes they are as science fiction to me as the word "satanism." On bad days, we mock one another. On good days, "love" and "life" are real and can be spoken.

Even after decades in recovery through psychotherapy and spiritual practice, this idea, that to be good is bad, wrestles within me constantly. As a child, I knew "good" as a lie because it was a mask for cruelty. As I grew up it became a more diffuse affliction. Goodness was rooted in hypocrisy. Fighting through this belief system has affected everything in my life – from harboring a hatred of my own worth to a penetrating mistrust in the good intentions of others. This is a dilemma of the soul. Knowing ourselves as meaningful, as belonging to life, as a natural part of a creative universe, as "good," means knowing ourselves soulfully. It is the recovery of our spirit that gives us, finally, our place in the world.

The skills that I developed to survive my childhood turned out to be spiritual skills. But it took many years and this trip to India to fully realize this, to get back my Self in all its peculiar grandeur, and to know not simply survival, but triumph. It is with those who have suffered, survived and triumphed where I find solace in this world. It's what His Holiness the Dalai Lama represented to me so many years ago when the news of his escape to India first reached my attention. It's what the Tibetan Elders represent as they, some with great difficulty, circumambulate the Lingkhor each morning. It's what I gleaned from the exuberant, joyful monk meditating in silence and solitude on top of the mountain. It's what the Khenpo warrior taught me with his fight for freedom and his passion for the language of freedom.

My own states of being often disintegrate into childlike parts and irrevocable sadness, grief that is unassailable. But when I get back from the brink of it all, it is always the stalwart in spirit who guide me, those whose lives have gone through the darkness and who stayed in faith and love on their spiritual path. My own ability to do so wavers on a daily basis. If the spiritual stalwarts weren't in the world, I wouldn't be. I know that completely. On this trip, I have found freedom for all of me.

India's rollicking diversity is exuberant with personal democracy. Yet there is also shocking discrimination and cruelty. Women are chattel, held behind bars and sold for sex. Children are oppressed and suppressed under the best of circumstances and raised and sold as sex slaves under the worst. Poor people grovel in unimaginable filth. The caste system, long illegal, still has a firm grip on the country's psyche. Yet behind it all, underneath it all, and in spite of it all, there is spirituality. Not the easy kind that sputters up from an over-fed, over-stimulated, over-indulged society in search of "meaning," but the kind that roars out in joy in the face of death and deprivation. It is an utterly nonsensical spirituality. It permeates the suffering. It is the suffering. It also permeates privilege and the privileged. Somehow, spirituality in India arrived before the people, took hold in the landscape, locked on to the very meaning of being, and hung on for dear life. And in India, life really is dear, just as it is expendable. The very deeply held bodily belief in reincarnation creates an almost giddy sense of acceptance of one's lot in life. Having a bad life in India is like having a bad day. Soon it will be over and there will be a new one.

So I have run away to India for Christmas and found an old colonial stone church on the edge of town where there's no priest, no pedantry, and no place to sit. The place is overflowing. I have to push my way inside where hundreds of people are crammed together in good spirits and bad singing. There are Tibetan monks, Indian families, European tourists and an array of Buddhists, Muslims, Hindus, Jews, Christians and a collection of those old Saint David's favorites—skeptics, non-believers, doubters and the gloriously confused. We sing carols in one another's languages and the buoyancy of hope and possibility is palpable in every breath. I am completely overcome. Tears flow down my cheeks like a river; I can't catch my breath. It feels as though we could light up the world.

The small Indian man who gave last week's sermon is bursting with pride and joy. He's surrounded up front by a crowd of people, mostly Westerners, participating in the service. He ushers them forward to read their favorite passages and to lead us in holiday songs from their countries. Two Indian women give a beautiful full-voiced rendition of "O Come, O Come Emmanuel," an elegant counter to our communal sing-along. There is a pretend birthday cake for Jesus where children put white candles and then stand gazing into the flickering lights.

The church darkness is also lit by colorful strings of lights and shining tinsel. As I watch the creative chaos amongst the group up front with the gentle Indian man, I realize that this is what he'd invited me to, the participatory process of this Christmas Eve tradition in which the company of strangers becomes a great gathering of spiritual friends.

It reminds me of the children's Christmas pageant back home. Years ago, I was asked to coordinate it and because I was saying "yes" to everything that was asked of me at Saint David's, where West Davis had opened my eyes to the possibilities and impossibilities within my own faith tradition, I took on the task. I knew I was in way over my head when the very children who showed up for rehearsal were the ones who knew they wouldn't be around for the performance. Going to rehearsal was better than nothing.

It all had to do with dressing up. Beards and wings and cloaks and loads of sparkling things made for a great get-up of one sort or another. But not making it to rehearsal had its consequences. Angels wandered the aisles in search of their parents, sheep sucked their thumbs, shepherds jousted with their staffs and Wise Men wisecracked their way through the script. Joseph was usually half as tall as Mary and Baby Jesus was a doll often handled with a startling and casual carelessness. The only role taken seriously was that of God. It was the only role that was fought over. My only requirement was that God showed up for both rehearsal and performance. God's costume was always a challenge and the solution was always more of anything gold. I knew it was sacrilegious to write words out of the mouth of God but it seemed to me that God deserved a voice in the pageant. After all, God was ultimately the real reason we were all there.

I grew to love those pageants. My favorite part was watching the parents dissemble as they realized there was no real organization other than their kids' on-the-spot desire to dress up and get attention. One year we had a real donkey for Mary to ride, and two favorite dogs as camels. There was nothing for a parent to do but sit back and pray.

I'd been so held captive as a child that I could never even begin to rein in the Christmas Pageant kids to whatever was deemed "good" behavior. My directorial inclinations held no weight whatsoever with me or them. But they knew I was on their side and I knew they were on the side of all that is good. So they rose to the occasion accordingly and honored the true nature of Christmas—birth of all that is beautiful, joyful and spirited. No matter what the bloopers were, the annual pageant-goers loved the blissfully spontaneous nature of things. And the kids, utterly unaware of their own grace, basked in the love and appreciation. They were directing us, me most of all, and it is something I will never forget. Out of their innocence I could see my own. And if they could do communion, so could I.

The children gave me courage and it was at one of those pageants, years ago, that I joined them for my first ritual of bread and wine. It was a moment infused with the innocence, wonder and rambunctious glee of childhood. Communion. It was a moment free of the gravitas of "meaning;" it was a moment of simply "being;" and "being" with those children was silly and sweet and sublime. That's all there was to it. But there is no communion tonight because there is no official priest on duty. It's simply our human communion that connects us, despite our divergent cultures, religions and beliefs.

After the service, there is much milling about outside in the dark and I get a whiff of coffee in the air. This is a shock as coffee is no staple here in India. I smell my way to a long table full of plates of cookies where cups of coffee are being served in honor of all us foreigners away from home at Christmas. I bump into Matt in the crowd. He's with a friend and they are on a mission. Someone he knows asked him to find the burial place of a woman who died here in Dharamsala and is buried in the cemetery at St. John's. They are to honor her gravesite for Christmas.

I start back along the road to town and find myself walking behind a family of five people, two Tibetan children, a Tibetan man, a Caucasian woman and another woman who might be her mother. They are all, including the children, speaking "American" English and exhibiting American exuberance. The two children are the ones I noticed gazing into the candles on Jesus' cake. It's clear and cold and I feel secure walking alone behind them. We've gone about a quarter-mile when an open jeep stops and offers the family a ride. The Indian driver waves at me to join them. I pile into the merriment of the crowded situation and the driver takes us all into town. All the way he wishes us a Merry Christmas.

All the way from the town square to the guest house, people wish me a Merry Christmas. They are delighting in recognizing that I am someone to whom Christmas has meaning. It is as though the occasion identifies me with spirit and it is something reassuring, familiar and trustworthy. I go to Jimmy's and get two pieces of banana toffee pie. One to eat tonight under the night sky of Christmas Eve, the other I'll eat for breakfast.

Nothing could have prepared me for Christmas in Dharamsala as my own personal convergence zone. All the loose ends of my long and convoluted life-journey have transformed themselves into a tapestry of faith that I can finally see and understand. The sense of isolation that has been my constant companion has been replaced by a deep and deeply reassuring sense of belonging. I no longer feel as though I need to be fixed. My "craziness" is the craziness of India. Nobody can fix it because in some profound way, there is nothing to fix.

I have always been guided towards faith and hope, even when I had none. Sustaining grace always intervened when life seemed inconceivable. It is a grace outside my control. It manifests itself in nature, in synchronicity, and in faith that everything that happens has spiritual meaning. These days it is not easy to confess to faith, to the religious impulse, to the possibility of encountering the Divine in ordinary life. Just as it does not make it easy to confess to an experience with evil.

But here in India, daily life is infused with celebration of the spirit and protection against evil. Buddhist and Hindu rituals, shrines, stories and temples are just a few of the ways in which religion sparks the sensibilities of day-to-day living. It is religion that lights up life and landscape with color and joy, even as so many Indian and Tibetan people's lives are rooted in terrible suffering. I am discovering that grief and love are the fundamental links to life, to the living, to healing and to belonging.

Weaving through these five weeks in India is a lifetime of longing, of continually starting over on the doorstep of my own life. I have finally crossed the threshold. I've experienced Hindus and Buddhists celebrating life and religion side-by-side, inclusively, with lots of room for a stumbling Episcopalian along the way. I've experienced the buoyancy of people and place as well my own buoyant and healed self in a place that I recognize and that recognizes me. It has been a spiritual, emotional and psychological homecoming, an epiphany from beginning to end.

The deepest truth is that every day is a profound and miraculous mystery. And we are gifted with the consciousness to know this. And we are gifted with the knowledge and the power to fix what's wrong in the world. Waking up to the truth is waking up to tragedy. It is also waking up to our responsibility to the world, to our place in the world and to our power in the world. A power fueled by spiritual truth.

What happened to me, and why, can be explained. The evidence abounds. But how I was protected, nurtured and sent along my spiritual way is an immense and majestic mystery. It is on this trip to India that I am recognizing what was always in attendance—an inextinguishable flame of spiritual guidance that knew me from the very beginning. It is why these words are on this page. It is why I am happy to be alive. It is why the very nature of being is sacred. We are here on earth to honor love—for our lives, our earth, and for one another. This is what I am waking up to in India. This is what I have known my whole life. It is beyond me. It is beyond us all.

On Christmas morning I wake to my small array of items on the table, the cards, the candle, the incense and the toffee pie. Dawn is just a hint in the sky. The Dalai Lama is back in town. He is here. This man, whose very life has been a guiding star to me for more than forty years, is less than a mile away. I know enough about his routine to know that he has been up since four, meditating and praying. That these days he wakes up in an earthquake protected room depriving him of his beloved view of the Dhauladhar Mountains. Perhaps, after his prayers, he goes outside to his gardens to hear the morning birds and watch the sunrise. He came back from south India to his Dharamsala home on Christmas Eve. Perhaps he, too, wanted to wake up here this morning, to know home on this sacred day, even if he is not a Christian. Yet, I know he is. He has been walking through the fire of human hatred and violence since he was a small boy, compassion firmly guiding his steps and his heart.

"Forgive them for they know not what they do." Reportedly, these were Jesus' first words from the cross. They speak the fundamental shape of compassion born out of understanding—whether from the earthly realizations of the Buddha under the Bodhi tree or the transcendent relationship of Jesus with His God. There is no other way to live. To defy this understanding is to choose death and destruction. When we forgive in the face of cruelty and brutality, whether of a regime, an institution, or an individual, we take the side of life, the unfolding miracle of creation that insists itself into light. Cruelty becomes an aberration, an indication of that which is less than life. Understanding and forgiveness is the high road—and the only road to a future.

The words in the poem that has accompanied me on this trip finally sink into my psyche. *To make injustice the only measure of our attention is to praise the Devil,* writes Jack Gilbert. It is a very terrible thing to keep suffering just because it proves I have suffered. It becomes another way of keeping my self imprisoned, of worshiping the Devil, of giving power to those who wished me powerless.

We must have the stubbornness to accept our gladness in the ruthless furnace of this world.

I will be stubborn.

If we deny our happiness, resist our satisfaction,
we lessen the importance of their deprivation.

I will not deny my happiness.

We must risk delight. We can do without pleasure,
but not delight. Not enjoyment.

I will risk delight.

Delight. It is bigger and brighter and stronger than us all. It delights in itself and in everything it reaches. It is everywhere in India. And it was here last night, in the old stone colonial church on the edge of town. We were directed through that which is always there, waiting for us to wake up to—grace, beauty and understanding.

This is precisely what I'm trying to remember to wake up to this morning. But of course I feel lonely and slightly dotty. There is no-one to share the morning with, no Christmas morning call from my son, nobody to fix dinner for, and no bacon to cook for breakfast—

which is one of my Christmas sins. Just the sun, rising brilliantly from the east, the birds singing, the dogs barking, and the monk circumambulating the roof.

Our Loseling monks have invited Matt and me to lunch today. It's for Christmas and there is also a Tibetan holiday to celebrate. They are excited because there will be three kinds of meat and meat is no staple in their lives. There will also be visiting monks chanting in the room behind the kitchen while we eat. Matt and I will give the monks the thanka we bought yesterday. I will give Dakpa some warm sweats, a dictionary, a notebook, some pens and some money. He'll be here for an English lesson this afternoon. In a minute I will go and walk the Lingkhor and the doors to the Dalai Lama's compound will be open for the first time since I arrived in Dharamsala. I could explore the possibility of a visit but I know I won't. Because it's finally time for me to learn what he has already taught me.

There are things wrong in this world. They manifest themselves in violence against the innocent. They are arrogant with power and rampant with greed. But even when evil gets its way, it doesn't win. Because what is good prevails effortlessly and takes hold naturally. There is always someone who will turn the other cheek and see the light. There is always life rising out of the ashes. There is always something to learn that will make a difference, and always someone to learn it from.

I sit with all this in a state of something akin to prayer. I'm waking up on Christmas Day in Dharamsala. I'm alone with it all. I miss my son. I had no idea why I was coming here and I discovered it was because I had to, that there was a pilgrimage to take and that it couldn't be taken without me. I miss Thrinley. I miss the company of friends and right now even of strangers. But the Dalai Lama is just across town and the Christmas card from Dakpa has a Tibetan Santa Claus and prayer flags across the top. The card from the dear Loseling monks says "Christ's Birth" on the front and shows Mary and Joseph in the manger.

So I will be a Buddhist and a Christian, too. I will go to church, to the gonpa, to the green cathedral of the outdoors, to wherever it is that stands up for the love of life and I will belong. I will live. I will be holy. I will be happy. And nobody can tell me otherwise.

I wrap myself up yet again against the morning chill and take my Christmas toffee pie out on the patio. There is no cloud in the sky, no protection from the onslaught of mountain beauty rising above the morning streets already filling with breakfast for the cows, monkeys and dogs. After their morning meal, the dogs will come out to stretch, sleep, and perhaps dream, in warm patches of sun. It's all happening all at once yet again. It's Christmas and I am here. The patio is fresh with new paint. In a while, Matt and I will meet for tea and perhaps discuss reality. In the meantime, my breakfast toffee pie is sweet and tasty. It is almost as good as bacon.

AFTERWORD

Early in 2009, I went back to visit India and all the places in this book. They are the same and they are different. As am I. India is still bursting at the seams with spiritual exuberance, too much poverty, and profound defiance in the face of any kind of expected, orderly, conforming behavior. I continue to try to live my life accordingly. But Mother India is a daunting teacher. Her accomplishments, throughout all her thousands of years of history, and throughout this very moment, are astounding in their brilliance and generosity. This is the 50th year that Mother India has provided a home and a government-in-exile for His Holiness the Dalai Lama and all the Tibetan people who risk life and loved ones to cross the Himalayas into freedom.

On this trip, I did try to get an interview with the Dalai Lama. But I was told that his health and his schedule preclude any private interviews. I was, however, at the Dalai Lama's temple in Dharamsala on March 10th, when he spoke on the 50th Anniversary of Tibetan Uprising Day. In the courtyard, hanging above him, was the biggest banner of all. It read: "Thank-you India." His Holiness spoke about the brutality of Chinese policies and his own failure to bring freedom, justice and peace to his beloved Tibetan people and their country. Yet, the very next day, the U.S. Congress voted almost unanimously to urge China to "cease its repression of the Tibetan people, and to lift immediately the harsh policies imposed on Tibetans." And the day after that, the European Parliament adopted a resolution on Tibet putting pressure on China to resume dialogue on "real autonomy for Tibet".

Like Mahatma Gandhi, Nelson Mandela, Martin Luther King, Jr., and Burma's Aung San Suu Kyi, His Holiness the Dalai Lama has honored, without falter, decades of peace and patience. It is this that ultimately we cannot ignore. It is this that the U.S. Congress and the European Union rose to support even as the Dalai Lama voiced the pain and frustration of "failure." It will take the entire world to prevent the genocide of the Tibetans and the destruction of a culture rooted in the beauty of being. It is a beauty that we are, perhaps, finally beginning to discover. And it is a beauty that I pray every day will be restored to the Tibetan people.

So, yes, I pray. It is an act I can neither define nor describe. Most of all it feels like a plea of body, heart and mind for some deep and abiding respect for all that lives and is alive. I, too, thank Mother India for giving me a home—in prayer, in complexity, in stark unadorned reality, and in the blazing glory and celebration of life. The 2004 trip to India took me into myself. The trip in 2009 took me out of myself. Who's to say where one journey begins and the other ends?

On this recent trip, I saw old friends and met new ones. I taught writing, went parasailing, drank lassi, (the forbidden yogurt drink for Western stomachs), wore Indian kurtas, smiled broadly as I said "No" to beggars, and relaxed into imminent death on the no-lane highways and byways of India. Dakpa, the young monk with whom I attempted English in 2004, came from Varanasi to Dharamsala to meet up with me. He spent two days chanting in the Dalai Lama's temple with many hundreds of other monks in Long Life Prayer for His Holiness. We both took part in the candlelight march for Tibet's freedom. Most of all, Dakpa wants me to help him finish the book he is writing about his life, his family, and his escape to India. But before returning to Varanasi and his studies in Buddhism, computers and English, Dakpa and I had a chance encounter with His Holiness the Karmapa in Delhi, where he was giving a teaching. As is usual in India, it was a chance encounter of sacred synchronicity.

I was buying Jack London's *The Call of the Wild* for Dakpa at a Penguin book exhibit at Delhi's India Habitat Center when I encountered a woman with a British accent at the checkout table. She was wearing a string around her neck attached to a name tag regarding her attendance at teachings with His Holiness the Karmapa. "What!" I burst out without thinking. "The Karmapa's here?!"

She smiled and said, "Yes, isn't that why you're here?"

When I stumbled over my words in surprise, she smiled again, took off her nametag and said, "Here, I've been here all day. Take it. I'm sorry there's not a lot of time with him left." And she put the nametag string over my head and led Dakpa and me off to where the Karmapa was teaching. I followed in a state of amazement. Then she waved and was gone.

The Seventeenth Karmapa, who is 23 years old, follows a line of enlightened teachers first acknowledged in Tibet in 1110. For much of his youth, the Karmapa was held under a form of house arrest by the Chinese in Tibet. He escaped to India in 1999 when he was 14 years-old and was joyfully received in Dharamsala by the Dalai Lama. I had heard of the distress of the Chinese at his escape and the resulting political awkwardness between China and India. China wanted him returned. Until recent years, the Karmapa has been rather sequestered, but now he journeys abroad, and throughout India, to give teachings.

As I slipped into the room where the Karmapa was teaching, it was question and answer time. (Dakpa, who was too respectful to enter while the session was underway, listened from the hall at a slightly opened door.) His Holiness radiated a penetrating awareness that seemed to pierce through each person's presence. There was nothing youthful about him. Questions were asked: Why is there such an important link between compassion and emptiness? His answer was quick: Because emptiness offers immediate opportunity and possibility for compassion. When we are "empty" of our own projections and obsessions, we can be open and compassionate to the needs of others. Compassion is not pity, he said. It is profound. He then went on to speak of the radiance of the awakened self upon which we were all seated. Compassion, he said, must be felt for those who cannot feel this radiance.

The next question was asked: What is the difference between intrinsic and ultimate reality? The people in the room murmured at the profundity of the question. But the Karmapa was not visibly impressed. His look and his body language appeared akin to:

Are you kidding me? I just gave you an answer to live within and you're asking me this piece of abstract nonsense? He paused, his eyes widened and his brows lifted. "There's a meeting going on right now of many scholars and translators," he said. "Perhaps they will be able to answer your question." As an afterthought, he said, "In your language, I think, no difference."

The last question was offered by a young Indian. "I am a teenager, he said, and terrible things are happening in the world. What advice do you have for us?"

The crowd tittered this time, perhaps because they thought the boy was so young and his question so naïve. The Karmapa saw it otherwise. He leaned forward in pointed concentration. "This past generation with its technology, speed and materialism has made everything very difficult. I am young, too. I relate to your feelings. Has technology been useful? Yes. Has technology been destructive? Yes. We are losing our environment. We are losing our time. Perhaps it is too late. Perhaps there will be balance. Is change possible? Yes. It is what we must pray for and work for."

Change is possible. But it's all a balancing act—whether we're working for or praying for personal peace or world peace. And that balancing act is precisely what I continue to learn about my own healing—every minute of every day. And all along, the earth continues to turn, unfurling its bewildering beauty, just waiting for me, and for all of us, to wake up yet again, and notice.

Acknowledgments

My deepest gratitude to His Holiness the Dalai Lama; his life in this world lit my way before I could name darkness.

My deepest gratitude to all my Buddhist and Christian teachers; they led me back to the heart of love.

My deepest gratitude to all the poets; they always get the last word.

My deepest gratitude to literary agent, Ned Leavitt; he deepened the spirit and the words in this book with his support, insight and guidance. He gave me the courage to keep on finishing it until it was really finished.

My deepest gratitude to my spiritual mentor, Andrew Harvey; his work brought me solace for two decades—and over the last few years his faith in the divine pulled me through when mine faltered.

My deepest gratitude to my son, Colin; his love and forgiveness made it possible to write this book.

My deepest gratitude to my sisters in Buddhism and in friendship, Thrinley DiMarco, Susan Campbell-Webster and Susanna Salsbury; they read this book as it was being written and kept me going with their prayers and friendship. I extend a special bow of gratitude to Thrinley who got me to India in the first place and supported my writing journey all the way through.

My deepest gratitude to good friend and superb editor, Emily Reed, who read every word at least twice and fixed them all accordingly; to inspired and skilful designer, Bruce Conway, who took tender care of this book and who also knows the story behind the story; and to John Soderberg who offered his help precisely when it was needed.

My deepest gratitude to the wildfire writers: Mary Kate Askew, Cady Davies, Beth Hetrick, Weyshawn Koons, Lisa Lawrence and Myah Thompson; they supported me with their language, love, laughter, and really good food as I nervously shared this book with them. A special thank-you to Weyshawn who got me there and kept me there.

My deepest gratitude to Dr. Michael Cohen who taught me the language of nature and introduced me to my 53 senses; to Diana Stone whose support was an anchor throughout the writing journey.

My deepest gratitude to Sandy Bishop, Chrys Buckley, Emily Connery, Barbara Cox, Alwyn Jones, Rhea Miller, Susan Osborn, Martha Scott, Jeannie Turner and Richard Wright who read this book as it was underway and offered insight and encouragement.

My deepest gratitude to all the students in my memoir classes on Orcas, Shaw and San Juan Islands; many a difficult day was brightened by their presence in my life.

My deepest gratitude to all my island friends, many of whom didn't know what I was up to during the years I was sequestered with this book; they patiently loved me anyways. A special thank you to Janice, who walked with me throughout; to the Sturdivants who fed me throughout; and to the canasta queens, especially Bridget, Louisa, Nancy and Vivian, who played with me throughout.

My deepest gratitude to my friends at a distance: John, Martha and Zoe Pappenheimer, Bonnie and David Snedeker, and Martha Brice and Martha Scott. I don't see them often enough but their presence is constant.

My deepest gratitude to the Tibetan people; they create hope out of despair; joy out of grief; bounty out of deprivation; and limitless gain out of unimaginable loss. May they prevail.

My deepest gratitude to my magnificent therapist, Brian. There are no words to convey the depth and breadth of our therapeutic journey together. He brought me to freedom and taught me its name. In his professional commitment to meticulous boundaries, he wishes to be identified only by his first name. To my Little Ones he will always be "Big Bryun." The best.

My deepest gratitude to all my multiple personalities and inner guides; their patience, love and acceptance towards me, even as I was impatient, unloving and intolerant towards them, are lessons I will always be learning.

Credits

"A Brief for the Defense" by *Jack Gilbert*, from *Refusing Heaven* (Knopf , 2005).

Excerpt from the poem "The Descent" by *William Carlos Williams* in *William Carlos Williams Selected Poems* (New Directions Books).

K.V.S. Thapar: Lines from "A Night on the Bank of River Beas" from the book of poems, *Cries of Anguish* (Writers Workshop Redbird Book, 2003, Kolkata).

Lhasang Tsering: *Tomorrow & Other Poems* (Rupa & Co, New Delhi).

"Late Fragment" *Raymond Carver,* from *All of Us–Raymond Carver, The Collected Poems,* Copyright Tess Gallagher (Vintage Books).

Lines from "Wild Geese" by *Mary Oliver,* from *New and Selected Poems–Mary Oliver (Beacon Press).*

Breinigsville, PA USA
30 November 2009

228341BV00003B/2/P